FAITH LIES

FAITH LIES

Seven Incomplete Ideas That Hijack Faith and How to See Beyond Them

Darrell Smith

ELM HILL

A Division of
HarperCollins Christian Publishing

www.elmhillbooks.com

FAITH LIES
Seven Incomplete Ideas That Hijack Faith and How to See Beyond Them

Published in Nashville, Tennessee, by Elm Hill, an imprint of Thomas Nelson. Elm Hill and Thomas Nelson are registered trademarks of HarperCollins Christian Publishing, Inc.

Elm Hill titles may be purchased in bulk for educational, business, fund-raising, or sales promotional use. For information, please e-mail SpecialMarkets@ ThomasNelson.com.

All Scripture quotations, unless otherwise indicated, are taken from the Holy Bible, New Revised Standard Version Bible: Catholic Edition. Copyright © 1989, 1993 National Council of the Churches of Christ in the United States of America. Used by permission. All rights reserved.

Scripture quotations marked KJV are from the King James Version. Public domain.

Scripture quotations marked THE VOICE are from The Voice™. © 2012 by Ecclesia Bible Society. Used by permission. All rights reserved.

Scripture quotations marked THE MESSAGE are from *The Message*. Copyright © by Eugene H. Peterson 1993, 1994, 1995, 1996, 2000, 2001, 2002. Used by permission of NavPress. All rights reserved. Represented by Tyndale House Publishers, Inc.

Library of Congress Cataloging-in-Publication Data

Library of Congress Control Number: 2018952583

ISBN 978-1-595557322 (Paperback)
ISBN 978-1-595558589 (Hardbound)
ISBN 978-1-595557308 (eBook)

CONTENTS

For Stacy

My beloved is to me a cluster of henna blossoms in the vineyards of En-gedi.

SONG OF SOLOMON 1.14

FOREWORD
Lynn Anderson

Two talking fish swim along, side by side.

Female fish: "You know, lately this water has become so polluted that it burns my eyes."

Male fish: *(after thinking for a moment)* "What the heck is water?"

Astonishing! He is totally surrounded by water, his life depends on it—water shaping the way he sees his world—yet he isn't even consciously aware of its presence.

So, the question for me—and for you—is, "What is the *water* in which I *swim*?" What is the prism through which I view my world? And you, yours?

For example, on a long flight, Sally strikes up a conversation with a stranger. At a lull in the dialogue, the stranger looks Sally in the eye and ventures to ask, "Tell me, Sally. Are you a Christian?"

Sally muses a moment then replies, "I haven't the foggiest idea what that question means!"

Sally is testing the water.

No wonder! She knows the word "Christian" may trigger any number of images—depending on the water through which one views it. The same is true of words like "Bible" and "faith," where the images evoked may be relatively harmless or enormously toxic. Our associations with the Bible or religion can be so hurtful at times that we feel tempted to abandon faith altogether.

Enter *Faith Lies*.

In this book, Darrell Smith helps us test our water. He calls out widespread, distorted ideas—myths that are sometimes actually attributed to the Bible. *Faith Lies* is not merely a critique of our water, however. Rather, Darrell guides us onward toward astonishing good news—a fresh perspective on the Bible and a healthier view of faith.

This book pursues the rich narrative and tradition of the God-Human dance. For Darrell, when we take the time to see our faith through clearer water, it is far from toxic. It is actually both fascinating and powerfully transformative.

Turn the page and dive in.

What comes into our minds when we think about God is the most important thing about us ... [as] no religion has ever been greater than its idea of God.

— A.W. Tozer
(The Knowledge of the Holy)

THE DISARMING

At the very beginning of Kevin Smith's satirical movie, *Dogma*, the writer and director many adore as Silent Bob offers this disclaimer on behalf of his production company, View Askew:

> Disclaimer: 1) a renunciation of any claim to or connection with; 2) a disavowal; 3) a statement made to save one's own ass.
>
> Though it'll go without saying ten minutes or so into these proceedings, View Askew would like to state that this film is—from start to finish—a work of comedic fantasy, not to be taken seriously. To insist that any of what follows is incendiary or inflammatory is to miss our intention and pass undue judgment; and passing judgment is reserved for God and God alone (this goes for you film critics, too ... just kidding).
>
> So please—before you think about hurting someone over this trifle of a film, remember: even God has a sense of humor. Just look at the platypus. Thank you and enjoy the show.
>
> P.S. We sincerely apologize to all platypus enthusiasts out there who are offended by that thoughtless comment about the platypi. We at View Askew respect the noble platypus, and it is not our intention to slight these stupid creatures in any way.
>
> Thank you again and enjoy the show.[1]

---

[1]   Kevin Smith, *Dogma*, DVD, Directed by Kevin Smith (Culver City, CA: Columbia TriStar Home Entertainment, 1999).

I'm not sure if reading that in a book is as funny as seeing it on the screen, but I hope that you are laughing—or at the very least, you are a little more disarmed than you were before reading it. While I clearly cannot disclaim as masterfully as Kevin Smith and the View Askew crew, that is really what I want us all to do here—be disarmed.

The explorative journey that follows in these pages may very well offend some trusted ideas and principles. Beliefs and thought processes may be challenged. You will be encouraged to be critically honest about the inherited stories and doctrines upon which your faith or spiritual life is built. You may find parts of this journey cause anger, fear, or frustration—most journeys worth taking do that at some point.

What I can promise you is that any struggle or discomfort you may encounter along the way will not be without meaning. This journey has a purpose, and that purpose is not to belittle faith or tear down God. Quite to the contrary, the purpose of this journey is to strengthen our faith and deepen our relationship with the driving force of the universe—the ultimate reality—what many of us call God. This journey should also place us in better relationship to one another. Like it or not, we don't do much of anything alone—we are in this together.

This is not a journey of answers. There will be no lines drawn in the sand. You will not be asked to adopt a belief or take a pledge. This is a journey of questions and conversation. This is an exploration that honors argument, dialogue, and discovery. Regardless of where you end up in and through this journey, you are and will be safe. You will not need to be armed or have your guard up. Instead, you will need to be open to having your life—your thinking and way of seeing the spiritual world around you—agitated and disrupted. And that is really the point—to subject the seemingly concrete way in which we behold the ever-changing universe to a shake-up. Why should our understanding be stagnant and singular when the reality in which we live is dynamic and even mysterious at times?

There is a wise rabbi in my life who repeatedly reminds me that there is growth in the disruption. To that end, let us disarm and journey toward disruptive growth together.

Disarm: 1) to lay aside arms; 2) to give up or reduce the means of attack or defense; 3) plagiarizing Kevin Smith's writing in an attempt to get people to relax.

Though it'll go without saying one chapter or so into this book, I would like to state that this writing is—from start to finish—a documentation of my experience with faith. Neither this book nor I insist that my experience is the right experience or the only experience. Rather, I hope that the questioning of my experience will help you to question your own.

So please—before you think about hurling this book across the room, remember: God is not afraid of questions. If God were afraid of questions, do you really think that God would have created you? Seriously. Since you have been able to speak, have you ever gone a day in your life without asking a question? See?! Right there, I just asked like three questions in a row—and I wasn't even trying.

This is not to intimate that questions are a bad thing in any way. If you are a questioner, then welcome. If you're not a questioner … why is that? Another question! Brilliant!!

Thank you and let the questioning begin.[2]

---

[2] My apologies to Kevin Smith and the fine people at View Askew for ripping off your brilliant disclaimer. Please remember that imitation is the highest form of flattery. I am not quite sure who said that, but I am sure happy to imitate them as well.

INTRODUCTION

Religion has given people great comfort in a world torn apart by religion.[1]

— Jon Stewart

That Which We Call a Lie by Any Other Name...

William Shakespeare's tragedy of *Romeo and Juliet* coined a number of famous phrases that still stick with us today. One such phrase happens in an exchange between the two star-crossed lovers from rival families. Juliet, lamenting that her Romeo bears the name of an enemy family, suggests that they drop their names, which, on the surface, seems to pose a problem. "What's in a name?" Juliet asks. "That which we call a rose by any other name would smell as sweet...."[2] In two lines, Shakespeare—via Juliet—nails this simple truth to the wall. What we call a thing doesn't really affect the characteristics of the thing or the impact it has upon us. Were we to call a rose an umbrella instead of calling it a rose, it would nevertheless still possess the characteristics of a rose. It would still look and smell like a rose. Calling a rose an umbrella

---

[1] *The Daily Show.* "Reza Aslan." Season 20, Episode 106. Directed by Chuck O'Neil. Written by Dan Amira, Steve Bodow, Travon Free, Hallie Haglund, Elliot Kalan, Matt Koff, Adam Lowitt, Dan McCoy, Jo Miller, Zhubin Parang, Owen Parsons, Daniel Radosh, Lauren Sarver, Jon Stewart, and Delaney Yeager. Comedy Central, May 13, 2015.

[2] William Shakespeare, *Romeo and Juliet*, Norton's Anthology. (Chicago: Hampton Publishers, 2004) 55-104.

would not enable it to keep us dry in the rain any more than it would prevent a rose from beautifying a garden or attracting a bee in search of pollen.

The same can be said of a lie. A lie is a lie no matter what we call it. A lie is an untrue, inaccurate, or incomplete statement or idea that misleads or deceives. With the power to conceal, limit, constrict, and imprison, lies can hurt people. And just like Juliet's rose, a lie doesn't change simply because we call it something else. We could call a lie doctrine ... or ortho- dox ... we could even call a lie biblical and that wouldn't prevent it from having the characteristics and impact of a lie. In the same way that a rose will fail to keep me dry in a storm even if I—and everyone around me— truly believe it is an umbrella, a lie will ultimately fail me even if I—and everyone around me—believe that it is true. The storm is an important part of that equation. It is often in the storms of life where we are truly able to separate those ideas and values that will help keep us afloat from those that will hasten our drowning. The harsh and complicated cir- cumstances in which we find ourselves during the course of our lives are the storms that reveal the true value of the ideologies and theologies to which we cling. Far too often, we find ourselves struggling to stay afloat in rough waters, grasping and pulling at the lifelines we have been taught to hold on to, only to find out that those lines are not tied off. We pull and pull, hoping that the line will bring us back to something solid and safe, but sometimes it just does not. We learn the hard way that certain ideas and philosophies weren't actually tied to anything helpful. Lifelines that should bring us back to a boat, a dock, or even another person on dry land turn out to be just floating rope.

Learning that the lifeline is not actually a lifeline while you're trying not to drown is like pouring salt on a wound. The timing of the lesson feels horrible. Nevertheless, it is in such moments that we seem to be the most open to education—to receiving new information. It is as if we have come to the end of an untied lifeline, realized that it will not help us, released it and cried out, "Throw me another line!" We become very open in such moments.

An exchange between two characters in the movie *American History X* ends with a very important question. The exchange takes place in a prison hospital where Danny, a young skinhead whose violent and racist ways have landed him not only in prison but now in the recovery room of the hospital following a gang attack, is trying to determine why the ideologies and philosophies upon which he built his life aren't working. Dr. Sweeney—Danny's former principal and a black man—comes to visit him, and Danny is ashamed. As Danny lays on a gurney crying in pain and fear, Dr. Sweeney identifies with his situation.

Dr. Sweeney: There was a moment when I used to blame everything and everyone for all the pain and suffering and vile things that happened to me—that I saw happen to my people; blame everybody, blame white people, blame society, blame God.
    I didn't get no answers because I was asking the wrong questions.
    You have to ask the right questions.

Danny: Like what?

Dr. Sweeney: Has anything you've done made your life better?[3]

Has anything you've done—any philosophy you've believed—any ideology you've espoused—made your life better? This is a hugely important question! This is the question we inevitably face when we pull on lifelines in the storm. Is this idea or value to which I am clinging helping me? Is the belief making my life any better?

As we undertake this journey together, this is the question to which we must return. Is this belief, this outlook, this idea, this theology making my life any better? Is it helpful? And if it's not helpful, then why am I holding on to it? Am I clinging to a lie because that is what is expected of me? Perhaps I hang on to unanchored lines because they represent a

---

[3]   David McKenna, *American History X*, DVD, Directed by Tony Kaye (Los Angeles, CA: New Line Home Entertainment, 1999).

tradition—hundreds, if not thousands, of years old? Perhaps I cling to incomplete ideas and unhelpful narratives simply because I have never been offered better alternatives. I don't know about you, but if I find myself in a storm and I have to choose between an unanchored line or nothing, I will always choose the unanchored line. It's better than nothing, right? Maybe if I hang on to it, I will find something to which I can tie it off?

Maybe not. Maybe holding tightly to a line that is not tied off to anything solid actually prevents me from being able to grasp something helpful. Maybe it is not enough to come to the end of the rope; maybe when I do, I actually need to let go.

Let me invite you to do just that. Let go. Loose your grasp on those lifelines to which you hold so tightly. You are safe. You don't have to permanently abandon anything to undertake this journey. If we get to the end and you have found nothing helpful along the way, so be it. You can pick back up the lines you know and go on with your life. The ideas, philosophies, and theologies with which you began this journey will be waiting for you at the end should you choose to hold on to them. It is not the intention of this book to tear down or subtract but to include and expand. Rather than seeing this exploration as something that will remove or threaten our existing and cherished beliefs, we can see it as adding to them—addition, not subtraction. And even the addition is completely up to you because not only are we safe, we are free. Both the goal and the mechanism of this journey is freedom—nothing less.

You are free...and so am I. Whether we always recognize it or not, freedom is the default reality in which we exist. Sure, there are a number of things that can limit, hinder, or remove our freedom—not the least of which is other people—but the reality remains: you are free. Freedom is how we get lies in the first place. We are free to tell lies. We are free to believe them. If we were not free—if we could not choose, could a lie even exist?

I realize that we may be moving into Yoda territory here, so let me quote his protégé, Obi Won Kanobi, who said, "You're going to find many

8

of the truths we cling to depend greatly on our own point of view."[4] Your point of view is free. It belongs to you. You, and only you, get to choose what to do with it.[5]

Well-Meaning Ideas

While we are on the subject of points of view, let me share a couple of mine that I think will help guide us on this journey. My first point of view is that each of the lies we will examine comes from good intentions. What does that mean? It means I don't think there is a conspiracy or a hidden agenda to create and promote lies that will hinder people's faith and freedom. Instead, consider that each of the lies we will explore came into existence and found continued life through the good intentions of faithful people who were doing the best they could in their circumstances. I don't think anyone was trying to poison the well. The lies or unanchored ideas with which we struggle are more likely the product of our acquiescence coupled with distance and interpretation.

Acquiescence, distance, and interpretation—three important words for us to remember as we navigate these waters.

Acquiescence is our accepting something without protest or investigation.[6] We do this quite a bit. It's nothing to feel shame about—we are incredibly busy people who are inundated with overwhelming amounts of information and stimuli. We are almost constantly asked to receive and make rulings on data that is coming our way. One of the ways we cope is to just accept those things that we do not feel we have either the time or

4   Lawrence Kasdan and George Lucas, *Star Wars: Episode VI – Return of the Jedi*, DVD, directed by Richard Marquand (Beverly Hills, CA: Twentieth Century Fox Home Entertainment, 1983).

5   Come on! You didn't really think you could read a book like this without running into a Jedi quote, did you? The force is with us!

6   *Ack·we·es·since*... yep, that just happened. I created my own pseudophonetic pronunciation of this $5-word in an effort to make sure we all know what we are saying. You may not need it. You may be completely familiar with this seventeenth-century French word and use it in your daily routine. If you do, *de toute evidence, vous êtes une personne belle et intelligente.*

the capacity to protest or investigate. We acquiesce. We just accept it and move on. This is not an isolated phenomenon, and it is not a new trend. We all do it.

And acquiescence is not even necessarily a bad thing. Consider traditions—those things that people before us have tried and deemed valuable, helpful, and worthy of passing on. Traditions can be a great thing. Regardless of our particular faith or religion, so much of our spiritual reality is built on tradition. There is something incredibly healthy and even encouraging about standing on the shoulders of those who have gone before us and trusting in their collective wisdom as we walk through this life. Traditions can comfort us, guide us, and empower us—and in such cases, simply accepting their existence in our lives is most likely what will lead to our own development and wisdom. My rabbi calls that "complete obedience without complete understanding," meaning that our understanding, growth, and development comes through our willingness to obey and follow first.

I get that. There have been plenty of times in my life when I needed to obey and follow a tradition in order to learn and truly grasp the wisdom it had to pass on. But what happens when we accept and embrace a tradition and, even on the other side of the looking glass, fail to reflect, investigate, or discern just what it is we are accepting and embracing? What if a tradition is corrupt? What if a tradition is bound to the time and place in which it was first embraced and simply cannot be applied in our times and places without adjustment?

This is where *distance* comes into the equation. Distance can be created by a number of things, including experience, time, geography, culture, and language. We understand this, right? If I am locked alone in a room with a person who only speaks a language I do not speak, we are going to have a distance between us. We will be linguistically separated. We will not be able to communicate with each other very well.

The same is true of time. When I try to explain to my children that there was a time in my life where I did not have a cell phone, a computer, or the internet, they think I'm making it up—it just does not compute. The distances of time and experience separate their childhood from mine.

Think of your favorite historical figures. Do you have them in mind? Whoever they were, they clearly did things or said things that resonate with you today. Their actions or words moved through time and space to impact you—which is really cool when you think about it. Parts of their lives *transcended* or overcame the distance between you to impact your life. Still, that same historical figure also said things, did things, and understood things in ways that did not transcend. There were parts of their existence that were bound to the times in which they lived, the places and cultures they lived within, the language they spoke, and the experiences they had. To really understand them in a holistic sense, you would have to do much investigation and research into the context of time, language, life experience, and culture. And even exhaustive investigation and research might not uncover it all. There would most likely still be parts of their experience and understanding that were lost to you. Distance is real, and it cannot always be overcome.

So what do we do when we can't overcome distances to clearly understand what was going on or what was being said? We make informed estimations. We do our best to bring together what data we can and try to make an educated guess. For the purposes of our equation, let's call that educated guessing *interpretation*. Interpretations are simply people trying to make sense out of things as best they can. People have been wading into the waters of faith for thousands of years and making interpretations based on their perspectives and experiences—their points of view. Sometimes, the aforementioned distances cloud those interpretations.

When we start looking at something like the Bible—written long ago by people of a different culture in a different place, who spoke different languages and had different experiences, all of those distances can be working against our understanding and our interpretations simultaneously.

Imagine a tribe of people who feel—without a compass or even the stars to guide them—they know how to locate true north. This feeling is based upon their combined perspectives and experiences. Over time, they have learned and proven they can find true north over and over. It is confirmed by their shared behavior and practices—it works for them. These people write down what they think is important about finding true north in the language and metaphor that makes the most sense to them. They note the landmarks. They tell the stories of the times they went the wrong way and learned where true north was not. They do this so that others may benefit from their collected wisdom and knowledge.

Now imagine a new tribe of people get a hold of these writings thousands of years later and in a different part of the world altogether. Do the writings still have value? Can the shared wisdom and knowledge still be helpful to these people of a different time, place, language, and culture? Probably—but it will take some work, right? There will be parts of the writings that represent timeless wisdom about true north. There will be other parts of the original tribe's writings that are particular to pursuing true north from their perspective and their location. To know the difference may require exhaustive research and investigation into the times, places, language, and culture of the tribes that created the writings and told the stories.

What if the new tribe of people simply acquiesced? Instead of investigating, they just accepted the original tribes' writings and traditions concerning true north. When they came upon something in the writings they didn't understand, they just made interpretations. Perhaps the new tribe even appointed some experts—whose job it was to understand and interpret the writings for everyone else—to tell them what they needed to know about true north? Can you see any danger or potential problems in this approach?

The landmarks aren't the same. The metaphors and narratives with which the original tribe communicated might not be readily available to the new tribe. That context the original tribe depended on may have been lost in the distances of time, geography, culture, and language. Can you see that without such study and deliberation over the context of the writings, the wisdom and knowledge they were meant to convey could be skewed or perhaps missed altogether? What if the original writings employed symbol, story, and metaphor that the new tribe misinterpreted and instead believed those writings contained literal or empirical information?

This is where we get into real trouble in our faith lives. We swallow whole ideas and beliefs as our own when what they really represent is the interpretative conclusions made by other people in other places at other times. We ignore distances of time, space, culture, and language. We surrender our own perspective and experience in favor of someone else's. And if we do this together in community—repeatedly, over the course of time—those ideas and beliefs become ideologies and belief systems. They become doctrine... orthodox... tradition... sacred.

While we can admit that such an approach certainly impacts our faith lives as those trying to function within a given religion, tradition, or denomination, we must also consider how this looks to the world around us. What story are we telling the world? How are we telling that story?

Let me put it another way. If I believe in a God that someone who knows me—who truly knows me—has trouble believing in, whom does that say more about—God or me? If the way I behave and live my life— the way I treat others—is one of the primary ways that my faith is shared, what does it mean that people are becoming more and more disillusioned? The truth is, the disillusioned among us are disillusioned with the story we are telling and the way we are telling it. Our atheistic and agnostic brothers and sisters are people of great courage. Against the very real pressure of societal norms, they are refusing to believe in the God that we are representing to them. Can we blame them? Perhaps, were we able to step outside ourselves and observe the God we represent to the world, we wouldn't believe either.

- Is our God for a specific country or ethnicity and against others?
- Is our God for a specific religion, denomination, or political party and against the others?

- Is our God harsh and vengeful—pouring out wrath on those deemed deserving of it?
- Is our God judgmental—a cosmic scorekeeper—or sadistic Santa Claus, watching for those who should be placed on the naughty list?
- Is our God disconnected or aloof—an absent-minded professor not always at the controls?
- Is our God a manipulative puppet master who is always pulling the strings and arranging things?

Whether or not we are always able to recognize it, our lives—the ways we behave and the things we say about God—don't always represent something desirable or compelling. If I can be honest with myself, sometimes my life—the ways in which I have behaved, the things I have said about God, my beliefs—has actually been quite repulsive to anyone paying attention. If there are people in my life who resist or reject my faith and my God, perhaps that says more about me than it does about God. Perhaps I am telling a story—representing a faith and a God—that is not consistent or compelling. Perhaps the narrative I have—the understanding to which I cling—is filled with misunderstanding and sketchy interpretation, and I just don't know it. Perhaps my faith and my God are important enough to deserve protest and investigation. Perhaps we are all, unknowingly, living under faith lies.

A Small, Tragic Example

I have worked in the church for a large chunk of my life. In doing so, I have run into honest and loving people who held tightly to some of the most skewed and hurtful ideas. And don't let me point any fingers here—I have lived the same way. More often than not, those of us holding onto faith lies don't recognize them as such. We just have them because we believe we are supposed to. We have inherited them—picked them up along the way—and have been unreflective about what they really say about God or about us.

Let me give you an example. In the last year, I have had conversations with faithful people who sincerely believed that those who aren't baptized before their death are sent to hell. To be clear, there are a number of bad ideas at work in that statement, not the least of which is the idea that hell is someplace people are sent upon dying if they haven't checked the right boxes—but let that one sink in for a moment. Think about what such an idea really means. Babies who die during childbirth, people who are never exposed to the concept of baptism, the person on his or her way to be baptized who is killed in a car wreck—according to such an idea, these people go to hell.

What does such an idea say about God? What does such an idea say about us? I don't know about you, but that is not a God or a faith of which I want to be a part. If that's God, I'm out.

Friends, do not misunderstand me. I do not bring up this example to mock or distance us from those who hold such a belief. They are not crazy, and they are not to be dismissed or ridiculed. Somewhere along the line they picked up a bad narrative. Maybe it was warped when they inherited it from someone they trusted. Maybe it skewed along the way based on interpretation. Regardless of how this faith lie came to be planted, what is needed now is investigation and protest.

For these people, a narrative of a vengeful, scorekeeping God whose idea of justice is so small that the unbaptized must suffer eternal torment and separation has hijacked the narrative of a loving God who cares more for people than rules. Baptism—a religious ritual practiced by Christians, inherited from Jewish tradition of *mikveh*—is certainly found throughout the Bible and the Judeo-Christian faith tradition. It has been an important symbol and place of intersection with the divine for thousands of years. Yet, who made it a rule?

- And if it is a rule, is there a right way to do it?
- Is there a way to practice baptism that doesn't count?
- What about the person John the Baptist baptized right before Jesus—did his or her baptism count?

- Who decided that baptism is a saving ritual that serves as your ticket into heaven?
- Who decided that without it, you go to hell?
- For that matter, where and when are heaven and hell?
- Is the point of our existence really to check-off some spiritual boxes that allow us to get a pass someday to someplace else?
- Is that really what baptism was ever intended to be—an escape clause to paradise?

The reason I offer this example is to demonstrate how pervasive even the smallest bad idea can be in our lives. Whether they realized it or not, the people who shared with me that the unbaptized go to hell were making declarations about who God is and who we are. They were acquiescing and subjecting understanding to decontextualized interpretations—submitting to faith lies.

The point of view I would invite you to hold on to is that none of the lies we will explore together came about because someone or something set out to deceive us systematically. Instead, they are the resulting weeds that grew up amidst the fertile soil created by acquiescence, distance, and interpretation. And weeds, if left unchecked, can take over a garden and kill off that which was originally intended to grow. Weeds must be pulled from a garden so that the sunlight, nutrients, and water can get to the sustaining crops we need to thrive. Similarly, lies must be investigated, protested, and discarded in order to preserve the helpful and freeing relationship into which we are invited. When we leave such lies uninvestigated over a prolonged period of time, a strange thing begins to happen. A folktale—a surface-level forgery of the original spiritual depth our forebears sought to preserve and pass on—replaces our faith. Instead of an inclusive, freeing narrative of love and acceptance and mercy, we descend into an illogical collection of fairy-tales and ideas that rarely make sense and aren't always helpful.

Come On In, the Water is Fine

My rabbi, David McNitzky, likens our acceptance of the folktale to hiking to a beautiful mountain lake.[7] Sure, while standing on the banks of the lake, there is much beauty to behold. It's a "Kodak moment." One may even find some sense of peace or sustenance just looking at the lake and beautiful scenery. But what if there is more? What if our eyes can deceive us as to what the lake really holds? What if we can't really see all there is from our point of view? What if we are invited not only to see the lake from the banks but also to get in the lake?

Swim, dive, behold the rich depths beneath the surface; taste the water and be restored as we drink; be sustained by the harvest of fish in the lake and vegetation around its banks; recline around a campfire on one of the beaches of the lake while listening to the stories of others who have explored the lake and are amazed at the wonders they have discovered. That's the experience I would rather have. I don't want to settle for standing on the shoreline and posing for a selfie. I want the total experience.

If that is you, too, then come on in—the water is fine. We will journey together. We will not pretend to have all the right answers or even that such answers exist. Instead, we will explore, investigate, and protest in search of freedom. We will attempt to get at the roots of the weeds in our gardens and pull them out. We will yank on lifelines that appear to be attached to something solid and, if they are not, then we will let them go and loose our grasp for something else. Does our faith deserve any less?

We will remember that the point of this journey is not to assign blame or to bring down faith, the Bible, or God. If we must assign blame for the presence of incomplete ideas or faith lies in our lives, then we need look

---

[7] *Rabbi* is the Hebraic word for "teacher." It is derived from the Hebrew word *rabi*, which means "My Master." It was and is the way a student of the Hebrew Bible would address the teacher or master of the Hebrew Bible from whom they were trying to learn. If "master" seems awkwardly strong to you, I get that—but the student-teacher relationship referenced here is much more than acquiring head knowledge. It is about following someone's life and example so closely that you can taste the dust kicking up from their feet as they walk along.

no further than the mirror. We are free. No one forced bad or incomplete ideas into our lives—we picked them up. For one reason or another, we let them in. Our intentions—just like the aforementioned faithful—were honorable. We did not set out to be deceived or enslaved by a lie. Nor does the presence of incomplete or bad ideas in our faith mean that we are stupid or gullible. Just like everyone else, we have been trying to survive. Along the way, we have picked things up—thinking that they would be helpful. At times, we were given things by people who swore up and down that the idea or belief they were giving us was not only helpful but required—as if without it, we would surely die.

This book reflects my experience investigating and protesting some of those seemingly "required" ideas. For one reason or another, I have had to ask the questions. I have pulled on each of these lines until the end wound up in my hand—revealing that it was never secured in the first place. Hopefully, you do not have to wait until you are at the end of the line to investigate and protest in search for freedom. That is my prayer for this book—that you will learn to ask the questions that expose the limitations and restrictions of the lies causing us to stumble and preventing us from being fully alive. Those kinds of questions are where I believe we can find God—that driving and unifying force of the universe—the ultimate reality ... and that is where the freedom is.

> Judaism is a protest in the name of human freedom and responsibility against determinism. We are not pre-programmed machines; we are persons, endowed with will. Just as God is free, so we are free, and the entire Torah is a call to humanity to exercise responsible freedom in creating a social world which honours the freedom of others.[8]

---

[8]   Jonathan Sacks, *Covenant & Conversation - Genesis: The Book of Beginnings* (Jerusalem: Koren Publishers, 2009), 26.

THE BIBLE IS ONLY THE
LITERAL WORD OF GOD

If it is true that the road to the future lies in the past, it is also true that when the past has been lost or neglected there is no certain future....When the past is lost, as it now is in our Western world, there is nothing left to focus on except the self.[1]

— Robert Webber

This may seem like a strange place to start, but if our goal is to come out from under the limiting lies of our faith, we must recognize that most of those misunderstandings begin in how we view, understand, and interpret the Bible. In fact, the work of removing lies from our faith necessarily involves the Bible. While it is not the only source of truth, it is a source with which we should constantly interact—and let me tell you, we humans have certainly interacted with the Bible! Millions of books have been written about the Bible. Each year, the Bible is the focus of movies, Discovery and History Channel specials, miniseries, debates,

---

[1] Robert Webber, *Who Gets to Narrate the World? Contending for the Christian Story in an Age of Rivals* (Downers Grove, IL: Intervarsity Press, 2008), 16–17.

conferences, classes, essays, articles, and more sermons than we could ever count.

People who trace their faith to any part of the Judeo-Christian scriptures have literally been arguing about what the scriptures were since before they were even scriptures. In acknowledgment of that reality, let me be clear as to my purpose in confronting this lie. It is not my intention or belief that the argument should cease. The argument—that is, the thoughtful debate over the scriptures and wrestling with the text—is a good and necessary part of our faith whether we identify as Jewish, Christian, Muslim, or none of the above. If anything, the conversation about the Bible should continue to expand—exploring different ideas and hearing from different voices.

It is also necessary to state, without reservation, that it is not my desire to bring low the Bible. Quite to the contrary, I believe that we should pore over the Bible and pour our lives into its story. The collected texts that comprise the Bible convey transformative truths that are applicable to every human life. What actually decreases the power and relevance of the Bible is when we insist it is only one thing—the literal dictates of God. Nevertheless, the point of this chapter will not be to offer the one "correct" view of the Bible and how it should be understood. In truth, I don't accept that there is one right way to understand the Bible. Rather, the point of exposing this lie is to remove the limitations we have placed on the Bible by declaring it to be only the literal word of God. If it were only the literal word of God, there would only be one way to understand it—literally.

My final disclaimer before we begin is to point out that this chapter will represent a 50,000-foot view of the ongoing conversation about the Bible. Were we to really delve into this topic in detail, it would consume this book and many more volumes. The good news is that there are loads of resources on this topic available to us all. There are many thoughtful scholars today, such as N.T. Wright, Ellen Davis, and Peter Enns, writing much more extensively on what the Bible is than I will accomplish in this chapter.

In spite of the summary nature of this chapter, I remember what it was like to have the curtain pulled back on the Bible. I realize that the peeling back of layers and seeming dissection of the Bible can cause anxiety and confusion. Accordingly, I invite you to hold on to these truths and trust that they will remain intact throughout our exploration.

1. The Bible is a gift of God through which God speaks to us.
2. The Bible is full of truth and informs our lives.
3. The Bible is of central importance to our faith.

It is my hope that these truths will provide comfort and peace for our journey. I hope that you will trust that it is not my intention to denigrate the Bible in any way. My hope is that we will loosen our grasp on the Bible and thereby allow it to flourish in our lives and in our world. I have learned the hard way that a tight grip on the Bible—seeing it only as the literal dictates of God—is actually a primary source of its denigration.

Quare Lateres?

One of my first jobs after my wife, Stacy, and I were married was working for my brother-in-law in the home-building business. When I went to work for my brother-in-law, my thought was that we would spend a lot of time wearing ties, sitting in a nice office, looking at blueprints—like Mr. Brady on *The Brady Bunch*.

I was so wrong.

My brother-in-law had just started out on his own as a custom homebuilder, and I was his first employee. I quickly learned that meant we were going to be doing a lot of the work ourselves—no office, no blueprints, no ties. We were hands-on. And when I say "we," I mean my brother-in-law—he was the skilled one; I was a construction idiot. My job consisted of loading tools, unloading tools, sweeping, cleaning, asking questions, and apologizing for whatever I messed up that day.

One day early in my tenure, my brother-in-law put me with the painters on a remodeling project he had been working. My assignment was to help the painters prepare the interior of the home for painting. That meant we were to move the homeowners' possessions and furniture out of harm's way and tape things off with plastic. I soon found myself in the living room of the home with one of the painters, trying to empty a closet of its contents so that the interior of the closet could be sprayed with paint. The closet was packed full of stuff and—like most closets—had a top shelf where long-forgotten things had been stacked for years.

I am a tall guy. I was able to reach the top shelf and take things down without any problem. The painter I was assisting was much shorter but was not going to be outworked by the construction idiot. As we emptied the closet and only the items on the top shelf remained, he would stand on his tiptoes or jump and reach until he could barely nudge something off the shelf so it would fall and he could catch it. We took a few turns like this. I would reach in and grab something off the top shelf. While I was storing that item safely away from the painting area, he would tiptoe, stretch, and jump to knock something off the top shelf and then catch it as it fell. That was his way of getting things down, and I was not going to question him.

After a few turns, I turned around to see him jumping to nudge a stack of items—trying to get them to fall into his arms. As they fell, the item on the top of the stack caught my eye right before it caught him in the head. I recognized it as a doorstop. At this point, you may be thinking, *What the heck is a doorstop?* Quite simply, it is a heavy object that people place in front of doors to keep them open. In this particular home, the doorstop was a brick that had been swaddled in a needlepoint cozy. It didn't look like a brick. It looked like a little rectangular pillow.

As it fell, I reached for it and exclaimed, "Watch out!" but it was too late. The cozied-brick tagged him right in the forehead and down he went—along with the stack of stuff he was trying catch. Since I know the painter is okay at the end of this story, I can tell you now it was hilarious. Seriously, you could not script a better pratfall. Dick Van Dyke, John Ritter, Will Ferrell, eat your hearts out—this guy dropped like a comedic champ.

Trying not to laugh, I asked, "Are you okay?" I began to pull off the items that had fallen on him as he rolled around, expressing his genuine surprise and displeasure. As I reached for the doorstop, he grabbed it away from me.

With his head in one hand and the brick in the other, he looked up at me, raised the brick and said, "What is this?!"

Realizing that if I told him it was a doorstop it might not compute, I said, "It's a brick."

His eyes widened in surprise. "A brick!?"

I was trying so hard not to laugh that I froze. As if he didn't believe me and thought it was some kind of cruel joke, he said it again, "A brick!?"

Then came the philosophical question that will haunt me the rest of my days. He looked at me with sincere bewilderment and shouted, "Why a brick?!"

Why a brick? His question contained all of his confusion, anger, and pain. Why would someone craft a needlepoint cozy for a brick? Why would they store that camouflaged brick on the top shelf of a closet? What the heck is the matter with you people? My painting counterpart could not understand at all. He had never seen such a pretty doorstop and never imagined that a brick would be waiting for him at the top of that closet. I tried my best to explain the concept of a brick for a doorstop and why people would put it in a cozy to make the brick pretty and keep it from scratching up the floors, but to my newly-concussed friend, I may as well have been speaking a foreign language. He didn't get it at all. His lifetime experience—his culture and context—had not yet introduced him to a needlepoint-covered brick. To him, it was a completely foreign concept. Why a brick? Indeed.

Is the Bible a Brick?

I cannot imagine a better metaphor to describe our relationship with the Bible. Many of us understand the culture and context of the Bible about as well as the painter understood why someone would wrap a brick in needlepoint.

For much of my life, I kept my Bible safely stored on the top shelf of the closet—out of sight, out of use, out of mind. And in the rare occasion that I would get it down, I couldn't understand most of it. There have been countless times when I have stretched and jumped in order to grasp the Bible, only to have it thump me in the forehead and leave me wondering, "Why a brick?"

Has that ever happened to you? Have you ever felt confident that you had the Bible under control—that you understood what was going on—only to end up confused, hurt, and unable to defend or apply the Bible to your situation? My guess is that everyone who has ever opened a Bible can identify with such an experience. In fact, I believe that most of us identify with the biblical "brick to the head" so much that we cope with the pain in one of two ways—either by leaving the Bible on the shelf, where it is irrelevant, or by attempting to take the Bible literally.

Some of us leave the brick up on the shelf because we believe it to be inconsistent, inapplicable, and useless. Much like the homeowners had decided long ago that the actual brick doorstop was no longer needed, we store the Bible and forget about it. We just don't need it. Coming to such a conclusion may have even involved using a ladder to get the brick down. We dismantle it—remove the needlepoint cozy and prove that it is just a brick. We dismiss the notion that it could be anything else—it's a brick, nothing more, nothing less. It's not needed. It's irrelevant.

Some of us leave the brick up on the shelf because we believe it to be beyond us. It is "Holy" after all, right? It is not to be questioned. It is—dare I say it?—infallible. It is to be accepted as the truth, and that's it. Perhaps we have tried to understand it, but it didn't go well. Now we see it sitting up on the shelf. Remember the last time we reached for it? Ouch. We remember the headache and decide to just leave it up high on the shelf. We "take it on faith" and assume that even though we don't under-stand it, that must be the way it is supposed to be.

Whether we find ourselves leaving the Bible on a high shelf out of faith and reverence or because we find it irrelevant and useless, neither response is helpful. There have certainly been times when I was most comfortable leaving the Bible up on its shelf. I didn't want to wrestle with it. Seeing contradictions within the Bible or ideas with which I did not agree made me uncomfortable. It made me feel as though my faith was weak. If I were a true believer, I wouldn't have to ask questions, and I wouldn't have doubts, right? So in those moments, I would hide my questions and doubts behind the idea that the Bible was the literal word of God. It is not to be analyzed. It is not to be contextualized. It just is, and that's it.

There have also been times in my journey when something in the Bible bothered me so much that I couldn't help but tear it apart and ultimately dismiss it as useless. We can all identify with dismissing parts of the Bible, right? Think about how much you enjoy bacon (Deut. 14:8)...or a cheeseburger (Deut. 14:21) ...or heaven forbid, a bacon-cheeseburger.[2] Do you really care if someone plants two different kinds of seed in their field (Deut. 22:9)? How many Christians have tried to cope with the Bible by assuming that the troublesome bits are only in the Hebrew scriptures—what most people call the "Old Testament"—and end up dismissing three-quarters of the story? In the "New Testament," Jesus teaches that to look on another person with lust in our heart is adultery (Matt. 5:27–30). Yikes! Five chapters into the "New Testament," I get slammed with the understanding that I have committed adultery simply because of my thoughts? It would seem that the troublesome bits of the Bible are not constricted to the "Old Testament."

Have you ever heard of the Jefferson Bible? Thomas Jefferson, the principal author of the Declaration of Independence and the third president of the United States, created his own version of the Bible. Following his time in office, one of the things Jefferson did was use a razor to cut out the parts of the Bible he thought relevant and paste them into another

---

[2] Seriously, you just sunk your teeth into a delicious double whammy by eating bacon and beef with cheese. You must pray. Right now. By the way, if you haven't noticed yet, not all footnotes are scholarly and boring.

book he titled, *The Life and Morals of Jesus of Nazareth*.[3] Jefferson precisely removed the miracles of Jesus and anything deemed supernatural in order to create a concise collection of the teachings of Jesus. Before we all judge President Jefferson too harshly, let's take a look in the mirror. We do this. We omit the parts of the Bible that trouble us and cling to the parts that encourage us. The only difference between Jefferson and us is that we have neither the time, the patience, nor the discipline to sit down and actually make our own Bible. But the truth is that those of us who engage the Bible in any way have our self-published internal versions— they exist in our heads and our hearts. For some of us, these versions of our favorite parts that omit the troublesome bits exist high on a shelf in the closet. For others, we interact with them daily and use them to frame our lives.

Fight, Flight, or Freeze

As I matured (read: got old), I realized that I would respond to the problematic questions of the Bible in one of three ways. Sometimes I would fight. I would declare that the Bible is the literal word of God and it is not to be trifled with. I would say things like "I take my Bible straight" or "The Bible says it. I believe it—that's it." Sometimes I would flee. I would recognize the contradictions and discomfort that the stories and the teachings of the Bible contained and distance myself from them—saying things like, "These are just the primitive stories of a primitive people," or "Jesus makes the Old Testament irrelevant." And sometimes I would freeze. I would find myself unsure of what was right or what I thought. In such cases, I was a Bible chameleon. If people who "took their Bible straight" surrounded me, I would try to blend in with them. If I found myself with people who dismantled and dismissed the Bible, I would mimic them. Either way, just like a kid in front of T-Rex at Jurassic Park, I was hoping

---

[3] Thomas Jefferson, *The Jefferson Bible: The Life and Morals of Jesus of Nazareth Extracted Textually from the Gospels in Greek, Latin, French and English* (Washington D.C.: Smithsonian Books, 2011).

that if I just held still, no one would notice me and recognize that I had no idea what to think.

When the Bible is a cozy-covered brick for which we have no cultural or contextual understanding, each of these three responses—fight, flight, or freeze—makes perfect sense. There are issues and ideas represented in the Bible with which we passionately identify. In such cases, we find it advantageous—if not easy—to **fight** and treat the Bible as the literal word of God. We rail against abortion or capital punishment, declaring the biblical principle of life and quote, "Vengeance is Mine, I will repay, says the LORD" (Rom. 12:19).[4] During such times, we leave the Bible high upon its shelf in the closet—where it can be detached, literal, and without nuance. It's easier to make our arguments that way.

There are also occasions where we think what the Bible says doesn't apply to our life, our situation, or our time, and we therefore dismiss it as irrelevant or inapplicable. In such times, we disassemble the Bible—like Jefferson—and say, "This part of the Bible doesn't matter to me." I am beyond whatever it is trying to convey. During such instances, we have an amazing ability to **flee** and perform whatever mental gymnastics are needed to allow us to feel good about sidestepping troublesome scriptures. "This may look like something else, but it's not. It's just a brick. Simply step around and keep moving."

Then, there are those times when we just don't have the foggiest idea what to think about the Bible. Even if we find ourselves surrounded by people who are certain they understand "the biblical perspective" on a particular issue, we just **freeze** and try to blend in—to remain unseen and unnoticed. We leave our Bibles high on a shelf because we're unsure, and we hope that people don't notice that our Bible is tucked away in the closet.

---

4   Unless otherwise specified, the Scripture quotations contained herein are from *The New Revised Standard Version Bible*, copyright © 1989 by the Division of Christian Education of the National Council of the Churches of Christ in the U.S.A. Used by permission. All Rights Reserved.

   While we are on the subject of Scripture quotations, how about that first biblical quote? Seriously, you are thirty or so pages into this book and the first time the Scripture is quoted it's "Vengeance is Mine… says the Lord." My, my, my—that is a strong opening!

Fight, flight, or freeze—three sides of the same coin—each revealing that the Bible befuddles us. Perhaps the largest problem of fight, flight, and freeze is that none of those responses work all the time. There are things in the Bible that even the most devout "fighter" has trouble reconciling as literalism. Similarly, there are truths in the Bible from which we can never escape—they just keep coming back—those parts that you just have to deal with. Ironically, the response of freezing might be the most exhausting option we choose. Dodging and blending in—hoping that no one will notice us—takes a great deal of energy. In all three instances, we are like my friend, the short painter—lacking the context, culture, and exposure to understand "why a brick?"

So if we agree that none of the three responses work all the time, we must ask ourselves, "Is there a fourth option?" What is the healthy response to the Bible?

In a word, dialogue.

The Bible is a developing story—a continuing conversation between God and the people of God. If you are looking for a simple rule as to how we should respond to the Bible, the rule is we should respond with conversation—and as I am sure you have already deduced, conversation cannot happen alone—at least not healthy conversation. If we find ourselves taking a stance on the Bible that terminates relationship or ends our conversation with each other or with God, we can be certain we have lost our way. It doesn't really matter if we lost our way by fighting for the acceptance of the Bible as literal, fleeing from the Bible as irrelevant, or freezing in uncertainty—each of those responses leads us away from God, other people, and therefore, away from truth. Hang on to that idea … we will come back to it in a moment. First, a few basic concepts of freedom for those of us trapped in one or more of the fight, flight, or freeze camps.

For the Times We *Fight* for Literalism

Coming out from under the lie of biblical literalism involves asking the question, "Is there such a thing as truth that is not literal?" When we say that the Bible can only be the literal word of God, we are placing our context and culture on top of its writings and assuming that it can only be understood through such a lens. To modern Western thinkers—like you and me—literal truth is important. Our government, our courts, our schools all value literal truth. We trust in those things that can be proven as fact. We like dates, measurements, precise times and GPS accuracy. We rest in knowing the exact details of an event that happened at a certain time in a specific location. We find comfort in dividing and organizing our world into exact categories: right and wrong, friends and enemies, healthy and unhealthy, normal and abnormal.

Such an approach looks at the stories of creation (that is not a typo—there are two creation stories in Genesis) and requires that we believe the LORD created the universe in six 24-hour days. Literalism requires a faith that traces the ages of the characters in the biblical stories against historical events in order to arrive at a conclusion that the Genesis creation story took place 6,000 years ago and, therefore, the earth is only 6,000 years old. Literalism contends that the truth of Noah's story lies in the fact that Noah literally put at least a pair of every animal in creation on a boat while God flooded the entire world—killing everyone except Noah and his family. People assume that the serpent that tempts Adam and Eve to eat the forbidden fruit in the garden is *satan*. However, that is not what the text says. The tellers and writers of that story told and wrote it for thousands of years with a talking snake. Not some evil, demonic counterpart to God—but a talking snake.

Are you uncomfortable with literalism yet? Do any of these ideas push your faith to an uncomfortable place where you feel you must turn off your intellect in favor of just believing? Friends, the Bible is not Santa Claus. We don't believe it into being real. In fact, I have found that my blind belief—that is, the suspension of my intellect—actually makes the Bible less real and more distant.

Nevertheless, I accept that there are people who have no problem with a talking snake, a 6,000-year-old universe, and a boat that holds every possible animal. I also accept that we are all capable of cognitive dissonance—making sense out of things that seem to be nonsense. In fact, over the last 400 years, biblical literalists have become very good at tying up what they perceive to be the loose ends of the Bible. In spite of our ability to force the Bible to fit into our literalism, let us consider a few **literal** facts about the Bible.

1. The Bible is not one book. It is a collection of books.

The word *Bible* literally means library. This work is a library of books created over thousands of years by people from different tribes who lived in varying places. It is a library that contains stories, genealogies, prophecies, poetry, laments, songs, symbols, and letters between friends and to entire communities. The contents of this library were written, copied, selected, compiled, and preserved by human beings according to a common divine thread—that of God's repeated intercession into human history toward a loving, inclusive, communal relationship between God and the people of God. In the case of Hebrew texts like Job, Exodus, and Genesis, the stories they contain were told and repeated for generations long before they were ever written down. Every step of the way—the text that we call the Bible—involved people. People told the stories. People wrote down the stories. People decided which stories would be preserved and canonized—meaning those books that would be considered Scripture and those that would not. This does not mean that God was not involved in the creation of what we call the Bible—quite to the contrary. God was at the center of it all. God was the reason the stories were being told. Don't miss that. God was **the** reason. God is the central character. It was because of God's interaction and relationship with people that they had stories to tell, to write down, and eventually to canonize. There is no question that without God doing all the things that God did, there would be no Bible.

The inescapable truth, however, is that there would also be no Bible were it not for people. Think about that for a moment. Without people, God would not have needed to do the things the Bible records. Without people, there would be no one to appreciate creation, no one for God to pursue and rescue, no one to tell the stories of what God had done, and certainly no one to write it all down and preserve it as Scripture.

While it may seem problematic to biblical literalism for people to be so important in the creation of the Bible, it is nonetheless brilliantly divine. This is totally the way of God. God desires relationship with us. God meets us where we are and invites us into the story. It makes perfect sense that God would invite people to tell the story. It makes sense that some of the words within the Bible will be considered "God's words"— meaning those words that people discerned God as actually having communicated to them in one way or another. It also makes sense that some of the words of the Bible will be the words of people—not God—but the people. Does that make them less relevant or true? The people who chose to write them down and preserve them clearly didn't think so.

> Already at the opening of the Torah, at the very beginning of creation,
> is foreshadowed the Jewish doctrine of revelation: that God reveals
> Himself to humanity not in the sun, the stars, the wind or the storm
> but in and through words—sacred words that make us co-partners with
> God in the work of redemption.[5]

I realize that this could be an abrupt summation to a truth that deserves reflection and time, so don't feel compelled to press on if you are not ready. Take some time to listen, pray, and think about what it means for God to have partnered with people in the creation of the biblical texts. Are you comfortable with the words of the Bible being the words of people? Talk with your friends, family, rabbis—ask questions— and remember that dialogue is the point.

2. There are no original transcripts of the biblical texts.

Here is a truth that the literalist in all of us can't escape: every Bible verse we have ever read or heard has been an interpretation—every single

---

[5]   Sacks, *Covenant & Conversation*, 25.

one. Not once in my life have I heard or read the original text—nor have you. By definition, the words of the Bible simply cannot be the literal words of God because we do not have any original, signed copies. Every transcript we have found and used to create the different translations of the Bible is a reproduction. No biblical scholar or translator is working from an original. Even if they were, we have to remember that the stories of the Hebrew scriptures were initially preserved orally—that is, the stories were told out loud and handed down from generation to generation. The idea that there is one correct transcript somewhere that represents the true words of God is simply false.

The whole history of the Bible is one of interpretation. Those who first wrote down the stories their mothers and fathers told made interpretative choices about what they wrote down and how they wrote it. The Hebraic rabbis and leaders who canonized the Hebrew scriptures made interpretative choices about which texts to include and which texts to exclude. The writers of the four Gospels made different interpretative choices about how to tell the story of Jesus—which is why we don't have four identical accounts of Jesus' life, death, and resurrection. Paul, Peter, James, and John made interpretative choices in their letters based upon the people and circumstances to which they were writing. Christians have yet to agree upon which books should be included in the Bible, historically making interpretative choices of inclusion or exclusion.

The interpretation doesn't stop with the closing of the biblical canon, however. The stories of the Bible needed to leave the confines of the ancient languages in order to reach the ends of the earth. While there are no original copies of any of the biblical texts, there are very old copies in Hebrew and Greek—and even a few portions in Aramaic. Early in the history of the Christian faith, those texts were translated into Latin. Every modern translation of the Bible—no matter what language—can be traced back to one of these early Hebrew, Greek, Aramaic, or Latin texts. In spite of this common and ancient origin, there remains this inescapable truth: every time the stories of the Bible were told, retold, written, rewritten, or translated, interpretative choices were made.

You may be thinking, *Big deal. So what if interpretative choices were made? The gist is still the same.* Really? What if I told you that the Hebraic pronouns that refer to God in the oldest Hebraic texts were not meant to assign gender in a literal sense? Does it impact how we view God if every divine pronoun is translated in the masculine "He" and "His"? Do we start to understand God to be a man—or at least masculine? The ancient Hebraic language of our oldest biblical texts did not seek to ascribe an actual gender to God in such pronouns. In much the same way that "the door" is referred to in Spanish as "la puerta," ancient Hebraic pronouns were not asserting that God was actually male any more than Spanish asserts that a door is actually female. Certainly there are texts in the Bible that refer to the masculine attributes of God, but there are also those that refer to the feminine attributes—all of them interpretative choices being made by the writers to communicate a greater truth about God than that of gender.

Consider these descriptions of God—one masculine, one feminine:

> The Lord is my strength and my might,
>   and he has become my salvation;
> this is my God, and I will praise him,
>   my father's God, and I will exalt him.
> The Lord is a warrior;
>
> (Exod. 15:2–3)

> You were unmindful of the Rock that bore you;
>   you forgot the God who gave you birth.
>
> (Deut. 32:18)

Is the point of these descriptions to convey that God is literally male or literally female? The reality is they can't possibly be literal—otherwise, one of them would be wrong. Instead, they represent deeper truths regarding the Lord's ability and eagerness to defend people as a warrior and God as the life-giver and birthplace of all humanity.

How about a "New Testament" example of interpretative choice? What do you know about the tax-collector Zacchaeus? You know he was short, right? As the Sunday School hymns and Vacation Bible School sing-alongs come rushing back, you remember, "Zacchaeus was a wee little man, a wee little man was he." But was he really wee?[6] The oldest Greek manuscripts of the story of Zacchaeus in Luke's Gospel don't indicate who it was that was short. The way the Greek writes out the sentence of Luke 19:3, an interpretative choice must be made. Was it Zacchaeus who was "short in stature" and therefore had to climb a tree to see Jesus, or was it Jesus who was "short in stature" and therefore could not be seen when surrounded by the crowds unless Zacchaeus climbed a tree to look over the crowds?

Whether we realize it or not, when we picked up our first Bible, we were picking up a library that contained hundreds, if not thousands, of interpretative decisions made for us by someone else. By definition, it is impossible for us to "take our Bible straight" because we have never been offered or had access to a "straight" uninterpreted Bible.

To even further wear you out with this point, as soon as we began to read the Bible, we cannot help but make our own interpretive choices. We decide what parts of the stories resonate with us and why. We interpret the events represented. We are part of the process. Is all this interpretation a coincidence? Is the fact that there is not one definitive, original transcript of any Biblical text simply a result of God's absentmindedness? I don't think so.

The continual involvement of human beings in translating and interpreting the Bible again points to our divine partnership. None of our interpretive efforts, however, exclude God from the process or devalue the truth of the biblical stories. God can be and, I believe, has always been part of the interpretative process. In fact, I believe that God loves interpretation—as any artist or creator of things would. I believe that God desires that the stories of divine love and intercession into human

---

6   Although short—pun intended—that was an incredibly fun sentence to write.

history be told and received in different ways. Interpretation only limits the power of the Bible if we believe that the Bible is limited to literal truth and therefore above interpretation.

3. The Bible is a 94 percent–98 percent Jewish library.

Okay, I am being a little cheeky here with the math, but the gist is that at least 62 of the 66 books Christians call the Bible were written by Jewish people and therefore should be wrestled with in a Jewish context. Scholarship seems to indicate that the book of Job was written before the establishment of the tribe of Israel and is therefore not technically Jewish. Similarly, the book of Ruth—if it was written by Ruth herself (unlikely)—would not be technically Jewish as she was not born a Jew. Lastly, the books of Luke and Acts—although most likely originally one continuous work—were written by a Gentile. At worst, that is 62 out of 66 books or 94 percent. I find that estimation to be low. I would argue that Job was a story told by and eventually written down by the people who became the Jews, and they are certainly the ones who preserved it. Likewise, that Ruth— while not initially featuring a Jewish-born character at its center—was most likely written by a Jew and is definitely a Jewish story. Add to that the notion that Luke-Acts is actually one book, and you arrive at 64 of the 65 books of the Bible being written by Jewish people—or 98 percent. Have I beaten this point to a pulp?[7]

We simply cannot grasp the truths of the Bible without looking through the lens of Judaism. Throughout this book, we will explore the inexorable tie between Judaism and Christianity. For now, we just need

---

[7]   If your answer was no, consider this: If we add the Deuterocanonical books—which were most certainly Hebraic—to our count of books in the Bible, the percentage Jewishness of the Bible goes to 99 percent. In the immortal words of Nigel Tufnel, the Jewishness of the Bible "goes to 11."

[7.1] Far be it from me to have a footnote for my footnote, but where else are you going to find a scholarly argument for the Hebraic nature of the Bible using a quote from *This is Spinal Tap*?

Christopher Guest, Michael McKean, Rob Reiner and Harry Shearer, *This is Spinal Tap*, DVD, Directed by Rob Reiner (Beverly Hills, CA: MGM Home Entertainment, 2004).

to focus on the impact this truth has on how we read and understand the Bible. We cannot understand the Bible without understanding the context of the Jewish people, places, culture, and context from which it came. To ascribe any other context—let alone that of our modern, Western context—will invariably leave us confused and disoriented. By the by, "Western" in this sense refers to the fact that most of us English speakers have been influenced and shaped by the western or Greek school of thought (Hellenism) versus Eastern philosophies. Judaism—and the writings of the Bible—occur in an Eastern context. What is the difference? I am glad you asked. Here are just a few of the more obvious differences:

- Our Western approach makes a distinction between the secular world and the spiritual world. The Hebraic understanding is that nothing is secular—everything is spiritual. Do we live our lives as though every situation is a spiritual situation? As though every detail is spiritual? As if every person whose life intersects ours is a spiritual being?
- Our Western approach values individualism and leads to a me-centered outlook while the Hebraic philosophy values community and leads to a tribe- or family-centered outlook. This is where all the Trekkies can apply the wisdom of Spock, "The needs of the many outweigh the needs of the one."[8]
- We Westerners view time as points on a straight line, subdivided into neat periods or segments of history—think timelines (you know you love them.) Our timelines are neat, orderly, and reflect when we have done something important or something important has happened to us. Hebraic thought perceives time as cyclical and organized by what God has done. This is much

---

[8] Harve Bennett, Gene Roddenberry, and Jack B. Sowards, *Star Trek II: The Wrath of Khan*, DVD, Directed by Nicholas Meyer (Hollywood, CA: Paramount Home Video, 1982).

Although that quote was originally spoken by Mr. Spock in *The Wrath of Khan*, it was remixed in the 2013 release of *Star Trek Into Darkness* because a quote that good has to be in the reboot—or perhaps because "there is nothing new under the sun" (Ec 1:9).

more messy and stressful to Westerners. Furthermore, it reflects what God has done for us—not what we have done.

- Western thought is based on words. Hebraic thought is based on images. "A picture is worth a thousand words." So goes the saying attributed to newspaper editor Frank Barnard—ironic that Barnard (a Westerner) made this point about the tangible power of imagery with words.

- Western thought is based on precise categories, cause and effect, linear equations like A + B = C. Hebraic thought is much more messy and blurred—based on contextual and relational logic. Everything is related and connected.

- Western thought holds that the worth of people is determined by their material possessions and power. Accordingly competition is good, and one's power over another is determined through business, politics, and organizations. In Hebraic thought, the worth of people is determined by their familial relationships. Material goods are a measure of God's blessing to be shared with one's community. One's power or status in the social structure is determined and ordained by God.

- Western thought sees faith as a blind leap, while Hebraic thought sees faith as knowledge-based and informed by one's experience. We hear this in our own vernacular, right? The way we discuss our faith makes it seem as though, at some point, faith didn't make sense and we had to take a blind leap forward anyway— that somehow the willingness to step out over the chasm is the measure of true faith. As admirable as we Westerners may find such "faith," the Hebraic understanding is much more integrated. Faith simply *is* to a Hebrew. God has been, is now, and always will be ... it is just accepted. There is no blind leap because faith informs the entirety of existence. Sure, one might not be able to see the path before her, but taking the next step—whether it results in success or failure—is not a blind leap. God informs and frames success and failure—not just success.

- We Westerners view money, power, success, and victory as blessings in and of themselves. Hebraic understanding holds that none of the above is a blessing until it is shared with others—given away for the benefit of the community. As Robert Webber wrote, "True joy is born of two encounters: with the fruits of the earth and with our brothers and sisters. Where one of these two is missing, (the fruits) change from being an end to being a means; ceasing to be an expression of life and becoming a means of obtaining satisfaction."[9] The ancient Israelite understood that they could not properly receive and enjoy the gifts of God without using them to serve and love others.

- Western thought holds that history should record facts objectively and chronologically. Hebraic thought sees history as an attempt to preserve significant truths in meaningful ways regardless of objective facts. This is especially important for us to remember as Westerners when we treat the Bible as though it is a history textbook. The Bible is not a history textbook. When we treat it as such, we end up confounded, confused, or corrupted.

- Eastern or Hebraic thinking holds that the truth continues to develop as God leads one into deeper understanding. The Western mind believes that the truth is static and unchanging.

This book that we call the Bible—the collection of works to which so many of us claim to build our lives upon—has a context. To be honest, it has many contexts—and why wouldn't it? Can you think of any other "book" that contains writings from people who are distanced by thousands of years, thousands of miles, different cultures, and different languages? Each story of the Bible has, at the very least, contexts of time, location, culture, and circumstance. In many cases, archeologists and

---

9   Robert Webber, ed. *The Complete Library of Christian Worship, Volume I, The Biblical Foundations of Christian Worship*, 1st ed. (Nashville, Tenn.: Star Song Pub. Group, 1993), 182.

scholars have been able to piece together much of the ancient context for us to study and understand today. In some cases, the context remains cloudy. Even when all the contextual details cannot be grasped, we are better off approaching the text as a Hebrew would. The Bible is a collection of Hebraic works. When we examine it and attempt to understand it with our Western mindset, we not only make interpretative choices but we also make poor interpretive choices.

For the Times We *Flee* from Irrelevance

In spite of the fact that we all join Thomas Jefferson in creating our own version of the Bible, we must address the question of why those things we deem irrelevant to our lives are preserved in the biblical text. Is it simply tradition? Have we simply passed down and preserved truths that were meant for a specific people in a specific time—or is there more to it than that?

I must confess that I do not believe that every truth in the Bible can be applied directly to my life and my circumstances. I perceive the Bible as containing truths that are timeless and truths that are time-bound. What that means is there are those stories and teachings in the Scripture that convey truths belonging to and instructive to all of us throughout history regardless of when or where we live. The simplest examples of timeless truths with which most of us are familiar are the *Instructions*—although most of us call them the Commandments (Exod. 20:1-17). Do not murder, do not commit adultery, do not take what is not yours, do not covet what your neighbor has—these are timeless ideas that are good for all of humanity regardless of time and space. Perhaps a better example is the *Shema* (Deut. 6:4–9)—which is arguably the basis for the *Commandments* and is certainly Jesus' response to the question of which commandment is the most important.

> Jesus answered, "The first is, 'Hear, O Israel: the LORD our God, the LORD is one; you shall love the LORD your God with all your

heart, and with all your soul, and with all your mind, and with all your strength.' The second is this, 'You shall love your neighbor as yourself.' There is no other commandment greater than these."

(MARK 12:28–31)

Can we all agree that regardless of our location on the timeline and on the planet, the ideas of loving God and loving our neighbor are good ideas? The truth, relevance, and application of these instructions are not decreased by the passage of time nor lessened by the distance of geography or culture. These are timeless truths.

I also think the Bible contains some time-bound truths. Such truths were true for a specific time, space, and culture but may not hold true in my time, space, and culture. Can you think of anything the Bible says that you think is out of place in your space and time? How about pigs? Do you eat bacon—or sausage—or a meat-lover's pizza with pepperoni, bacon, ham and sausage? What about football? Do you enjoy tossing the old pigskin around—or are you a fantasy footballer? Leviticus 11:7–8 instructs the people of God not to eat of the flesh of the pig or touch the carcass of a pig lest they become unclean. Certainly, those of us who eat pork or enjoy football do a little Jeffersonian trimming of the Bible when it comes to this verse. Maybe shellfish are your thing, and you can be found passed out in a booth at Red Lobster during Shrimp-Fest. Sorry, Leviticus 11:9–12 rules shrimp as out of bounds. Bacon, football, lobster, shrimp ... these rules that form the basis of kosher law are only the beginning. Leviticus is full of instructions that most of us have no trouble dismissing as irrelevant.

What if rather than being irrelevant, such instructions were the time-bound or culturally-bound principles of a people trying to live for God and each other? What if these instructions were not irrelevant? People made choices to record and preserve these instructions for thousands of years. The words of Leviticus 11 were formative in their faith—their relationship with God and with each other. When we find ourselves confronted by a biblical text that seems irrelevant, we have a choice—discard it and move on, or wrestle with it. You know what I am going to say, don't you? We have to wrestle!

When we wrestle with a text that seems time-bound, taking the Bible literally just doesn't work. We have to ask different questions. To start, why was this written down? Why was this important? In the case of the injunctions against touching pigs and eating shellfish, how would that have helped the people who first received it? What does this particular Scripture tell us about who God is and who the people of God are called to be?

Leviticus is a text that reveals a God who is different from all the other gods represented in that time and place. When we look at Leviticus in context, we remember that God had delivered the Hebrews from Egypt. These people had been slaves and servants for 400 years. They understood how to be slaves. They had absorbed Egyptian culture and knew how to serve Pharaoh as taskmaster. They did not know how to be a nation. They had no idea how to be in relationship with a God who loved them and was calling them to be something different. God gives them steps—little steps—that are going to help them practice becoming a different people—steps that will set them apart and make them unlike those around them. Steps that will teach them to trust that, unlike Pharaoh, God loves them—and will protect and provide for them.

Let me ask you to consider another possibility. Think of a game or sport that you have played. If possible, consider a game or sport with a lot of rules or regulations, like chess or basketball. Do you remember the first time you tried it? Did it only take one explanation of the rules for you to completely grasp it? Or did you experience what is called progressive apprehension? Progressive apprehension simply means that as we progress, we apprehend or understand more and more. For example, I remember when my father was teaching me to play chess. There were so many rules. Each piece on the board moved in a different way and could only move in its specific way. Although my dad carefully walked me through all the rules, what stood out to me was the fact that the knights were on horses and that they moved in an "L" shape. Accordingly, my first few attempts at chess were all about the knights. I would move my knights around the board one L at a time until they were captured. That was the regulation that I could wrap my mind around. When awash in the "new" ideas and concepts of chess, I grabbed a hold of one idea that I understood and rode it into the ground. Overtime, I progressed. I was able to absorb more and more of the game and see the different pieces working together in harmony. Strategies began to emerge. There were complex offenses and defenses, gambits and techniques. Eventually, I could see more than just rules and regulations. I could see the artistry and beauty of the game. Chess may not be your game—but I am hopeful that however you apply this metaphor, you begin to consider progressive apprehension.

Every human being who has ever lived experiences progressive apprehension. We are all in the midst of progressive apprehension every day in numerous ways. My wife can surely attest to my progressive apprehension of her needs and of our relationship during the course of our marriage. My children could talk at length about my development as a parent—especially my two boys who got me as a neophyte father with no experience at all. Our education, our relationships, our occupations, our faith—every aspect of our life—reflects our progressive apprehension. If that is the case, can we also allow it to apply to the writings of the Bible?

The people who told, wrote, and preserved the stories of the Bible also lived with progressive apprehension. They developed through time and experience just like we do. Is it really that much of a stretch to assume that their stories are also subject to progressive apprehension? Have you ever completely changed your mind based on something you experienced? What if you had written down a story about something you understood or learned ten years ago—would you still agree with your conclusions today? Might your understanding have changed somewhat throughout the last ten years?

There is no doubt that the people who wrote, selected, and preserved the teachings of Leviticus believed them and practiced them. The ancient Israelites did not eat pork—nor touch the dead carcass of a pig. The ancient Israelites did not eat shellfish. I also have no trouble believing that these injunctions made them different and distinguishable as a nation of people—unlike those around them. Perhaps abstaining from shellfish and pork was safer for them given the cleanliness and food preparation knowledge of the time and culture from which these writings came. Whatever the case may be, progressive apprehension allows me to see the seemingly odd instructions of Leviticus in the context of a people who are learning to become the people God has called them to be. These instructions represent their understanding at that time. When I try to bring them forward in literalism—detached from context and progression—they make little sense in my life, and I am forced either to dismiss them or to twist them and myself all up in an effort to make them make sense.

When I allow the time-bound truths of the Bible to come forward through progressive apprehension, unencumbered by the limits of biblical literalism, they can grow and develop—sometimes even within the Bible itself. Peter, the student and follower of Jesus, tried to live and practice the life of a good Jew. He followed the instructions of Leviticus and accepted them as true—no shellfish or pork for Peter. Then, in Acts 10, Peter has a dream.

> He saw the heaven opened and something like a large sheet coming down, being lowered to the ground by its four corners. In it were all kinds of four-footed creatures and reptiles and birds of the air. Then he heard a voice saying, "Get up, Peter; kill and eat." But Peter said, "By no means, LORD; for I have never eaten anything that is profane or unclean." The voice said to him again, a second time, "What God has made clean, you must not call profane."
>
> (ACTS 10:11–15)

This story in Acts 10 deals with much more than what is okay to eat. It deals with progressive apprehension. God gives Peter a vision, inviting him to grow and develop—to leave the literalism of the rules and grow into new understanding. God challenges Peter's literalism and asks,

"Will you trust that I am good and that I know what I am asking you to do?" Peter is changed—right within the biblical text. He progresses and understands on a deeper level because of what he has experienced. If we can allow for the biblical characters themselves to experience progressive apprehension and move beyond their initial understanding of scriptural instruction, why would we not extend ourselves the same grace and freedom?

What's the bottom line? None of it is irrelevant. If someone feels that Leviticus 11 is filled with specific timeless instruction about what is healthy to eat and what is not, then I say go for it—eat a kosher diet. If another feels that it is okay to touch and eat the flesh of a pig, I point to Peter's dream in Acts 10 where he is instructed to eat of animals that were not kosher and say go for it—enjoy that bacon cheeseburger. What we should agree upon is that none of it is irrelevant. Every piece of the story was remembered and written down for a reason. Each sentence helps to craft the progressing story of a loving God who rescues, delivers, shapes, provides for, and partners with his children.

For the Times We *Freeze* in Ignorance

Repeat after me, "*I don't know* is an acceptable answer and an opportunity to explore." So many times we find ourselves in situations where we cannot explain or justify some part of the Bible for which we are called to account. Sometimes, the questions we can't answer are our own—we are the ones criticizing, objecting, and pushing back on our own faith. Regardless of whether the questions and criticism come from within or from others, we tend to freeze in fear when we don't know. The fear is that if we can't explain or understand a part of the Bible, then maybe it's "wrong." And if part of it can be "wrong," then maybe the whole thing is at risk. Such situations can make our faith seem fragile and subject to withering under the slightest of scrutiny. Our solution? Avoid disagreement, avoid scrutiny, avoid confrontation, avoid discussing the parts of the Bible we don't understand and can't explain.

In my brief and ridiculous tenure as a salesman, I was taught that questions and objections are a sign of interest. Sure, this was basic sales training that was trying to get me to keep selling even when people wanted to shut me down, but there is a truth in there, nonetheless. If people are genuinely disinterested, they don't ask questions or argue—they just move on. Questions and pushback are the telltale signs of someone who is interested in wrestling... and what do we know about wrestling? The Bible is built for it! When we are confronted with aspects of the biblical texts for which we cannot account, we should not freeze. We should see it as an opportunity to explore, learn, grow—to progress our apprehension. We just need to pause, take a deep breath, and remember that the text is designed for wrestling. Get those disconcerting scriptures out in your community and examine them from all sides. Repeat after me, "*I don't know* is an acceptable answer and an opportunity to explore."

There's No Such Thing as "The Right Way"

The stories of the Bible were told, written, selected, and preserved by people. Every bit of the Bible we have ever read or heard is an interpretation. The Bible cannot be truly understood outside of its Hebraic context. Any one of these truths by itself upends the idea of biblical literalism. Yet perhaps the greatest argument against biblical literalism is that it ultimately asks us to believe in and decide upon one right way. Does your life show that to be true? In the midst of an infinitely diverse creation as perceived by infinitely diverse human experiences, do you believe there is only one right way to anything? Moreover, do you want to be responsible for deciding what the right way is? I sure don't. And to be honest, I don't want you to decide for me either.

I do want to add your understanding to my own. Rabbinical tradition teaches *Shiv'im Panim l'Torah*—"The Torah has seventy faces." Don't miss this truth: the Hebraic forbearers of our faith did not believe that there was one correct way to interpret Scripture. The very people to whom the biblical stories happened—the people who told the stories, wrote them down, preserved them, and passed them on to us—understood each Scripture to have seventy faces. Our Jewish brothers and sisters hold the scriptures like a diamond that presents a different image of light and beauty depending upon the angle at which it is viewed. Can you see how ridiculous it is that Christians take those Hebraic scriptures out of context and insist that there is one right way to understand them? Yet, that is exactly what we do. Even worse, sometimes we criticize those who do not ascribe to our "one right way" as having weak or no faith.

My experience thus far has taught me that holding on to something too tightly kills the thing. Those things that we hold most dear should be given freedom and room to grow and flourish. In the wise words of the clearly theological rock-and-roll song by 38-Special, "Hold on loosely but don't let go. If you cling too tightly, you're gonna lose control."[10] No one benefits if we believe in and pursue one way to understand, process, and wrestle with the Bible. Biblical literalism, by definition, "clings too tightly" and ends up constraining and killing the very stories that exist to inspire and encourage our relationships with each other, with freedom, and with God.

There are a number of statements that well-meaning believers have made in the history of the faith that deserve to be vaporized and never heard again. One of those follows the idea that it is a sin to question God—ergo, it is a sin to question "God's Word." You may have heard the same idea expressed slightly differently, but the gist is that we are not to question the Bible—that we are to follow blindly and without criticism or complaint. Friends, I cannot put this delicately—that idea is pure, concentrated GUANO.[11] The Bible exists for our questions. It is there for our criticism and our doubt.

---

[10] Don Barnes, Jeff Carlisi, and Jim Peterik, "Hold on Loosely," performed by 38 Special, *Wild-Eyed Southern Boys*, CD Track 1, A&M Records, 1980.

[11] First off, guano is a highly underutilized word—that is simply a fact—deal with it. Secondly, if you don't know what it is, stop what you are doing right now and get yourself to your local cavern tour. You won't regret the tour…although you may regret your time around guano.

Can you accept that? Can you let go of any shame that you have felt for criticizing, questioning, or doubting the scriptures? The scriptures exist to give us a place to bring our doubt—they are designed for criticism and questioning! Let me ask it to you this way: do you really want to give your heart, soul, and strength to a faith that is based on writings that don't stand up to criticism, questioning, and doubt? I sure don't. I want my biblical text to be able to withstand continual beatings. While those who would challenge us to not question and simply accept may be trying to do a good thing and strengthen our faith, the truth is such suggestions require us to surrender our brain. If you can forgive the football metaphor, to swallow the Bible without critical examination is to mentally punt the ball away. We humans are reflective. We are critical thinkers. We ask questions, expose inconsistencies, and search for truth. What kind of God would ask us to stop all that—to stop being human—when we approach the scriptures? Nevertheless, fear that our faith cannot withstand criticism and laziness from doing the work of exploration keeps us from examining it. We surrender the Bible to literalism and allow it to find a place on a shelf in the closet—a place of reverence, irrelevance, or somewhere in between.

Be at Peace

Is your head spinning yet? If you are starting to feel the frustration and exhaustion of culture shock, you should know that you are on the right track. This should be frustrating to us as Westerners; we should feel exhausted. We are learning a new language, which can be a humbling and daunting task. We are trying to use muscles that we have used very little or not at all. We are asking ourselves, "Will it all be worth it?" As we consider that question, we must remember that we are not called to figure it all out in one day. We are invited into progressive apprehension—a lifetime of relationships and experiences that grow and inform our understanding of who God is and who God calls us to be.

Reading through this chapter may have unsettled some things for you. It is possible that you find some of these ideas enlightening, exhausting, encouraging, or infuriating. Please remember that while we have explored, we have not strayed from our original center.

1. The Bible is a gift of God through which God speaks to us.
2. The Bible is full of truth and informs our lives.
3. The Bible is of central importance to our faith.

We have not upended our faith. We have not brought low the Bible. Instead, we have considered the possibility that there is more going on within the biblical texts than literalism. The Bible is not simply the literal dictates of God. The Bible is the collected progressive apprehension of God's people as they experienced God and each other. Nevertheless, the integral role that people have played and continue to play in writing, collecting, interpreting, and understanding the biblical narrative does not obscure or diminish the role of the divine. The Bible is still supernatural—it is still something more than a collection of books. In his insightful Tumblr exploration—that ultimately became an insightful book—entitled *What is the Bible?*, theologian, Rob Bell wrote:

> To believe that the Bible is both a library of books and also more than just a library of books takes faith. You have to believe that there's something else going on in these pages, something just below the surface, something that unites all those writers writing over all those years and then all those people making all of those decisions about which of the things those writers wrote belong in the particular arrangement of writings we call the Bible.[12]

I couldn't agree more with Bell. There is something just below the surface that unites all of the storytelling, writing, preserving, and interpretation. Consider that what lies beneath the surface is similar to the

[12] Rob Bell, *What is the Bible? Part 11: How We Got It*, robbell.com, accessed March 5, 2015, http://robbellcom.tumblr.com/post/67479672681/what-is-the-bible-part-11.

mass of an iceberg. Most of us are building our lives around the visible piece of the iceberg when we should get beneath the surface and behold the entirety of it all. What if, like an iceberg, 90 percent of the spirit and power of the Bible lies beneath the water—beneath that small "surface breaking" piece?

When we begin to take in the whole iceberg, we also begin to understand that the iceberg is not a random piece of ice adrift at sea. It is connected to a larger system that defines and shapes the entire environment. It helps align the world. If the icebergs melt, the climate will change and ultimately the earth's axis will change and life will be extinguished. Perhaps that is true of the Bible. Regardless of our interpretations of the small surface-breaking piece, more is going on. There is more beneath the surface—more for us to investigate and wrestle. And like the iceberg, the Bible is not a random book adrift in the abyss. It, too, is connected to a larger system—something Jesus called the Kingdom of God. To be sure, the Kingdom of God cannot be destroyed, but how we behold it and interact with it defines our reality, our existence—it, too, aligns our world.

Exposing the Bible to our questions and criticisms does not weaken it. Pursuing the context of the biblical stories does not demean them. Loosening the grasp of biblical literalism does not remove the power of the Scripture. On the contrary, these are the ways that we dive beneath the surface to behold more.

The Bible is not a history book ... but there is history within.
The Bible is not a rulebook ... but it does contain instructions for being free and fully alive.
The Bible is not simply the literal word of God ... but God has chosen to partner with people to tell the literal story of God's love.

Our engagement—literal or otherwise—of the stories of the Bible have built and shattered nations, imprisoned and released millions, brought death and given life. The purpose of this chapter is to deal honestly with the impact our understanding of the Bible can have. Do we position it in ways that end relationship and conversation—ways that lead to destruction, imprisonment, and death? Or do we hold it in ways that encourage relationship, start conversations, release the captives, and give life? If nothing else, I pray that we will all remove the brick from the shelf and begin wrestling with not only what it is but also where it belongs—in front of a door, keeping it open.

LIE 2

GOD IS ANGRY AND DOESN'T LIKE ME— ESPECIALLY WHEN I SIN

The God that holds you over the Pit of Hell, much as one holds a Spider, or some loathsome Insect, over the Fire, abhors you, and is dreadfully provoked; his Wrath towards you burns like Fire; he looks upon you as worthy of nothing else, but to be cast into the Fire;[1]
— Jonathan Edwards

What happened to you as you read through the Jonathan Edwards quote above? How do you respond? Is there something in you that rejects the philosophy behind Edwards' sermon "Sinners in the Hands of an Angry God?" If you are like me, perhaps you have picked up a milder version of this philosophy. You may not think that God holds you over the "Pit of Hell" like a loathsome spider, but you may believe that

---

[1]   Jonathan Edwards, "Sinners in the Hands of an Angry God. A Sermon Preached at En eld, July 8th, 1741." Reiner Smolinski, editor. Electronic Texts in American Studies. Paper 54, accessed October 29, 2015, http://digitalcommons.unl.edu/cgi/viewcontent. cgi?article=1053&context=etas

God disapproves of you—or is disappointed with your life. Whatever our response may be to the idea that God is angry with us and doesn't like us, we probably need to unpack this lie to really understand all the ways it may be affecting how we think about God and our relationship to God. The truth is too much of the Christian faith in the last few centuries has been built upon this lie. It is foundational—it's just not a solid foundation. It is a foundation that leads to a world where punishment must be meted out for all bad behavior. It is a foundation that not only empowers but demands judgment. It is a foundation that distances children from their loving parent as they begin to believe what gives them divine value is the way they behave.

Behind the lie "God is angry and doesn't like me—especially when I sin" is the idea that your relationship with God—God's affection for you—is based on your behavior. The better person you are, the more God likes and loves you—the more God will bless you. The more mistakes you make and sins you commit, the less God likes and loves you—the less God will bless you. Whether we recognize it or not, this lie requires God to have anger—or even worse, the dreaded biblical wrath—over the sinful behavior of people. This lie characterizes God as the cosmic scorekeeper watching our every move and shaking the Godhead in disappointment— wondering how we could repeatedly be so bad. Actually putting these words to it may make this idea seem silly and easily dismissed, but bear with me. This idea that God is angry and doesn't like us when we sin is too prevalent and too important to leave unexamined. It must be exposed in all the little nooks and crannies of our lives.

A Bad Foundation

Have you ever prayed for something or wanted to pray for something but were overcome with the thought that you did not deserve to ask God for anything? Have you ever felt as though you were unworthy or unqualified to even be in a conversation with God? I sure have. Here's another one— have you ever tried to barter or make a deal with God? "Dear God, if you will please let me get this job, I promise you that I will stop (insert questionable behavior here)." For many of us, the idea that we have to behave in a "good" way or stop behaving in a "bad" way to earn God's love and blessing is central to our faith.

This is known as a *transactional relationship*. Such thinking sees our relationship with God as a transaction. We give God something and then get something in return. If we give God good things, we get good things in return. If we give God bad things, we get bad things in return. The problem is that this thinking is diametrically opposed to the biblical narrative. The overarching story of God as told in the scriptures is that God refuses to let our relationship be transactional. We try, mind you, very hard to maintain a transactional relationship, but God will have none of it. Throughout the Bible, when God's people obey and are good, they are met with relationship and mercy. And when God's people disobey and are bad, they are met with relationship and mercy. This doesn't mean that God's people never experience consequences—just that their relationship with God does not exist based on their behavior. Their relationship with God exists because God wants it—no matter what they do.

If this sounds familiar, it should. This should resonate with you in your familial relationships. There is a reason that the relational metaphor between God and God's people throughout history is that of a family. Your family—those whom you love and do life with be they biological or otherwise—is your family. They can disappoint you and hurt you, but they are still your family. The relationship just is. Your relationship with your family is not transactional, or at least it should not be.

Yet, transactional thinking is everywhere. We still behave as though it is true. It is something we don't really even think about—like breathing. We just accept it and move on. In fact, even reading this right now and realizing that I am going to call this central idea of our faith a lie might make you a little anxious.

When we adopt a narrative or story line as "the way things are" and build our lives upon or around it, we will eventually live as though it is true—even if we knew it was a lie in the beginning. Lies become buried in our stories so deeply that we lose touch with how they got there in the first place and have a hard time even considering what we or the world would look like without them.

This lie—the idea that the great "bearded man" in the sky sees our bad behavior, is disgusted with us, frowns upon us, and is keeping a record of every single mistake we make so that we will be ultimately held accountable, shamed, and punished—is a narrative that I picked up as a child. My life was built upon this foundation. That foundation generated thoughts like these:

> *I must strive to do good things or else I'm going to get it.*
> *I must try to get rid of and control my bad habits or someday I am*
> *going to pay for all of them.*
> *The reason things aren't going the way I want them to go is because*
> *I am getting what I deserve.*
> *I hope God wasn't paying attention when I did that.*
> *God, I know that was wrong and I am sorry that I did it. Please,*
> *forgive me. I'll never do it again.*
> *I deserve to be punished.*

Do any of those thoughts seem familiar to you? If so, you are not alone, and you are not weird.

A Convicted Button Pusher

When I was five years old, I went on one of my father's business trips with my mother and older sister. One day while Dad was off at work, my mother took my sister and me to the swimming pool at the hotel where we were staying. Near the swimming pool was a covered patio with vending machines. It wasn't long before my sister and I were begging our mother for money to go get candy and soda. My mom gave us some change and returned to the book she was reading poolside. After my sister and I had spent what we were given, I continued to push the buttons on the candy vending machine—if for no other reason than because buttons are fun to push and you never know, you might get lucky. Well, we got lucky. The machine was broken and no matter what we pushed, it just kept spitting out candy. It was a dream come true for a couple of sugar junkies. Without missing a beat, we grabbed a hotel towel and began to load it up with our spoils.

We emptied the machine. I think the only thing we left in there were a couple of Almond Joy candy bars because neither of us liked our chocolate to be distracted by coconut—just give us the straight sugar. Later, when our mother took us back to our adjoining hotel rooms, my sister and I went into our room, spread the towel out on the bed, and began to divide and enjoy our treasure. Somewhere in there my mom happened by the adjoining doorway, saw the Costco-sized load of candy we were gorging ourselves upon, and the nougat hit the fan.

As she grilled us with questions of where the candy came from and what had we done, I slowly began to descend from my glistening sugar buzz and consider the possibility that we had done something wrong. Just as I was about to make a very logical argument about it not being our fault, I heard the words that came with a foreboding soundtrack and a pit in my stomach—"What will your father think?" My sister and I both panicked, "Wait! Mom, we don't have to tell Dad—we'll go put the candy back in the machine!" We knew that if she was bringing Dad into the situation, we must have really screwed up—and now we were going to get it.

I have no idea how much time passed between when Mom caught us and when Dad got back to the hotel, but I can tell you that it was an eternity to my sister and me. We sat and waited, doomed as convicted felons awaiting punishment with a pile of sweet, chocolate evidence between us. When Dad arrived, we could hear Mom in the next room telling him what we had done. With disappointment and restrained anger, he came in and questioned us for our version of the afternoon's events. When we had thoroughly allocuted to our crime, our father calmly instructed us to wrap the candy back up in the towel. He was way too calm for my liking.

I was waiting for the boom to be lowered. Where was the yelling? What about our punishment? Don't leave me hanging—let's have it!

And then … boom. Dad announced to us that we would be taking our spoils to the front desk where we were to confess our crime to the hotel staff and suggest that they call the police so that we could be punished for our thievery. Go ahead and sit in that for a moment as a five-year-old would—and don't miss that last bit because it's true. Dad told us we were to ask the desk clerk to have us arrested for stealing. All I could think was, *I finally did it. I found the line that is too far for my parents. They're giving me up to the police.*

Do you have this picture in your head? A five-year-old and an eight-year-old go up to the front desk of the hotel and unwrap a towelful of candy, confess to stealing it from the pool vending machine, apologize, and then suggest to the front desk clerk that she call the police to come and get us—all while my father stands behind us with his arms crossed. My sister may have been old enough to know they were not going to call the cops, but I was not. I was sure that I was going to jail. I had just confessed and handed over the incriminating evidence, for crying out loud!

The euphoric relief that washed over me when the desk clerk laughed and said, "That won't be necessary," was like nothing I had ever felt before. What? I am free?! I am not going to jail! I immediately knew that this woman was the coolest person I had ever met. How about that, Dad? I bet you weren't planning on the desk clerk being so cool! Your plan to send us to prison has been foiled!

Of course, my father knew they would not call the police. Of course, my parents were just making sure that we learned a lesson that we would not forget. In hindsight, I can look back at that episode and see it as incredibly fair and effective parenting. My sister and I were not punished or grounded any further after we returned the candy. Neither of my parents ever raised a hand to us, but they did make sure that we realized our actions had consequences and that we met those consequences head-on. I don't fault my parents one bit for how they handled it. In fact, I think it was quite brilliant.

Here's the problem: I didn't connect the dots. At five, I didn't realize that my parents had just helped me understand that the behavior I choose will always have a consequence that I cannot escape. I didn't grasp that I had truthfully displayed the normal five-year-old behavior to a candy machine that spits out candy. What I learned is that when a vending machine dispenses free candy, I am not supposed to take it. I am supposed to be stronger in the face of temptation. I thought I had messed up—that I had been weak when I should have been strong. I had pushed the buttons and I had taken the candy. I was a failure.

What my parents and the hotel clerk saw that I did not see was that I had behaved like any five-year-old would have. None of them actually expected me to act any differently than I had in that moment. Have you ever seen five-year-olds in the presence of a button—any button—that they did not push? Can you imagine a kid who would stop pushing the buttons on a vending machine that keeps giving out candy? Of course not! My parents knew that. The gracious desk clerk knew that. I didn't know that. What I picked up was that I had made a mistake and that I deserved to be punished. I had stolen candy, and I deserved to go to jail. The only reason I had not gone to jail was because the woman behind the desk decided to have mercy on me.

Jesus, Friend of Button Pushers

For the longest time, this is exactly how I saw my relationship with God. I knew I was not living a sinless life. I frequently made selfish mistakes, hurt others, and did things that I should not do. If given an opportunity to steal some candy, I would take it. Therefore, I concluded that I was a sinner who deserved to be punished, and the only reason that I would not be punished is because someone decided to have mercy on me—Jesus. Just like the hotel clerk, Jesus would forgive me. That was the foundation of my faith; I was a candy thief who did not have the strength to stand up to temptation and Jesus was the gracious hotel clerk. I needed that clerk to forgive me because there was no way I could ever be worthy otherwise.

I had heard enough preachers and religious folks reference "judgment day" and the scriptures about judgment to have an unsettled feeling about what awaited me. I believed that if Jesus wasn't standing with me on "judgment day," I was going to prison. God was going to come settle accounts, and Jesus was going to defend me. It would be as if the clerk at the hotel who forgave my sister and me for pillaging the candy machine was going to stand next to us on the day we checked out of the hotel and stood before the hotel manager.

"So these are the two thieves who stole from me?" the manager would say. My sister and I would stand ashamed with our heads bowed.

"Yes, sir," the desk clerk would answer. "But I have forgiven them."

The manager would question, "You have? Then who is going to pay for the damage they have caused?"

"I will," the clerk would say. "I will take whatever punishment is necessary on their behalf."

This act of the hotel clerk standing before the manager on our behalf is what theologians call *punitive substitutionary atonement*. The idea is that we sinners—by our misbehavior—have separated ourselves from God and must atone or make reparation for our wrongdoing. This theological belief holds that we deserve to be punished. Jesus stands before God as our substitute. He takes our place in atoning for our mistakes. Theologians who align with this thinking will point out that substitutionary atonement takes place frequently in the scriptures. For example, when Adam and Eve commit the "original" sin and become ashamed of their nakedness, God kills an animal to provide skins for their clothing (Gen. 3:21). During the pinnacle of the Exodus narrative, the Hebrews are commanded to kill a lamb and mark the doorposts of their homes with its blood so that the Spirit of God will know to "pass over" their homes as it travels through Egypt, killing the firstborn (Ex. 12:13). Throughout the times of the Tabernacle and the Temple in the Hebrew scriptures, God's people are offering sacrifices of slaughtered animals, first fruits, and grains in order to get right with God. Christian theologians point out that all the preceding sacrifices are shadows of the ultimate atonement offered by Jesus on the cross.

If you are like me, there is something about punitive substitutionary atonement that you don't want to question. In a way, my Christian upbringing has created in me an expectation for that story. I have been taught that whatever punishment I might deserve, Jesus stands between that punishment and me. That heroism draws me to Jesus—it makes me love him. Why would I want to question that? I am humbled that Jesus took the punishment for me just as I was humbled by the desk clerk who said, "It's all right. It will not be necessary to call the police."

I don't want to question that Jesus atoned for my sins because I have been taught that it was Jesus' actions that cause my release from punishment. Jesus is my merciful substitute. He erases my sins. Through his sacrifice, I become justified. "Justified to do what?" you might ask.

Justification is another theological concept that overlaps with substitutionary atonement. The basic idea behind justification is that the death and resurrection of Jesus justifies his followers before God. His righteousness is bequeathed upon his followers, and they become justified before the LORD. If my sister and I had really been required to stand before the hotel manager, it would have been the substitutionary atonement of the desk clerk that allowed us to stand before him or her blameless. We would have been justified because of the actions of the clerk. If the hotel manager or police showed up looking to punish us, we would have pointed to the clerk and said, "She said we were forgiven." In essence, her mercy justified our moving on from our mistake and not being arrested. Similarly, we, as selfish and sinful people, are supposedly justified to have a relationship with a selfless and holy God because of Jesus' sacrifice as our substitute.

Does this all sound about right? Do these concepts of substitutionary atonement and justification sum up any part of your understanding of Jesus and God? If so, you may be wondering, *Then, where is the lie?* That is a good question to ask. Before we look at a possible answer, consider the following questions:

*How do punitive substitutionary atonement and
justification make you feel about Jesus?*

How do they make you feel about God?

*As much as these ideas may resonate with your faith,
do they feel like a complete representation or is something missing?*

The Half-Truth

There have been a few parenting moments in our home that sound like this,

Abby:	"Mommy, Sammy pushed me!"
Mommy:	Sammy, did you push Abby?
Sammy:	Yes.
Mommy:	Abby, why did he push you?
Abby:	I don't know … because he's mean?
Mommy:	Sammy, why did you push Abby?
Sammy:	Because she kept sitting on me and thumping me in the head.

Now I don't want to single out our daughter as being the only child who utilizes this technique. All of our children employ the self-promoting technique of the "half-truth." It is a fairly pedestrian method of lying that obscures the big picture in an effort to highlight the information one feels is more important. In the scenario above, it is much more important to our daughter Abby that we know how corrupt her older brother is and that he be punished. After all, she is the one who brought my wife into the altercation in the first place.

All parenting skills aside, we do not accept the half-truth in our home. A half-truth is a lie. To be honest, a half-truth isn't a truth at all. It is a misrepresentation of the truth. Consider a historian who represents the Nazi party during World War II as having been a group of patriotic Germans who fought zealously with a sense of national pride in an effort to benefit their country. Would you accept that as the truth of who the Nazis were? Of course not! Yes, the Nazi party was in part comprised of those who thought they were taking patriotic action for the benefit of Germany, but those actions were maniacal and genocidal. The Nazi party murdered millions of innocent Jews in the Holocaust—a truth that should never be underrepresented or forgotten.

I realize that jumping from my children's arguments to the atrocities of the Nazi regime is quite a drastic leap. The point of leaping such a chasm is to show the real impact a half-truth can have when we allow it to stand. Half-truths create a distorted picture of reality that is not true at all. When we fail to receive or strive for the entire picture, we end up with a reality that is horribly out-of-focus. The truth is so distorted that we are tempted to draw conclusions from an incomplete representation. What if my wife was not the sage mother that she is and did not ask my son why he pushed his sister? What if, instead, she determined her course of action in disciplining our son based on the half-truth presented by our daughter? She would have formulated certain beliefs about our son and his behavior and then based her actions on those beliefs. This may sound like a basic idea, but unfortunately, human beings do this all the time.

You will not have to look very far to find a person who is certain they have ascertained the entire picture of a given situation and is willing to stake their reputation—their very life—upon their conclusion. The aforementioned Nazi example—that hypothetical historian I mentioned—exists. There are those who are certain that the Nazis were just patriotic Germans and that the Holocaust is a fabrication—that it never happened. The whole, horrible truth eludes them, or perhaps they choose to ignore the whole horrible truth. Those of us who grasp a more complete picture of World War II and the reality of the Nazi regime might consider such a myopic view foolish and ultimately dismiss such people as insane and irrelevant. While these people may very well be sociopaths, they are not irrelevant, and they are an extreme example of people who cling to distorted views and half-truths. Unfortunately, they are not alone. We do the same thing with our faith.

So what is the half-truth behind the lie that God is angry and doesn't like us when we sin? What incomplete representation has led millions of faithful people to the conclusion that their relationship with God is based on their ability to act right?

Jesus Christ died for my sins.

The Incomplete Idea

Now, take a deep breath and relax—we're all going to be okay. Remember, I am not saying that Jesus did not die for our sins; it's just not a complete idea. It represents a distorted picture upon which millions of people—including me—have based their lives. In fact, it is a half-truth so firmly grasped that it has led to war, devastation, and great loss of life.

Yeshua ben Yosef (Jesus son of Joseph) lived on earth for approximately thirty-three years. His dedicated and purposeful ministry lasted between one year and three years (depending on differing Gospel accounts). He loved. He healed. He helped. He taught. His disciple John concluded his Gospel account of Jesus' life, death, and resurrection by saying, "There are also many other things that Jesus did; if every one of them were written down, I suppose that the world itself could not contain the books that would be written." (John 21:25)

That is a bold statement. All the books of the world could not contain all that Jesus did? Then why in the world do we think we can contain Jesus in one sentence? In a very basic question, we must ask ourselves: was the whole point of Jesus' life to die for our sins? Is that really what he was all about? Was it all just so that we would be *justified* by Christ's *substitutionary atonement*?

Jesus did not seem to think so—at least, that is not the truth as presented in the Gospel accounts. Jesus loved "sinners." I'm not talking about the reality that he had no choice because every human makes mistakes.

I'm saying Jesus gave his time, energy, and love to flawed people—both the "down and out" and the "up and in"—the connected and the marginalized. Not once did Jesus have his disciples haul someone off for being an outsider, irreligious, or impure. Every time the crowds of religiously behaving people haul "sinners" before Jesus in the Gospel accounts, Jesus declares their sins forgiven.

What's that about? If Jesus repeatedly declares the sinners that are dragged before him in the gospels as forgiven, why was the cross even necessary? Was he serious when he told people that their sins were forgiven? Or was he just being dramatic? Were their sins really forgiven? If they were—and we are to believe that Jesus had the power to forgive sins with a statement, why didn't he just speak forgiveness over the entire world and retire to the countryside? Why the cross?

I want to invite you to begin loosening whatever grasp you may have on punitive substitutionary atonement as a complete explanation of the crucifixion of Jesus. I assure you that my intentions here are not to remove your beliefs and ideas but only to open them up to new information. For example, did you know that punitive substitutionary atonement is not the only explanation Christians have offered for the cross throughout history? It wasn't even the first explanation. Truth be told, the theory that Jesus had to die on the cross in order to appease God's wrath against you did not experience wide acceptance until Anselm of Canterbury penned *Cur Deus Homo* (*Why God Became a Man*) in 1098 CE. Consider this summation offered by Franciscan priest and author Richard Rohr:

> After Anselm, Christians have paid a huge price for what theologians
> called "substitutionary atonement theory"—the strange idea that before
> God could love us God needed and demanded Jesus to be a blood sac-
> rifice to atone for our sin-drenched humanity. With that view, salvation
> depends upon a problem instead of a divine proclamation about the
> core nature of reality. As if God could need payment, and even a very
> violent transaction, to be able to love and accept "his" own children—

a message that those with an angry, distant, absent, or abusive father were already far too programmed to believe.[2]

Without abandoning your current beliefs about substitutionary atonement or getting lost in the varying theories Christians have developed over the last 2,000 years to explain the cross, I want to ask you to consider the possibility that sin is our problem and not God's.

So What?

Let me ask you a question that someone once asked me in order to expose the lie that God is angry and doesn't like me when I sin.

Is it possible for someone to lead a life without mistakes?

That is, if you tried really hard, could you do it? Could you lead a mistake-free life? My experience tells me that it is not possible. In fact, my life screams out from the top of its lungs that I cannot live without mistakes. My mistakes are too numerous and too recurring to think otherwise. The apostle Paul, who wrote most of what is known as the New Testament, didn't think a perfect life from start to finish was possible either. In his letter to the Romans, he stated, "You see, all have sinned, and all their futile attempts to reach God in His glory fail." (Rom. 3:23 VOICE)

Years ago, I had a theology professor who taught that the most important question to ask of any idea or statement about God is always, "So what?" The purpose of asking this question of our theology is to reveal what happens next. If someone tells you that God is love—the next question should be, "So what?" What am I supposed to do with that statement? How is that idea supposed to change me? Often, asking the "So what?" question can reveal the incomplete and fearful human

2   Richard Rohr, *Jesus: Human and Divine*, Richard Rohr's Daily Meditation, accessed March 20, 2015, http://myemail.constantcontact.com/Richard-Rohr-s-Meditation-Love–Not-Atonement.html?aid=iXa_UNn2YaQ&soid=1103098668616

thinking behind our statements and ideas about God. If someone tells you that God hates homosexuality, asking the "So what?" question reveals that such a bigoted statement actually invites you to join in hating homosexuals. You are being invited—if not expected—to align your thinking with that God.

Here's the problem—theology is literally our thoughts or words about God or the ultimate reality. Our thoughts. Our speech. Our writing. Theology doesn't fall down from Heaven. It doesn't come from some secret and pure place; it comes from us—people. You may not think of yourself as a theologian, but you are. We are all theologians. We all have theological ideas and words—things we think, say, or write about God. Every theological statement or conclusion that has ever been written down, said out loud, turned into a sermon series, or inspired a book (insert wink emoticon here) has come from a human being. And while we humans are certainly capable of some wonderful thoughts and ideas, our thoughts and speech will always include some reflection of our own junk. Our baggage, our pain, our fear—they all find their way into our thoughts and speech about God—into our theology.

In short, our best efforts are always going to be biased and incomplete. To be sure, with the wisdom of history, the help of community, and some divine guidance, we are capable of grasping some really solid and helpful ideas. But we will never fully grasp the infinite with finite minds. We will never adequately express with words that which is beyond expression. The great theologian Dallas Willard once told my father that theology is like a dog watching a chess match. This is an incredibly humbling reality. Dallas Willard may very well have been one of the wisest theologians of our time, and he equated his own masterful understanding and insight to a dog's understanding of chess.

"So what?" you ask. So it is helpful for us to have a proper perspective on both the theology we confront and the theology we create on our journey. We're all just dogs trying to understand what chess is all about. Jonathan Edwards wanted his parishioners to understand how vile and wicked they were compared to a pure and holy God—and that the difference between them and God angered God. God's wrath burned against their sin. The Apostle Paul—in the aforementioned theological statement of Romans 3— seemed to want the readers of his letter to the Romans to understand that sin was inevitable and inescapable to every human life. Paul wrote that everyone makes mistakes and that even our best behavior can't equip us to reach God. A theological statement like that demands at least one follow-up question. Any ideas on what the next question should be?

So what?

So what if all people sin and fail to gain relationship with God through good behavior? What does that mean to us here and now? What does that mean for our lives? I think it means Paul wants us to consider that our behavior—our ability to live without mistakes—is not supposed to define our relationship to God. I think it means God is not surprised by our mistakes or the fact that we all make them. Consider a few questions generated from Paul's statement. If Paul is right and God is not surprised by our mistakes—God even expects our mistakes—then why would God be angry? If Paul is right and it is impossible for any human being to live a completely perfect life but our relationship with God is based on our ability to avoid sinning, where does that leave us?

In a word, *screwed*. There are two ideas that are contradicting each other here. One idea tells us that God is angry and doesn't like us when we sin—that we are sinners with whom God is wrathfully disappointed. The second idea tells us that no one can lead a sinless life. The two ideas do not work together at all. What kind of God would say to you, "Our relationship will be defined by **your** ability to act right. Oh, and by the way, it is impossible for you to act right all the time ... so, good luck!"?

At best, if God bases God's relationship with us on how we behave and it is impossible for us to live a sinless life from start to finish, we end up with a continually transactional relationship with God—a relationship that has us trying to behave well enough or ask forgiveness enough times to secure God's love. In this scenario, we see our blessings as a result of our good behavior and our troubles as a result of our bad behavior. We hold God in a distant relationship of voodoo, hoping and praying that if we mix the right combination of prayers and behavior, God will be appeased. At worst, we end up with a God who we believe is responsible for our impossible circumstances—a God that has set us up to fail. This God can be seen as a cosmic jerk who has placed us like rats in a laboratory maze to study us or be amused by us—or as or a nutty professor who set everything in motion but then neglects the details.

When I began to pray and think through these questions, it became clear that even if that God did exist, I did not want to believe. I did not want to be in relationship with a God who would create a no-win scenario and then punish me for not being able to win. I didn't want a relationship that was based on my ability to be perfect because my life had already taught me that I couldn't do it. I found myself dissatisfied with God. It all seemed so pointless and exhausting.

The closer I came to giving up on God, something strange began to happen. It was as if I was being cheered on to follow my questions through to exhaustion and surrender. Something was encouraging me, saying, "Yes! Ask that question! See how ridiculous that God is and let it go!" For the first time in my faith, I came to the point of giving up. *I don't get you, God—and if you're like this, I don't want to get you. I am tired of trying to make you make sense—so I give up.* As I did, I could actually feel a response well up inside of me. It wasn't just a thought in my head. It was sensory. It actually felt true.

It was as if something had fallen off me and opened me up to receive the notion that the God I was giving up was not God at all. I was giving up a cosmic scorekeeper. I was giving up a transactional deity who would set me up to fail. It was as if God was happy that I had given up on that god because now I could enter into a new relationship. This relationship, however, would be different. This God—the God Paul seemed to write about—came with the disclaimer that our relationship would not be based on my ability to live a perfect life. This God wasn't surprised by my mistakes. This God wasn't angry. This God did not require a transaction of blood in order to be near me.

What if Paul's aforementioned statement in Romans declaring, "All have sinned" and "failed to reach God in His glory" is not a statement of how disappointing and infuriating we are to God but rather a statement of the human condition? What if Paul is saying sin has never been what our relationship with God is about?

Proclaiming Favor

Let's consider a few things in our continued exploration of this half-truth that Jesus died for our sins. First, in the Gospels, it's the people—us—who are repeatedly obsessed with sin and "bad" behavior, not Jesus. Jesus is interested in forgiveness, freedom, life, and love—all of which make up the Kingdom of God. Second, following the resurrection of Jesus, do you know how many times Jesus speaks to his disciples about their sins or mistakes? Not one time. In all of the times that witnesses recount post-resurrection encounters with the risen Jesus, not once does Jesus say, "I have a bone to pick with you people." Not once does Jesus complain, "I just went through hell for you people, so straighten up and stop sinning!" The only time Jesus even mentions sin following the resurrection is to instruct his disciples to proclaim the "forgiveness of sins to all nations" (Luke 24:47). There it is again! Jesus is once again demonstrating that the forgiveness of sins is something that is declared out loud—something he did with his words and now empowers his disciples to do with theirs.

There is even an interesting exchange between Peter and Jesus following the resurrection where Peter is clearly burdened by his mistake of denying that he knew Jesus on the night of his capture—in essence, rejecting him at the moment of truth. Nowhere in that exchange does Jesus let Peter's behavior separate him or cause distance in the relationship. John's Gospel records Peter as having denied that he knew Jesus three times on the night of Jesus' arrest. Following the resurrection—when Peter should certainly pay up for the biggest mistake of all, Jesus asks him three times, "Do you love me?"—once for each of his denials—and tells Peter, "Then, take care of my sheep." Jesus does not reject him. Jesus does not let Peter's behavior define their relationship. Jesus accepts Peter—bad behavior and all—and charges him with taking care of the family business.

Consider the words from the prophet Isaiah that Jesus quotes at the beginning of his ministry on earth.

> The Spirit of the LORD is upon me, because he has anointed me to bring good news to the poor. He has sent me to proclaim release to the captives and recovery of sight to the blind, to let the oppressed go free, to proclaim the year of the LORD's favor [3]
>
> (Is. 61:1–2)

This is how Luke records Jesus as declaring his mission statement. Jesus says that he has come to bring good news to the poor, to release captives, to give sight to the blind, to set the oppressed free, and to proclaim the favor of the LORD. Wait, he didn't mention dying for our sins. In fact, he didn't even mention sin.

Now I realize that we can read between the lines and metaphorically deduce that we are the "captives" who are released from our sin through Christ's death and resurrection. But if that is all that was going on, why didn't he just say that? If the whole point of Jesus' life, death, and resurrection was to save us from our sin, why not just say, "The Spirit of the LORD is upon me, because he has anointed me to come and rescue you from your mistakes and sinful lives"? The simple answer is because that is not all that was going on. Jesus could have quoted any Hebrew Scripture at the outset of his ministry. Why did he choose this one? Why not quote the prophet Ezekiel?

> As I live, says the LORD God, I have no pleasure in the death of the wicked, but that the wicked turn from their ways and live; turn back, turn back from your evil ways; for why will you die, O house of Israel?
>
> (EZK. 33:11)

---

[3] The words of Jesus presented in Luke 4:18-19 are a direct quotation of Isaiah 61:1–2.

Or why not quote Moses?

> Remember and do not forget how you provoked the LORD your God to wrath in the wilderness; you have been rebellious against the LORD from the day you came out of the land of Egypt until you came to this place
>
> (DEUT. 9:7)

There are numerous scriptures in the Hebrew Bible that deal with human rebellion and sin—and the distance that our unholy behavior puts between our holy God and us. Why didn't Jesus quote any of those? Why, instead, did he talk about the favor of the LORD? For that matter, what exactly is the favor of the LORD?

The Hebrew word used in Isaiah 61:2 is transliterated as *ratson*. Besides favor, *ratson* means acceptance, goodwill, pleasure, delight, and desire. The Greek word found in Luke's Gospel account where Jesus quotes Isaiah 61 is *dektos*. *Dektos*, as you can imagine, has a similar definition: acceptance, pleasing, welcomed, received. So Luke records Jesus as stating the purpose of his ministry is to bring release, freedom, and sight, and to declare to the people that they are acceptable, pleasing, and desired by the LORD—that they are the LORD's desire and delight.

What?!

That doesn't sound anything like Jonathan Edwards' sermon. According to Jesus' mission statement, God is not angry with me. Jesus proclaims that God favors me! If that's the case, then why do we believe that sin defines our relationship with God? Why do so many people—including "church" people—seem to live lives that indicate our relationship with God is based on our behavior? Why do we think the whole thing is about sin?

Let me say this again—sin is our problem. We are the ones who bring it into our relationship with God. Throughout the story of God, when people bring their sin into the divine relationship, God repeatedly and consistently says, "That is not who you are." Consider the possibility that

God did not need Jesus to die for our sins. Consider the possibility that God has never been surprised or hung up on our sin. That may seem counterintuitive—but hold that thought for a moment. We will come back to it.

For now, let's think through these questions:

Who am I if I am not defined by my sin?

What if my purity and perfection aren't what governs my close-
ness to God?

If God doesn't look at me and see my behavior, then what does
God see?

Who am I?

Now, receive this answer and let it get all over you.

> *You are a beloved child of the Most High God.*
> *You are God's delight and the joy of God's heart.*

The Whole Truth

If this idea seems incredible to you, it's because it is an incredible idea. This was a radical notion to the first-century faithful, and it is still just as radical for us today. You are God's child. That is what God sees when God looks at you—a beloved daughter, a treasured son. God could choose any metaphor to represent the relationship God desires with people, and people have certainly used a number of different metaphors to describe God. Yet, the primary position God takes with us is that of a loving parent.

Now there are certainly some bad parents in this world, but most of us who have ever cared for a child in a parental or guardian capacity understand what it is like to love a child. We know what it is like to look at a child and have joy well up inside—to be overcome with love, compassion, and protection all at the same time. We know that if our child comes to us and makes a negative self-declaration like "I am stupid" or "I am ugly," that every fiber of our being unites to reject that lie and shout, "That is not true! That is not who you are! You are brilliant! You are beautiful!"

Can you get into that headspace? Think about a relationship you have or have had with a child for whom you care. Now, remember something they did that let you down. Think of a time when they hurt you or disappointed you. Did that selfish behavior make you love them less? Did your love for them diminish? I can personally attest to the truth that my children continue to discover new and inventive ways to disturb me, and they frequently make mistakes—but never has their behavior made me stop loving them—not even close. Every moment of our relationship makes me love them more than the last—which doesn't seem possible, but the love that I think is as big as it could ever be continues to grow and grow. It's amazing.

Here's the rub. I'm not that great of a father. Don't get me wrong. I'm not throwing myself under the bus—I do all right, but I am a selfish human being capable of putting my kingdom before all others. I continue to discover new and inventive ways to disturb and let down my kids. I get grumpy. I get tyrannical. I get fed up, and my behavior towards my kids displays these realities. In spite of all of that, I never stop growing in my love for my kids—even when their behavior is at its worst.

Now, if that is a true statement for me—a selfish, sometimes grumpy, sometimes tyrannical father—why would we expect less from our perfect, loving parent in God? Both Matthew's and Luke's Gospel accounts record Jesus speaking to this very reality.

Think of it this way: if your son asked you for bread, would you give him a stone? Of course not—you would give him a loaf of bread. If your son asked for a fish, would you give him a snake? No, to be sure, you would give him a fish—the best fish you could find. So if you, who are sinful, know how to give your children good gifts, how much more so does your Father in heaven, who is perfect, know how to give great gifts to His children!

(MATT. 7:9–11)

Some of you are fathers, so ask yourselves this: if your son comes up to you and asks for a fish for dinner, will you give him a snake instead? If your boy wants an egg to eat, will you give him a scorpion? Look, all of you are flawed in so many ways, yet in spite of all your faults, you know how to give good gifts to your children. How much more will your Father in heaven give the Holy Spirit to all who ask!

(LUKE 11:11–13)

God is our perfect and loving parent. Nothing we do makes God love us less. The forbearers of the Christian faith understood this truth. They didn't try to sum up all that Jesus was in one statement like, "Jesus died for our sins." They knew there was more going on.

Here Comes a Lion, Father

Remember those questions we asked earlier?

*How do punitive substitutionary atonement and
justification make you feel about Jesus?*

Think about my merciful hotel clerk. I loved her as much as a five-year-old boy can love. I had nothing but praise for her—and still do to this day. Her substitutionary atonement on my behalf—the way she justified me not going to prison—made me love her. It made me want to give back to her. But what about her boss? What about the hotel manager?

*How do substitutionary atonement and
justification make you feel about God?*

Do they make you feel all warm and fuzzy inside about the Father? Or do they create a distance between you and the Cosmic Scorekeeper? Does Jesus standing with us to take the punishment for our mistakes make us feel closer to the one who gives out the punishment? As we have said, the picture this paints is one of an angry God whose holiness is offended by our stinky behavior and must be appeased. As much as we might love Jesus for standing in there and taking it on our behalf, this does not draw us closer to God. This does not paint a picture of God as a loving parent … unless … there must be something that we are missing.

What if justification is not all that is going on in the life, death, and resurrection of Jesus? What if there is something more—without which God's narrative skews and distorts into the lie that God is good and I am not so I must have Jesus to make me tolerable to God? Does that sound like a loving parent to you? I love my child, but they're just so stinking bad that I can't stand to be in relationship with them unless they clean it up? Again, I realize this seems ridiculous, but that is exactly where our faith devolves if we follow the half-truth of Jesus dying for our sins.

Justification in and of itself is a half-truth. It cannot be the whole story because the story it tells is the corrupt story of an unjust God who sets his children up to fail and is subsequently distanced from them by their behavior.

Do you know the story of Simba the lion as popularized in Disney's *The Lion King*?[4] If you don't, I will summarize it, but I highly recommend that you watch the movie—or the play—if you have the opportunity. Simba, a young cub, is born to Mufasa, the Lion King. During his upbringing, Simba's uncle, who is jealous for Mufasa's throne, plots to kill Mufasa and frame Simba for his own father's death. The plot successfully places Simba in danger, and Mufasa's efforts to rescue Simba actually get him killed— right before Simba's eyes. Simba wrongly believes he is responsible for the king's death and runs away in shame. He leaves his kingdom, his family, his land, and disappears into a scavenging existence of anonymity.

We, too, believe the lie that we killed the King. We wrongly believe that our sins led our King to his crucifixion. As a result, we fail to live

---

4 Irene Mecchi, Jonathan Roberts, and Linda Woolverton, *The Lion King* DVD, directed by Roger Allers and Rob Minkoff (Burbank, CA: Buena Vista Home Entertainment, 1995).

into the truth of our family line and land and, instead, settle into lives of scavenging and anonymity. The problem with that reality for Simba and for us is that it's based on a lie. We didn't kill the King. Once more, enabling us to run away is not why the King sacrificed himself. The King sacrificed himself for his child—his blood—his royal offspring—his heir. Herein lies an important clue to a fuller truth.

Justification and Adoption

In order for justification to make any sense, it must be united with *adoption*. Adoption is the part of the story that we have lost. Adoption is exactly what you think it means—that we are part of the family. We are daughters and sons, brothers and sisters, heirs to the Kingdom of God.

God loves you more than you can possibly imagine. God loves you so much that you are given the freedom to choose whether or not you will love God back. But God doesn't stop there—no way, no how. God sees that we are blinded and imprisoned by our sin. We just can't see past our failures to believe that a perfect and selfless God would be in relationship with a flawed and selfish people. So God makes a way. God creates a path, declaring that we are not only justified—we are family.

There is this great moment in *The Lion King* when Simba's rabbi, Rafiki, leads him to a pool of water in the jungles where he has been hiding in shame. Simba hasn't seen his reflection while he has been growing up as a scavenger. The last time he saw himself, he was a scared little lion cub. Now, listening to the spirit of his father, he sees himself in the water and sees his father looking back at him. His reflection—that of a grown lion who looks like Mufasa—reminds him of who his father really is and therefore who he really is. He is not a scavenger. He is not anonymous. He is the beloved son of Mufasa, the Lion King. He is the royal heir to the throne.

We too have neglected to see our divine reflection. We have been imprisoned, oppressed, and blinded from seeing ourselves as God sees us—as children of God. We have settled into a theology that tells us we killed the King and are therefore unworthy. It's not true. You are not a scavenger. You are not anonymous. You are the beloved child of the Most High God. You are a royal heir to the throne. You are part of the family.

My Father and Your Father

When Mary Magdalene meets the risen Savior outside the tomb, Jesus tells her, "Go to my brothers and say to them, 'I am ascending to my Father and your Father, to my God and your God'" (John 20:17). Go to my "brothers" and tell them that I am going to "my Father and your Father." This is not ambiguous speech; this is family.

Why would God sacrifice so much to justify rebellious and unworthy people? Because we are worthy; we are God's children. The story of the Judeo-Christian faith is one of God continually justifying us and creating a path from our mistakes to relationship. Ephesians 1:5 states, "He destined us to be adopted as His children through the covenant Jesus the Anointed inaugurated in His sacrificial life. This was His pleasure and His will for us."

Justification is important. I am not denying that I sin. I behave in ways that God says are not good for me or for others. As Paul reminds us, we all bring sin into our relationship with God. We are the ones who lose sight. We are the ones who get imprisoned. We are the ones who are held captive, unable to see our identity independent of our failures. If the story of God affirms anything, however, it affirms that God can always see us for who we really are. God can see even when we cannot. Therefore, we are justified. But who needed to know that? Did God not think we were justified before Christ died on the cross or was that our thought? Could God really not bear to look at us—let alone be in relationship with us before Jesus made the ultimate atonement for our sins, or was it us who could not bear to look? Is it God who defines and justifies people by their behavior and therefore requires substitutionary atonement or is that something we require?

God notices and condemns bad behavior in the stories of the Bible.

God even allows the consequences of those bad behaviors to be painfully and fatally experienced on numerous occasions. Does God ever use those bad behaviors to terminate relationship? I humbly submit to you that the answer to that question is "No!". Death and failure are renewable resources in the Kingdom of God. That is to say, God does not allow people's mistakes—and the consequences that accompany them (including death)—to terminate relationship.

God is not concerned with my sin because it makes me unbearable to God. God is concerned with my sin because it wounds me, and it wounds others. Richard Rohr offers this insight into a more complete understanding of the crucifixion and the importance of abandoning transactional thinking.

> Jesus did not come to change the mind of God about humanity (it did not need changing)! Jesus came to change the mind of humanity about God. God in Jesus moved people beyond the counting, weighing, and punishing model, that the ego prefers, to the utterly new world that Jesus offered, where God's abundance has made any economy of merit, sacrifice, reparation, or atonement both unhelpful and unnecessary.
>
> When we begin negatively, or focused on the problem, we never get out of the hamster wheel. To this day we begin with and continue to focus on sin, when the crucified one was pointing us toward a primal solidarity with the very suffering of God and all of creation.[5]

Don't miss that last thought—"the crucified one was pointing us toward a primal solidarity with the very suffering of God and all of creation." What in the heck is he talking about? That quote started off as a nicely worded summary of our journey thus far—reminding us that our relationship with God is not and never has been transactional. But then it took a weird turn there at the end—a weird but important turn.

---

[5] Richard Rohr, *Jesus: Human and Divine*, Richard Rohr's Daily Meditation, accessed March 20, 2015, http://myemail.constantcontact.com/Richard-Rohr-s-Meditation-Love-Not-Atonement.html?aid=iXa_UNn2YaQ&soid=1103098668616

If My Bad Behavior Didn't Nail Jesus to the Cross, Then What Did?

Clearly Rohr is agreeing that our sin did not nail Jesus to the cross and rejecting the notion that the whole point of Jesus' death was a transactional payment for our sins. But what is he saying did nail Jesus to the cross? Come to think of it, what are we saying nailed Jesus to the cross if it was not our sins?

Before we go any further, let me say clearly that I am not sure that the crucifixion can be boiled down to any one thing. I don't know that one idea, one theory, or one explanation can capture it all. It is a transcendent event. The history of the Christian faithful over the last 2,000 years has generated and embraced numerous theories and explanations of what exactly happened at the crucifixion. There seems to be something right about that plurality. It makes sense that it is not one thing. Theologian and author Tony Jones equates the historical theories of the atonement to lights at the foot of the cross—each one shining up from a different angle and point of view—all of them drawing our attention to this amazing and unparalleled event.

Still, Jones and Rohr would have us consider one more layer of affection at the cross—one more light shining up, revealing something about God and about us. Rohr says the crucifixion of Jesus points us toward "a primal solidarity with the very suffering of God and all of creation." What does that mean? How would the crucifixion of Jesus provide solidarity between our suffering and God's suffering?

In his book, *Did God Kill Jesus?*, Tony Jones writes that throughout history, the crucifixion has been an answer in search of a problem. To the earliest Christians, the problem seemed to be a need for God to triumph over the devil. Moving forward in history through theologians like Augustine and Anselm, the problem became that God's holiness required a payment for all of our debauchery. Other theories of the crucifixion have determined the problem was the sacrificial system, death, and even our competitive rivalry and propensity to exorcise the tension of our rivalry onto a scapegoat third party.

My upbringing seemed to take from many different theories of the crucifixion. It was kind of a mash-up of all of the problems Christians have decided the crucifixion happened to solve. As we have already discussed, I was certainly taught that Christ died for my sins. I was also taught that through the cross, Jesus triumphed over evil and death and that Jesus was the ultimate scapegoat.

But what if the crucifixion wasn't an answer to a problem? What if the crucifixion was not a reaction but a relationship? Jones writes,

> From the beginning of time, God has practiced humility and self-limitation. Maybe it's the only way that God could be in an authentic relationship with finite creatures, or maybe it's because God simply thought it best, but in either case God started by retreating enough to create the cosmos. Then God withdrew enough to let Israel chart its own course, for both good and ill. And ultimately God was humbled in a way that neither the Hebrews nor the Hellenists had thought possible, by inhabiting a human being—for that matter, a human being of humble origins. God built a bridge between humanity and divinity, and then God walked over it.
>
> When God fully entered the human experience in Jesus, new vistas of understanding were opened. Joy, pathos, trial, temptation, happiness, grief—God went from observer to participant in the whole gamut of human existence.
>
> And then some things you'd never expect God to experience— existential loneliness, god-forsakenness, atheism, death—even that became part of the life of God.[6]

Tony Jones, like Richard Rohr, is asking us to consider that the cross was God fully identifying with humanity. God joined us in solidarity of

---

6   Tony Jones, *Did God Kill Jesus?: Searching for Love in History's Most Famous Execution* (New York: HarperCollins Publishers, 2015), 245.

suffering—in every agony we experience—including the agony of being abandoned by God.

The night before his crucifixion, Jesus pleads with God for any other outcome than the cross. He receives no answer. After suffering through the false arrest, the mockery of justice in his hidden trial, the horrific torture of being whipped to the point of death, the grueling pain and shame of crucifixion—just before his death—Jesus cries out, "My God, My God, why have you forsaken me?" (Matt. 27:46) God experiences the agony of crying out to the universe, "Where are you, God?!"

This idea paints the cross not as a defensive reaction by God to sin, evil, or death that changes humanity but as a purposeful, initiated act of love, empathy, and identification with humanity that changes God. The crucifixion of Jesus forever builds a connection of suffering between God and humanity—a connection that nothing can separate. Jesus went to the cross to obliterate every possible shred of distance between God and us. The cross, then, is not God's response to our bad behavior. It is relationship. It is connection. It is understanding.

And the cross is not even the end of the story. Jesus rose. Even abandonment and death could not constrict God's relationship with God's people. The presence of God's Holy Spirit serves as an advocate and counselor to God's people. As Jones writes, "Everything after the crucifixion is meant to ensure that we never again feel forsaken by God. We may at times feel alone, but since the crucifixion, God has made sure that we aren't alone."[7]

Dirt + Breath

Our ancient Hebrew forefathers and foremothers told and wrote down a poem of creation that seemed to speak to the familial nature of our relationship with God from the outset. "Then the LORD God formed man from the dust of the ground, and breathed into his nostrils the breath of life; and the man became a living being." (Gen 2:7) We come from God.

---

[7] Jones, *Did God Kill Jesus?*, 246.

But that wasn't enough. We found numerous ways to reject, disappoint, and forget our very breath. So God came to us. God self-limits yet again and is poured into a human being. God dwells among the breath-filled dirt as breath-filled dirt. God joins us completely, reconnects us once and for all to our familial identity—not because we are wonderful, but because God is wonderful. God loves us as parents love their children. Nothing in all of creation—not even our mistakes—can threaten the connection God made to us on the cross. Paul said it this way in his letter to the Romans:

> It is God who justifies. Who is to condemn? It is Christ Jesus, who died, yes, who was raised, who is at the right hand of God, who indeed intercedes for us. Who will separate us from the love of Christ? Will hardship, or distress, or persecution, or famine, or nakedness, or peril, or sword?
>
> No, in all these things we are more than conquerors through him who loved us. For I am convinced that neither death, nor life, nor angels, nor rulers, nor things present, nor things to come, nor powers, nor height, nor depth, nor anything else in all creation, will be able to separate us from the love of God in Christ Jesus our LORD.
>
> (ROM. 8:33–35, 37–39)

Nothing can separate us from the loving God who justifies us. Nothing can break the connection we have to a God who experientially knows everything we feel and suffer. No behavior we ever exhibit—no matter how bad—can leave us as sinners in the hands of an angry God.

Don't just read that. Do you trust that it is true? Do you know that those moments when we are at our worst—when we did those things that we will never tell anyone about—when we said that thing of which we are so ashamed—when we hurt other people, we were still being loved by God? At those very moments—during those very moments—while you were in the middle of the sin, you were still being loved as a daughter or a son by God.

Listen

Let's make this real. Go to one of those moments in your mind right now. Pick the behavior of which you are most ashamed. Remember it; bring back the details of the event from your memory. Can you see it? Can you feel the shame and distance? Do you hear a voice condemning you, telling you that you cannot be forgiven? Do you hear a voice that says that behavior proves you are not worthy? Do you feel that you have to keep that behavior or transgression locked away so that no one else will ever know about it? That voice is not God.

That moment, event, or behavior you are remembering is not who you are. Let me say it again. That is not who you are. That is not how God sees you. Your identity is not found in your mistakes, your sin, or your failure. Your identity is found in the breath that you carry inside of you—the breath of God. Your family resides in the one who endured the abandonment of the cross to show just how related you are. You are God's daughter. You are God's son.

Listen to the voice of a loving parent:

> Then the LORD said, "I have observed the misery of my people who
> are in Egypt; I have heard their cry on account of their taskmasters.
> Indeed, I know their sufferings, and I have come down to deliver
> them from the Egyptians, and to bring them up out of that land to
> a good and broad land, a land flowing with milk and honey...
>
> (Ex. 3:7-8).

> For the Eternal is listening, and nothing pleases Him more than
> His people; He raises up the afflicted and crowns them with His
> salvation.[8]
>
> (Ps. 149:4 VOICE)

---

[8] *The Voice Bible: Step Into the Story of Scripture,* Chris Seay, ed. (Nashville, TN: Thomas Nelson, Inc., 2012).

The father replied, "My son, you are always with me, and all I have is yours."

(LUKE 15:31 VOICE)

Listen to the voice of your brother Yeshua:

Indeed, God did not send the Son into the world to condemn the world, but in order that the world might be saved through him.

(JOHN 3:17)

The Father judges no one but has given all judgment to the Son, so that all may honor the Son just as they honor the Father. Anyone who does not honor the Son does not honor the Father who sent him. Very truly, I tell you, anyone who hears my word and believes him who sent me has eternal life, and does not come under judgment, but has passed from death to life.

(JOHN 5:22-23)

Are not five sparrows sold for two pennies? Yet not one of them is forgotten in God's sight. But even the hairs of your head are all counted. Do not be afraid; you are of more value than many sparrows.

(LUKE 12:6–7)

Listen to the voices of the faithful who have gone before you:

Therefore, now no condemnation awaits those who are living in Jesus the Anointed, the Liberating King, because when you live in the Anointed One, Jesus, a new law takes effect. The law of the Spirit of life breathes into you and liberates you from the law of sin and death.

(ROM. 8:1-2 VOICE)

As I will show you, it's important that the One who brings us to God and those who are brought to God become one, since we are all from one Father. This is why Jesus was not ashamed to call us His family....

(HEB. 2:11 VOICE)

We all did it, all of us doing what we felt like doing, when we felt like doing it, all of us in the same boat. It's a wonder God didn't lose his temper and do away with the whole lot of us. Instead, immense in mercy and with an incredible love, he embraced us. He took our sin-dead lives and made us alive in Christ. He did all this on his own, with no help from us! Then he picked us up and set us down in highest heaven in company with Jesus, our Messiah.[9]

(EPH. 2:3–6 MSG)

I AM ... What are you?

Do you hear an angry God who doesn't like you? The voice of those statements doesn't sound like the half-truth of justification. Summing up our faith lives with the statement "Christ died for my sins" leaves so much out of the picture. I get it—even the half-truth can be a compelling picture. In fact, we could probably build lots of churches, empower lots of programs, and raise lots of money based on that picture. It is strong enough to motivate millions of people into religious action. But in the end, it is still a half-truth—and half-truths aren't true.

Hopefully, we have come out from under the incomplete idea that Jesus had to die for our sins. Yes, God needed to set us free from our mistakes. But we have seen that could be done without human sacrifice. We have also seen that our mistakes were our problem—blocking our view

---

9 E.H. Peterson, *The Message: The Bible in Contemporary Language* (Colorado Springs, CO: NavPress, 2002).

and our reception of our true identity as God's daughters and sons. We are family.

God does hope that we will learn from our mistakes. In fact, I believe that God takes action to help us grow in and through our failures. God does not turn away from our mistakes. God meets us right in the middle of them. God is not angry. God loves us—even when we sin.

The picture God has painted and is painting is much grander than just substitutionary atonement and justification. The relationship God offers every son and every daughter is much richer than a relationship governed by "good" behavior. This truth is much more comprehensive. It removes the narrow and imprisoning idea that the whole point of our relationship with Christ is because we needed to be forgiven.

God loves you. Period. In your most sinful moment, in the times when you feel completely alone and abandoned, God's love for you does not decrease or disappear. We must carry the full truth of our relationship with God and each other. We must shine the light of love, family, belonging, and freedom upon every lie that tells us we must perform in order to receive. As my rabbi has taught me, we do not work *for* God's approval—we work *from* God's approval.

The beautifully complex picture such truths paint must guide the rest of our ideas about God and each other. Accordingly, let us be plain and clear with the truth.

Read these statements out loud. Okay, make sure you are alone first. Or maybe not—perhaps you are about to cause the best kind of scene wherever you are. Whatever the case may be—hear these words. Don't just read them in your mind—let the favor of the LORD be proclaimed out loud over your life.

I Am not my sins and mistakes.
I Am God's child.
I Am acceptable to God.
I Am pleasing to God.
I Am welcomed.

I Am received.

I Am God's delight.

I Am God's desire.

I Am a child of the Most High God—a beloved (daughter or son).

I Am the delight of God's heart and God's joy.

I Am so loved that God endured the abandonment of the cross
to identify with me.

I Am God's favorite. So is my neighbor. So is my enemy.

"You were a million years of work,"
said God and His angels, with needle and thread.
They kissed your head and said,
"You're a good kid
and you make us proud.
So just give your best
and the rest
will come, and we'll see you soon."
We are made of love,
and all the beauty stemming from it.
We are made of love,
And every fracture caused by the lack of love.[10]

---

10 Ryan O'Neal, "Needle and Thread," performed by Sleeping at Last, *Keep No Score*, CD
Track 3, Sleeping at Last, 2006.

THE DEVIL IS GOD'S COUNTERPART

I am quite sure I am more afraid of people who are themselves terrified of the devil than I am of the devil himself.[1]

— Teresa of Ávila

When I was a young boy, my first best friend was named Ben Fay. Ben and I were buddies through preschool, church, and the most important reason of all: our mothers were friends. Ben and I were much like any other young children—capable of mischief on our own but capable of so much more when we combined our talents. Somewhere along the path of my relationship with Ben Fay, I discovered that he was a handy person to have around … even when he wasn't around. Now you're asking, "What the heck does that mean?" It means that I crafted an imaginary friend for the times I was alone, and I named him after my very real friend Ben Fay. Are you with me? There was a real Ben Fay—an actual little boy—my buddy whom I would play with. There was also an imaginary Ben Fay—not real—that I would utilize as needed.

---

[1] Saint Teresa of Ávila, *The Life of Teresa of Jesus; The Autobiography of Teresa of Ávila*, translated by E. Allison Peers (New York: Image Books, 2004), xviii.

At this point, you might begin to wonder if you have committed some of your very valuable time to reading the theological musings of a dolt who is so dense he could not think to name his imaginary childhood friend something original. I understand this wondering, and I want to assure you that my motivations in creating an imaginary Ben Fay were thoughtful and duplicitous. You see, I didn't set out to create an imaginary friend.

One day after the real Ben Fay and I had been playing and he had gone home, my mother was upset about a mess we had made and left for someone else to clean up. In the middle of my scolding, it dawned on me that I was not alone in my guilt, so I blurted out a phrase that I would go on to repeat numerous times in my young life: "Ben Fay did it!" My mother, knowing that Ben Fay had helped make the mess, eased up and recognized that I alone was not to blame. I couldn't believe it. It had worked! She was not mad at me!! When I realized that Ben Fay didn't have to be around to accept some or all of the blame for my actions, the imaginary Ben Fay was born. From then on, any time I faced an inquisition, consequence, or punishment that felt like more than I could handle on my own, I would just throw Ben Fay under the bus.

Mom: "Who made this mess?!"
Me: "Ben Fay did it."

My Sister: "Who ate all the cookies?!"
Me: "Ben Fay did it."

Dad: "Darrell!!"
Me: "Ben Fay did it."

It kind of rolls off the tongue, doesn't it? Four sweet syllables to move the focus off me and on to someone else—a simple phrase to paint me as the victim.

I feel it necessary to digress for a moment and acknowledge that while it has been thirty-five years or so since I have seen Ben Fay, I assume he is still out there somewhere. If you know Ben Fay, please don't think less of him for being my unknowing accomplice in crime. And, whatever you do, please do not blame your own troubles on Ben Fay!

So where am I going with this? How does Ben Fay relate to the lie that the devil is God's counterpart? I want to invite you into the tension between the real Ben Fay and the imaginary Ben Fay. What I mean by tension is that we are going to stay in between without coming to resolution one way or another. Ben Fay was a real person. Ben Fay was also a creation of my imagination that I used to explain and deal with my own behavior and the consequences thereof. To decide on which Ben Fay was to blame for all my misbehavior is not the question. To decide on whether or not Ben Fay was real is not the point either. We need to stay in the tension and ask the more important questions.

The lie that oppresses us and limits our faith is not even about the "realness" of evil. Let me be very clear here. Evil is real. I have yet to meet someone whose life has not been scarred by evil. Right now, all over the world, real people are experiencing very real pain and very real oppression caused by the presence of evil in this world. Our pain and our oppression are not to be dismissed as delusions. They are real and are to be validated and fought against.

What is at stake here is not whether evil is real. It's not even whether the devil is real. It's whether or not that evil, or the devil, can stand against our God. The question we need to ask is who have we said the devil is and how does that distort our view of God and of ourselves? The purpose of this exploration is not to decide one way or the other if the devil is real. Rather, I am hopeful that we can agree not to decide on the "realness" of the devil and instead decide that the problematic lie is that the devil is somehow God's counterpart or opposite. This is a lie about a good God versus a bad god—what is known as *dualism*. *Dual* means two opposing forces. Good versus evil, dark versus light, right versus wrong. This is a lie that allowed me to divide my childhood existence into the good and innocent Darrell and the bad and mischievous Ben Fay.

God Versus *Satan* ... Wait, Who Is *Satan*?

The primary example of dualism in our world is the idea that there is a good, supernatural force guiding the universe battling an evil, supernatural force corrupting the universe. And unlike the blurry lines of Batman *vs.* Superman—where both seem to be for good, and we all just want them to get along and fight crime together—God versus *Satan* is neat and orderly. It makes sense to us because it successfully divides and organizes our reality for us. It just seems simple to think that everything that is good and right is because of God and everything that is bad and wrong is because of the devil.

As much as we might feel that such thinking is neat and orderly, it falls apart really quickly as soon as something that is bad and wrong touches our life. When evil or corruption really hits home and affects us personally, we want answers. "Where were you, God?" "Why did you let that happen to me?" In turn, those questions shine a bright light on the misleading idea of dualism and lead to questions like, "If God created everything, why did God create the devil?" or "How did God lose that battle to the devil?" Is that what happened? God somehow lost a match with the devil? Were God and the devil really fighting over your life, and the devil somehow snuck a sucker punch in? What originally seems orderly about dualism becomes confusing and disordered really quickly as soon as we start talking plainly about the devil.

To be honest, we have every right to be confused. The history of our faith is rife with misunderstanding and misapplying information about the devil. The truth is we don't have a clear and consistent picture about the devil—not even within the pages of the Bible. Don't miss that. The Bible itself does not offer a clear picture about the nature, state, or identity of the devil.

This is the point where you're thinking, *What?! Then how in the heck did we come up with all those ideas about the devil?*

That is a great question. In fact, it is the best question to ask.

Have you ever seen one of those brainteaser paragraphs that show just how much your brain is concluding on autopilot without you really being aware of it? Something like this:

> Aoccdrnig to a rseearch sduty at Cmabrigde Uinervtisy, it deosn't mttaer in waht oredr the ltteers in a wrod are, the olny iprmoetnt tihng is taht the frist and lsat ltteer be in the rghit pclae. The rset can be a toatl mses and you can sittll raed it wouthit porbelm. Tihs is bcuseae the huamn mnid deos not raed ervey lteter by istlef, but the wrod as a wlohe.[2]

Now, I get that you may have read through that a little slower than the rest of this chapter, but I'm guessing you got through it and were able to make sense of it. The reasons that we are able to make sense out of that gibberish does have to do with the placement of the first and last letters of each word—as the paragraph itself indicates—but it also has to do with our ability to extract information from the larger context of the paragraph. As we read, we understand more and more what the topic is, and we begin to expect certain words. We scan the paragraph and find identifiable markers and elements that allow us to make assumptions and conclusions about what each sentence should be saying.

Believe it or not, a similar phenomenon can happen with our theology—or in this case, angelology—when we are confronted with a disjointed and incomplete narrative. We fill in the holes. We smooth out the roughness. We look for contextual clues and seek to make sense out of something that does not make sense on the surface. In short, we interpret—or worse, we allow someone else to interpret for us. Just like the jumbled paragraph above, when we take the biblical texts traditionally understood as referring to "the devil" and piece them together, we arrive

---

[2] brainHQ, *Scrambled Text*, brainhq.com, accessed October 1, 2015, http://www.brainhq.com/brain-resources/brain-teasers/scrambled-text.

   I must confess that neither I nor my spell-check, enjoyed typing that paragraph. I have a sense that my computer is deeply disappointed in me. There are so many red underlines that I refused to correct. Every time my computer tried to convince me that I was spelling those words wrong, I had to go to great lengths to convince it that I wanted the misspelled version. It may never trust me again.

at a nonsensical narrative that clears up very little about the devil—especially not whether the devil is a real, singular being working against God.

The very fact that I have thus far in this exposition referred to the devil as "the devil" reveals an interpretive implication that there is a singular being that is "the devil." Why else would one refer to "the devil" as such were "the devil" not a real singular entity? Wouldn't we simply speak of abstracts, like *evil* or *sin*? In order for us to get to the truth about the devil in relation to God, we must first clear away some of the clutter that we have picked up about the devil.

Let's start with the Bible. If we understand the Bible not as a monolith or static report but as a library of books that tell the progressing story of God and God's people, we should not be surprised to find that different writings from different people in different places from different times would reflect different ideas about the devil. Let me be blunt—there simply is not a consistent idea throughout the Bible about who or what the devil is.

Let's look at a few examples of "devil-referencing" Scripture, each of which uses the Hebraic word *satan*.[3]

Numbers 22 tells the story of Balaam, his donkey, and an angel of the LORD who stands as a *satan* or adversary against them.

> Then the LORD opened the eyes of Balaam, and he saw the angel of the LORD standing in the road, with his drawn sword in his hand; and he bowed down, falling on his face. The angel of the LORD said to him, "Why have you struck your donkey these three times? I have come out as a *satan*, because your way is perverse before me.
>
> (NUM. 22:31–32)

---

[3]   I must point out that the inherent interpretation of *satan* as a single entity is so prevalent that it is even found in the very word processing program with which I am writing this book. Every time I type *satan* into the document, it is underlined in red to indicate my failure to use a capital "S" in writing the name. Even my word processing software has been coded to represent *satan* as a single being with the name *Satan*! As mentioned in the last footnote, this may very well be the chapter that causes my computer to break up with me.

The beginning of the Book of Job paints a peculiar picture of *satan* as being a heavenly being who serves at the discretion of God.

> One day the heavenly beings came to present themselves before the LORD, and *Satan* also came among them. The LORD said to *Satan*, "Where have you come from?" *Satan* answered the LORD, "From going to and fro on the earth, and from walking up and down on it." The LORD said to *Satan*, "Have you considered my servant Job? There is no one like him on the earth, a blameless and upright man who fears God and turns away from evil." Then *Satan* answered the LORD, "Does Job fear God for nothing? Have you not put a fence around him and his house and all that he has, on every side? You have blessed the work of his hands, and his possessions have increased in the land. But stretch out your hand now, and touch all that he has, and he will curse you to your face." The LORD said to *Satan*, "Very well, all that he has is in your power; only do not stretch out your hand against him!" So *Satan* went out from the presence of the LORD.
>
> (JOB 1:6–12)

Zechariah 3 describes the fourth vision Zechariah received where *satan* acts as an accuser against the high-priest Joshua.

> Then he showed me the high priest Joshua standing before the angel of the LORD, and *Satan* standing at his right hand to accuse him. And the LORD said to *Satan*, "The LORD rebuke you, O *Satan*! The LORD who has chosen Jerusalem rebuke you! Is not this man a brand plucked from the fire?".
>
> (ZECH. 3:1–2)

Wow! What a mess! Any one of these verses by themselves can turn our ideas about the devil upside down. Where do we begin?

Let's start with the word *satan*. *Satan* is a Hebraic word that means adversary or accuser. In each of these instances, *satan* is precisely the Hebraic word that is used. In fact, if we are looking for any reference to "the devil" in the Hebraic scriptures, *satan* is all we are going to find. There are no other references to any kind of "devil" or "antichrist" in all of the books that comprise the Hebrew Bible. You may be thinking, *Well, duh! Of course, the Hebrew Bible doesn't talk about the Antichrist because the Christ had not yet come.* That is a very valid point, but don't miss that there is also no labeling of *satan* as Lucifer, Mephistopheles, or Beelzebub in the Hebrew Bible either—at least not as we understand it.

Historically, some have looked to the Isaiah 14:12 reference of Lucifer in the King James Version of the Bible as a descriptor of a singular, supernatural, evil being.

> "How art thou fallen from heaven, O *Lucifer*, son of the morning!
> How art thou cut down to the ground, which didst weaken the
> nations!"
>
> (ISA. 14:12 KJV)

If we keep reading in the New Revised Standard Version, however, the continuing description doesn't jive very well with a single, supernatural being.

> Those who see you will stare at you,
>   and ponder over you:
> "Is this the man who made the earth tremble,
>   who shook kingdoms,
> who made the world like a desert
>   and overthrew its cities,
>   who would not let his prisoners go home?"
> All the kings of the nations lie in glory,
>   each in his own tomb;
> but you are cast out, away from your grave,
>   like loathsome carrion,

clothed with the dead, those pierced by the sword,
　　who go down to the stones of the Pit,
　　like a corpse trampled underfoot.
　　You will not be joined with them in burial,
　　because you have destroyed your land,
　　you have killed your people.

(Isa. 14:15–20)

To be sure, there are elements in this description that sound a lot like what many of us have come to think of as "the devil." Yet, there are other portions—like the fact that this description states that Lucifer is a "man"— that don't seem to make sense. In fact, these verses don't only describe Lucifer as a man but as a "dead" man that is "cast out" from his grave like "loathsome carrion." How does that work? If the point of this story is to warn listeners and readers of the continuing presence of a supernatural, evil-incarnate being, then why does this story say that he is dead?

The simple answer is that this story was never about the devil at all. This description is an indictment of a cruel Babylonian king, a very real and very dead human being. And friends, this is no mystery or Bible code. The verses immediately preceding this passage state:

"When the Lord has given you rest from your pain and turmoil
　　and the hard service with which you were made to serve, you will
　　take up this taunt against the king of Babylon..."

(Isa. 14:3–4)

The whole thing is a taunt. The Scripture itself tells us that this whole section is a thumb-your-nose at the king of Babylon poem. So if this passage was never about the devil, how in the world did we get to thinking that Lucifer was the name of the devil?

You know the answer before you even read it. Interpretation.

People interpreted this passage to be about the devil and, in so doing, concluded that Lucifer must be the proper name of the devil.

Watch this interpretive journey!

In the entire Bible, the name Lucifer is only used in this single location—Isaiah 14:12. As our oldest copies of the Book of Isaiah are written in ancient Hebrew, we should note the Hebrew word that is used in Isaiah 14:12—the very word that has been translated as Lucifer—is *helel*. *Helel* means to shine or bear light. Over a thousand years after this taunt of a Babylonian king was first written, a fourth-century priest and historian named Jerome translated the entire Bible into Latin—a translation that is known as the Vulgate. In his translation, Jerome interpreted the "shining" and "light bearing" of *helel* as the "morning star"—also known as the planet Venus. Can you guess what the Latin word for the planet Venus is? That's right—Lucifer.

Come forward another 1,100 years or so and we find the writers of the King James Version of the Bible using Jerome's Vulgate to translate the Scripture into English. Guess which word they brought forward from the Latin? That's right, *Lucifer*. Still, this interpretive timeline only explains the insertion of the word *Lucifer*. Neither Jerome nor the King James writers asserted that Lucifer was *Satan*. The suggestion that this passage was describing a supernatural, evil being and not a Babylonian king developed later through even more interpretative choices. Over time, people read meaning into the text. The taunt of the Babylonian king was no longer relevant to them; they had no concept of Babylonian kings because Babylon had faded into history. When they read these very real, very contextualized verses in Isaiah, they didn't have the context, so they interpreted. These weren't bad people; they were just like you and me—meaning-making machines. Instead of letting the text say just what it said—that this was to be a taunt of a dead, Babylonian king—people assigned a meaning to this passage about the devil—a meaning that this passage was never meant to convey. Thus, the belief formed that the unflattering description of a ruler in Isaiah 14 was referring to a singular, supernatural evil being—and that his name must, therefore, be Lucifer.

Dramatic pause.

Did that blow your mind? If it doesn't, that's okay, but don't miss this prime example of how time, context, translation, and interpretation can drastically impact our understanding and shape our world. Seriously.

Think about it. How has that interpretative journey impacted you? Have you been thinking and living as though the Bible itself validated the existence of a singular, supernatural, evil being—whose name was Lucifer? How did that make you feel? Did it make you fear the devil? How did it make you think about God? Whether we want to admit it or not, so much of our faith is based upon our misunderstanding of other's interpretations—and their interpretations may have been very misguided.

How about some of the devil's other names? Did you learn that Mephistopheles and Beelzebub were also names for the evil one? Not according to the Bible. Mephistopheles is a name first applied to a devil character in German folklore in the late sixteenth century. Even then, Mephistopheles is seen as a demon who works for the devil and not as the devil himself. Beelzebub or Beelzebul, like Lucifer, is a name that does appear in the Bible—both in the Hebrew scriptures and in the New Testament—but not as a name for the devil. Instead, Beelzebub is representative of a different "evil being—a Philistine god, the god of Ekron (2 Kings 1:2-3). Calling this Philistine god Beelzebub was the Hebraic way of putting him down—literally referring to him as "lord of the flies" and likening him to a pile of dung.

To be sure, the name comes up again as the Gospel writers quote the crowds accusing Jesus as saying that he is in league with Beelzebul (Matt.12:24, 27; Mark 3:22; Luke 11:15, 18). This usage may represent a continuing belief that Beelzebul exists and is a singular, supernatural, evil being, but Jesus' response to his accusers does nothing to validate such a belief. In fact, the point of Jesus' response to his accusers seems to be to ridicule the idea that such an evil being has anything to do with what is going on.

But some of them said, "He casts out demons by Beelzebul, the ruler of the demons." Others, to test him, kept demanding from him a sign from heaven. But he knew what they were thinking and said to them, "Every kingdom divided against itself becomes a desert, and house falls on house. If *Satan* also is divided against himself, how will his kingdom stand? —for you say that I cast out the demons by Beelzebul. Now if I cast out the demons by Beelzebul, by whom do your exorcists cast them out?"

(Luke 11:15–19)

Beelzebub, Beelzebul, Mephisopheles, Lucifer, the Evil One, the Antichrist—none of these titles appear in the entirety of the Hebrew scriptures as a reference to the devil. Each of these titles represents a later development. The ancient Hebrews, the storytellers and authors of the Hebrew Bible, only use the word "*satan*" when dealing with the devil, and they don't even use that word consistently. Sometimes, as in the case of Job 1, *satan* does seem to refer to a single being—albeit one who works for God. Other times *satan* refers to an agent of the Lord who stands as an obstacle to human will, as in the case of Numbers 22.

So where are we left when we go looking to understand the devil in the Hebrew Bible? We are left knowing that the word *satan* means accuser or adversary. In the instance of Balaam, *satan* is used to describe an angel of the Lord on a holy mission. The books of Job and Zechariah use *satan* to describe an angel who is not only in the presence of God but is subject to God's direction. Job and Zechariah also point to *satan* as one who stands ready to accuse humans—not God.

This is really the point I would like us to grasp here. The Hebrew Bible does not set *satan* up as an adversary to God but only uses the term *satan* to describe an adversary to or accuser of human beings.

You may be thinking to yourself, *Okay, fine … the Hebrew Bible portrays* satan *as an adversary of humans and not of God. So what? What's the big deal?* My response to you would be, "Exactly! So what? What is the big deal?" That is exactly the right question to ask. What does it mean that the authors of the Hebrew scriptures did not see God as having an adversary? What does it mean to believe—as many faithful people do now—that God and the devil are opposing forces … or that there is a battle between

God and the devil for control of the world ... or your life ... or your soul? These are the right questions to ask, and they are enough to make your head spin. So before we run headlong into some supposed "answers" to those questions, let's take a look at how we got from a Hebraic people whose conceptualization of *satan* was of angels who, under the ultimate authority of God, stood as accusers or adversaries of people to a modern faith that believes the devil is a singular, opposing being to God.

Devil-Obsessed

I recently heard a Google executive on NPR discussing some of the more fascinating statistics Google has gathered on Americans through Google search. When the executive was asked about the top searches related to Christianity in America, his answer disturbed me: *the rapture, Antichrist,* and *hell.* Those are the three most-searched "Christian" topics according to Google. Can you believe that?! If you will forgive the horrible pun, what in the hell is wrong with us? Why are we so devil-obsessed? Why do we think the most important and fascinating story of the Christian faith is the one where there is a "god" of evil who will ultimately battle the good "God" in the rapture in an effort to take as many souls to hell as possible?

Think about it for a moment. Consider the vast canon of stories, artistic expression, television shows, movies, and books dedicated to the devil. Can you even count the number of exorcism or demon-related movies that have been released in your lifetime? Our culture is obsessed with God's counterpart. To be sure, one of the reasons we love to bring up an evil counterpart for God in our writings and movies is so that God's enemy can be crushed and we can all cheer as good wins out over evil. Would you be surprised to find out that such a storyline is ancient? That people have believed in such a story about God for thousands of years? My guess is no, you would not be surprised. But you might be surprised to find out that the ancient storyline of God versus the devil is not from the Bible. It is not a Judeo-Christian story.

The idea that God is pure good and has a counterpart that is pure evil is not a new idea, and (let me be very clear here) it is not an idea that comes from the scriptures of the Hebrew or Christian Bible. In fact, the stories of the Bible paint a drastically different picture. One of the reasons the stories of the Bible—the stories of Abraham, Isaac, and Jacob, the stories of the Exodus, the stories of Jesus and the early Christian faith—stood out from every other religion at the time is precisely because they presented a God that had no equal—no counterpart. The God that is presented in the texts of the Bible is so singular and so powerful that the thought of an opposing force is ridiculous. How could the Creator of all things have a created counterpart?

The ancient idea of opposing divine forces—of a divided cosmos where all that is good comes from the "good" God and all that is bad comes from the "evil" God—is *theological dualism*. Theological dualism conceptually divides the supernatural into two opposed or contrasted forces: Good versus Evil. Dualism is an ancient religious concept that existed in religions all over the world, especially the world in which the Hebrew people and, later, the Christian faithful lived. The Assyrians and Babylonians—two nations that conquered and exiled the Hebrew people in 722 BCE and 586 BCE, respectively—held theologically dualistic ideas. At the time when the Hebrews were exiled into Babylon, Zoroastrianism was the predominant spiritual philosophy. This Zoroastrian faith in which the Hebrew people were immersed during exile held there was a good god of light named *Ahura Mazda* and an evil god of darkness named *Angra Mainyu*. This, folks, is not just dualism. It is dualism that directly touched and influenced the lives and ideas of the forbearers of the Judeo-Christian faith. Furthermore, this is just one example of the many ancient dualistic ideas present during the same times and in the same places as many of the biblical stories.

The ancient Canaanites believed in a demon named *Mot*, who was the god of the underworld and death. Ancient Egyptians believed in *Set*, a storm god who resembled a jackal, had a forked tongue, and was associated with scorching heat and death. In ancient Greece, *Hades*, the son of Zeus, lived in the land of the dead and was a hideous and fearsome god of death. Many of the ancient gods of evil, death, and the underworld in the various cultures surrounding the Hebrew people were characterized by their hideous appearances, including horns and tails. Do such descriptions bring anyone else to mind?

Here is the problem: none of that is found in the books that comprise the Bible. Nowhere in Scripture is a singular evil being set up as the god of the underworld or death. Even in the instances when the biblical texts seem to indicate that *satan* is a singular being, there is no point at which that being is understood to be God's counterpart or opposite. As much as we may force the dualism of our history and of our culture on the Bible and thereby misinterpret and misunderstand its story, there remains a resounding message within its pages. The God of Abraham, Isaac, and Jacob has no equal, no counterpart, no opposite. The LORD our God is One; the LORD alone. (Deut. 6:4)

Consider these words of the prophets; they do not leave room for the existence of an evil god that counters the good God.

> I am the LORD, and there is no other;
>> besides me there is no god.
>> I arm you, though you do not know me,
> so that they may know, from the rising of the sun
>> and from the west, that there is no one besides me;
>> I am the LORD, and there is no other.
> I form light and create darkness,
>> I make weal and create woe;
>> I the LORD do all these things.
>
> (Isa. 45:5–7)

> Is a trumpet blown in a city,
>> and the people are not afraid?
> Does disaster befall a city,
>> unless the Lord has done it?
>
> (Amos 3:6)

For the inhabitants of Maroth
    wait anxiously for good,
      yet disaster has come down from the LORD
      to the gate of Jerusalem.

(MIC. 1:12)

Similarly the story of Job, which does introduce a singular *Satan* character, still leaves no ambiguity as to the sovereignty and singularity of God.

> Then Job arose, tore his robe, shaved his head, and fell on the ground and worshiped. He said, "Naked I came from my mother's womb, and naked shall I return there; the LORD gave, and the LORD has taken away; blessed be the name of the LORD."

(JOB 1:20–21)

> Then his wife said to him, "Do you still persist in your integrity? Curse God, and die." But he said to her, "You speak as any foolish woman would speak. Shall we receive the good at the hand of God, and not receive the bad?" In all this, Job did not sin with his lips.

(JOB 2:9–10)

> Then there came to him all his brothers and sisters and all who had known him before, and they ate bread with him in his house; they showed him sympathy and comforted him for all the evil that the LORD had brought upon him.

(JOB 42:11)

Friends, I hope you are catching some of these phrases. These are some big, hairy, undeniable theological statements. These statements are about God—not the devil.

They comforted him for all the evil that the LORD had brought upon him.

Does disaster befall a city unless the LORD has done it?

I am the LORD and there is no other—I form light and create darkness, I make weal and create woe; I the LORD do all these things.

To our Western minds, these are incredibly heavy and confounding ideas that stand in direct opposition to dualism. It makes me quite uncomfortable to sit in these texts. I would much rather believe that the devil is responsible for everything bad and God is only responsible for the good stuff. Yet the texts of the Bible do not direct me to such a conclusion. They ask me to stay in the tension of the one God—the God of those things that I consider beautiful and light-giving as well as those things that I consider destructive and dark.

Get Behind Me, *Satan*!

At this point, you may be ready to give up on this journey. You may be thinking to yourself, *Whatever, Darrell… you're just nuts. This is all Old Testament-Hebrew stuff anyway—what about the New Testament? What about the story of Jesus being tempted in the wilderness by* satan? *What about all those times in the New Testament where* satan *is referred to as a singular being?* If you are thinking such questions to yourself, let me be the first to say, "Yippee!" Those are the right questions to ask. What do we learn about *satan* from the way the Christian canon deals with the devil? Does the message change at all?

The short answer is not really—at least, not the important message. To be sure, the New Testament does reference *satan* more than the Hebrew Bible, which is interesting given that the New Testament canon is considerably shorter than the Hebrew Bible. The New Testament also contains a greater number of references to *satan* as a singular being.

Satan (proper name) -

"And no wonder, for *Satan* himself masquerades as an angel of light".

(2 COR. 11:14)

The devil -

"Then Jesus was led by the Spirit into the desert to be tempted by the devil".

(MATT. 4:1)

Your enemy -

"Be self-controlled and alert. Your enemy the devil prowls around like a roaring lion looking for someone to devour".

(1 PET. 5:8)

The father of lies -

"You belong to your father, the devil, and you want to carry out your father's desire. He was a murderer from the beginning, not holding to the truth, for there is no truth in him. When he lies, he speaks his native language, for he is a liar and the father of lies".

(JOHN 8:44)

The evil one -

"But the LORD is faithful, and he will strengthen and protect you from the evil one".

(2 THESS. 3:3)

These examples are but a few of the many instances in the New Testament where the singular, evil entity of the devil is referenced. With such prolific usage of this persona in the New Testament, it is no wonder that we have picked up the banner of dualism and carried it forward in our faith. Is it possible that the surrounding dualism of the cultures in which Christianity was birthed infiltrated the Christian faith? The scholarly term for this phenomenon is *syncretism*. Syncretism, simply put, is when different religious ideas or schools of thought meld together over time.

There is a strong scholarly case to be made that the progression of the biblical *satan* from a nonspecific adversary to a singular, supernatural, evil being is an example of syncretism. But again, whether or not the devil is a real being is not the lie we are trying to dismiss. The lie that warps our relationship with God is the notion that *satan,* in any form, is God's counterpart. Regardless of why the New Testament seems much more comfortable with presenting *satan* as a singular being, the reality is that no passages in the New Testament assert that the devil is God's counterpart or opposite. Just as is the case in the Hebrew Bible, not one single Scripture in all of the New Testament positions *satan* as outside or beyond the authority and control of God.

This is not to assert that the New Testament is unified or resolved to presenting *satan* as a singular being either. Just like the Hebrew Bible, the New Testament contains many confusing representations of *satan*. Consider the following references from New Testament texts.

> Then Jesus began to teach them that the Son of Man must undergo great suffering, and be rejected by the elders, the chief priests, and the scribes, and be killed, and after three days rise again. He said all this quite openly. And Peter took him aside and began to rebuke him. But turning and looking at his disciples, he rebuked Peter and said, "Get behind me, *Satan*! For you are setting your mind not on divine things but on human things."
>
> (MARK 8:31–33)

Mark's Gospel seems to indicate that Jesus accused Peter of either being a *satan* or being possessed by *satan*. Both Matthew and Luke echo this same story and conclusion in their Gospel accounts. The Gospel of John, however, has Jesus calling Judas a devil during the events of the Last Supper.

> So Jesus asked the twelve, "Do you also wish to go away?" Simon Peter answered him, "LORD, to whom can we go? You have the words of eternal life. We have come to believe and know that you are the Holy One of God." Jesus answered them, "Did I not choose you, the twelve? Yet one of you is a devil." He was speaking of Judas, son of Simon Iscariot, for he, though one of the twelve, was going to betray him.
>
> (JOHN 6:67–71)

The muddied waters of what *satan* is aren't even limited to the Gospels. In 2 Corinthians, Paul suggests that, just like Job, *satan* is tormenting him for a holy and divine purpose.

> But if I wish to boast, I will not be a fool, for I will be speaking the truth. But I refrain from it, so that no one may think better of me than what is seen in me or heard from me, even considering the exceptional character of the revelations. Therefore, to keep me from being too elated, a thorn was given me in the flesh, a messenger of *Satan* to torment me, to keep me from being too elated.
>
> (2 COR. 12:6–7)

Paul's writing to Timothy suggests either employing *satan* or surrendering to *satan* the teaching or training of unfaithful individuals that they might develop better behavior.

> I am giving you these instructions, Timothy, my child, in accordance with the prophecies made earlier about you, so that by

following them you may fight the good fight, having faith and a good conscience. By rejecting conscience, certain persons have suffered shipwreck in the faith; among them are Hymenaeus and Alexander, whom I have turned over to *Satan*, so that they may learn not to blaspheme.

(1 Tim. 1:18–20)

So according to the New Testament, Peter and Judas were at one point either *satan* or possessed by *satan*, Paul is being tormented by *satan* in order to keep him humbly focused on his calling, the misbehaving faithful should be turned over to *satan* for training, and *satan* is a singular, fallen angel who prowls about seeking to devour someone. Does that clear it all up?

Ask the Wrong Question, Expect the Wrong Answer

Are you with me yet? We cannot possibly look to the books of the Bible—Hebrew or New Testament—and arrive at a singular, inclusive answer of what or who the devil is. There are scriptures in the Hebrew Bible that call good and obedient angels on direct orders from God *satan*. There are scriptures in both the Hebrew Bible and the Christian texts that refer to human beings as *satan*, or devils. There are also biblical texts that seem to indicate the presence of an accusing, adversarial angel that is interested in oppressing and tempting humanity. So which is it?

Is *satan* really an angel agent of God, doing only the will of God?

Is *satan* a singular demon who opposes and accuses humanity?

Is *satan* a general term for those who oppose and accuse—be they human or otherwise?

Is *satan* a singular, evil being or a metaphor that represents the progressive apprehension of the people who lived and told these stories?

The answer according to the Bible is yes. This strange library simultaneously asserts that *satan* is all of the above. *Satan* is a roaring lion looking for someone to devour. Human beings can be a *satan*. *Satan* is the accusing force that plays the role of bringing us face to face with the consequences of our actions.

If we posit a singular understanding or representation of the devil—no matter what it is, we are choosing to omit the texts that stand in contradiction to our singular point of view. In short, we are cutting up our own Jefferson Bible on the topic of *satan*. If we ask the wrong question, we will get the wrong answer.

The Bible simply does not singularly answer the question of who **satan** is. But there is a singular representation of who *satan* is **not**. *Satan* is not God's counterpart. Whether *satan* is an angel on a holy mission, a fallen angel, the accuser, the tempter, the trainer, Peter, Judas, or a metaphor for our struggle with the evil within, at no point is *satan* outside of the authority and power of God. At no point is *satan* God's adversary.

Now, friends, let me be clear once again. The point of coming out from under this lie is not to question whether or not the devil is real. Was Ben Fay a real boy—my tangible, knowable friend? Yes. Was Ben Fay an intangible symbol of my struggle to justify some of my behavior and a safe figure behind which I could hide? Yes. Is *satan* a singular being who tempts, accuses, and opposes humanity? Yes. Is *satan* a metaphorical representation of those forces that stand in opposition to our relationship with God—including our own behavior? Yes. It is not an either-or question according to the biblical texts—it is a both-and. We are invited to stay in that tension. In fact, the only way we can escape that tension is by lying to ourselves and each other through mental gymnastics and bad biblical interpretation.

Yet, there is a place where the tension stops. Nothing—and, friends, I mean nothing—in the Bible communicates that *satan*—be he singular and tangible or symbolic and intangible—stands in opposition to God. The movie *The Usual Suspects* is often quoted for its line that states, "The greatest trick the devil ever pulled was convincing people that he didn't exist."[4] While that is a great line in the context of that movie, it is never-theless dualistic thinking. The truth is the greatest trick that the devil ever pulled was convincing people that he was God's equal—and that we have something to fear.

Whether the devil exists or not is the wrong question to ask. The right question is whom does *satan* oppose? Whom does *satan* accuse? You already know the answer before you read it. The Bible is consistent in its stance that none can oppose God. God has no counterpart. *Satan*, in whatever form we want to embrace, is our adversary—not God's. *Satan* is our accuser—not God's. *Satan* is our enemy—not God's. God may not have a counterpart, but we sure do.

So What?

Do you feel discord stirring in your belly? I sure do. I find wrestling with my own dualism to be very disconcerting—and sometimes physically uncomfortable. As the tentacles of any lie release their grasp on my think-ing, I can sometimes physically feel my fear. What do I do now? What am I supposed to believe? I'd rather not turn away from ideas with which I have become comfortable—especially if I have no idea of what I should turn toward. Can't I just pretend that I don't have these questions? What would be wrong with just remaining blissfully ignorant and going back to the way things were? I mean, really, what difference does it make if I view *satan* as my adversary instead of God's? How does that really change anything?

If you are feeling this way, you are not strange and you are not alone. Believe it or not, at the end of this long and arduous journey are a few simple truths that will hopefully resonate with our spirit if we have come out from under the confusing mess of dualism.

---

4   Christopher McQuarrie, *The Usual Suspects*, VHS, Directed by Bryan Singer (New York, NY: PolyGram Video, 1995).

1. God stands unopposed and is on your side.

If God has no counterpart or adversary, then nothing that comes against you—no circumstance, no tragedy, no pain, no attack—is bigger or more than God. The God who is for you, the God who delights in you, who celebrates you, who loves you beyond understanding, is never overpowered or outmatched. None of it scares God or sends God packing. Whatever it is, God will be … and God will always be for you.

2. *Satan* opposes us and that makes us responsible.

If *satan* is our adversary and not God's, then we stand as adversaries to the ways of *satan*. We are the opposition of *satan*—regardless of whether we understand *satan* as a singular, evil being or a metaphor for wrestling with our own evil. If *satan*, in any form, claims a victory in this world, we bear the responsibility. I know this is a tough one to grasp, but knuckle down here. If *satan* is that which stands in opposition to humanity—that which tempts, accuses, and seeks to destroy us—then we are responsible for falling to those temptations, for believing the accusations, and for being subject to attack.

To be blunt, evil does not get into this world—it does not get expressed in our reality—without us. We are not innocent victims. We are complicit. Recognizing that God has no counterpart moves us into a place of growing accountability. We cannot hide behind dualism and pretend there is a cosmic battle being waged between God and the devil and we are just bystanders who have no control.

The cosmic battle is over, and God won—rest in that truth. But the battle was never between God and *satan*. The battle that God won was between our freedom and our eternal consequences. Even if we reject our true identity, even if we believe the lies and the accusations of the enemy, even if we use the very freedom God provides to attack God, we are still beloved and we still have a home. The God of the Bible fights to set people free from the very oppression they cause. That battle is over. God won.

This same God who fought the cosmic battle and won on our behalf invites us to join in the continuing redemption of creation. God invites us to partner in restoring the very *shalom* (peace) we disrupted in the first place. We are once again—and continuously—given a choice. Standing in opposition to our reception of that invitation…*satan*. Whether we understand *satan* as the singular evil being with a legion of demons in tow or some internal struggle with temptation and evil, both stand in opposition to our acceptance of God's invitation to join in the restoration of all things. If evil is released on this earth, it is because we either let it happen or we caused it to happen—not because the devil snuck one in while God wasn't looking. The devil is our adversary, not God's. We are called to oppose *satan*. We are called to live in the truth of who we are and who God is. We are called to love.

3. We have nothing to fear.

Whatever *satan* may be in our lives at any given moment (a temptation, an oppression, an accuser), none of it can oppose the good God who loves you and fights for your freedom. This is really the kicker of it all. This truth may seem so easy and so obvious that it may actually seem counterintuitive. *Satan*, in whatever form, is our adversary, not God's. God has no adversary and is for us. So while we are called to stand in opposition to *satan*, we do not do so alone. We stand in opposition to *satan* with the Creator of all things, the Sovereign of all creation going before us. *Satan*—no matter what *satan* may be—doesn't stand a chance. If we are living into the loving relationship God offers us, we have nothing to fear—not demons, not a singular fallen angel, not evil, not even death.

> So who can separate us? What can come between us and the love of God's Anointed? Can troubles, hardships, persecution, hunger, poverty, danger, or even death? The answer is, absolutely nothing. As the psalm says,
>
> On Your behalf, our lives are endangered constantly;
>   we are like sheep awaiting slaughter.

But no matter what comes, we will always taste victory through Him who loved us. For I have every confidence that nothing—not death, life, heavenly messengers, dark spirits, the present, the future, spiritual powers, height, depth, nor any created thing—can come between us and the love of God revealed in the Anointed, Jesus our Lord.

(ROM. 8:35–39)

The apostle Paul who wrote those words was not a dualist. His worldview did not have room for a battle between a good God and a bad god. Paul clung to the One God—the God of light and darkness—the God of everything. Paul's God had no counterpart. Paul's God had no equal. Paul certainly wrote about *satan*, but to Paul, just as it was with Jesus and just as it had been throughout the entirety of the scriptures, *satan* was an adversary to humans—not to God.

This is the truth to which we are invited to return. No matter what forces may seem to tempt us, accuse us, or oppose us; regardless of whether those forces are perceived as the evil one or the evil within, we are not alone, and we are never outside of the realm of the One God. Nothing can separate us from the love God has for us—not our death, our life, our past, or our future. No spiritual power, however it may be understood, can overcome God. With that kind of truth behind me, I am not afraid. With that kind of truth leading me, I can be honest and deal with the evil I create on my own. With that kind of truth inside me, I can love.

I Am Supposed to Protect and Defend God and My Faith

We are not enemies, but friends. We must not be enemies. Though passion may have strained, it must not break our bonds of affection. The mystic chords of memory, stretching from every battlefield and patriot grave to every living heart and hearthstone all over this broad land, will yet swell the chorus of the Union, when again touched, as surely they will be, by the better angels of our nature.[1]

— Abraham Lincoln

Do you know who Stephen Hawking was? If not, you should. Stephen Hawking was a renowned theoretical physicist. He served as the Lucasian Professor of Mathematics at the University of Cambridge for thirty years and served as the director of research at Cambridge's Centre for Theoretical Cosmology. Are you impressed (or intimidated) yet? Dr. Hawking wrote a number of books discussing the nature and fabric of

---

[1] Abraham Lincoln, *First Inaugural Address*, abrahamlincolnonline.org, accessed April 22, 2015, http://www.abrahamlincolnonline.org/lincoln/speeches/1inaug.htm.

the universe and received numerous awards, including the Presidential Medal of Freedom—which is the highest civilian honor awarded in the United States. Are you getting a picture of Stephen Hawking? He was a serious man. For most of his life, Stephen Hawking could very well have been the most intelligent and most reflective human being on the planet. I think Dr. Hawking was smart enough to deserve my attention and consideration.

Shortly before his death, Dr. Hawking was asked in an interview to clarify some remarks he made about the existence of God and how those remarks were to be understood compared to an earlier statement made in his book *A Brief History of Time*.[2] In the 1988 work, Hawking wrote that a unifying theory of science would help humanity "know the mind of God."[3] This was a riff on a quote often attributed to another theoretical physicist—Albert Einstein—who supposedly said, "I want to know God's thoughts; the rest are details."[4] Coming forward twenty-five years or so from Hawking's statement in *A Brief History of Time*, he was given an opportunity to further expound on the subject in an interview with the Spanish paper *El Mundo*. Hawking stated, "Before we understand science, it is natural to believe that God created the universe. But now science offers a more convincing explanation. What I meant by 'we would know the mind of God' is, we would know everything that God would know, if there were a God, which there isn't."[5]

---

[2]   Stephen Hawking, *A Brief History of Time* (New York: Bantam Books, 1988).

    By the by, if you haven't read *A Brief History of Time*, you should. It will absolutely tweak your bean—and if we are not open to having our beans tweaked, we close ourselves off to wonder. Don't be afraid to get neck-deep in something you don't understand or with which you disagree. You will be okay, and God will not fall off the throne.

[3]   Hawking, *A Brief History of Time*, 193.

[4]   Stephen B. McSwain, *The Enoch Factor: The Sacred Art of Knowing God* (Macon, GA: Smyth & Helwys Publishing, Inc., 2010) 82.

[5]   Ellisha Rader Mannering, "Stephen Hawking Says He's An Athiest," WebPro News, Accessed September, 30, 2014, http://www.webpronews.com/stephen-hawking-says-hes-an-athiest-2014-09

Bam! That is one of those drop-the-microphone-and-leave-the-room quotes, isn't it? There was no uncertainty, no ambiguity. "There is no God. See ya later, Hawking out." What are we supposed to do with that? One of the most intelligent thinkers to ever live said that science proves that God is not real. What does that do to you? What is welling up inside of your gut? Is one of those fight, flight, or freeze responses taking root in your faith right now? Do you feel yourself beginning to perform mental gymnastics to make Hawking's thoughts jive with your own? Maybe not. Maybe you feel your mind throwing up a wall to keep such arguments out. Maybe you find it easier just to dismiss Dr. Hawking as a lost soul who didn't really know what he was talking about. Do you want to argue with Dr. Hawking? Do you want to forget about him? Do you want to prove that God does exist?

If I'm honest with myself, I can admit that I have felt all of these responses at different times when I am faced with people, opinions, and worldviews that do not seem to fit into my understanding. As strange as it may seem, it is in our reaction to this benign story where we find our next lie—the idea that we, in some way, are responsible for defending or protecting God—that we need to be able to explain God and prove God in any situation at any time. Let's state some truths clearly in the first person:

1. I am not responsible for defending or protecting God—and that is a good thing because I need God to defend and protect me.
2. God will not falter or disappear if I do not argue correctly, fight for, or stand up in the name of God—and that is a good thing because if God could falter or disappear, God wouldn't be much of a God.
3. God does not need my protection or defense—and that is a good thing because if God did need my protection or defense, we would both be screwed.

Now, go back and read those three truths out loud—let them sink in. They just make sense, don't they? It is not my job to protect God. I couldn't even if I wanted to. And even if I could, would I want to protect and defend a God who needs protecting? Once again, I need to invite you to push through any resistance you may feel to doing the work and digging into this lie.

As much as these truths may ring true in our minds, there is still something in us that feels that it is right and good to stand up to Dr. Hawking—to straighten him out. You may believe, as I certainly have before, that it is your duty as a person of faith to fight back against those who would attack your faith. Even if you don't feel you need to attack those who oppose your worldview and faith, you may feel that you are nevertheless called to defend what you know to be true. Even worse, we all possess this ultimate capability to terminate and discard. If we feel we have done what we can to stand up to Dr. Hawking or even to persuade him of our viewpoint, and it has not worked, then we will dismiss him. We will declare him irrelevant, unreachable . . . an enemy.

In that incredibly swift moment, we make a horrible trade. As quickly as neurons fire in our brains, we are capable of making a distinction that looks at one of God's children—the delight of God's life and the joy of God's heart—as an irrelevant distraction to our faith or an enemy to our God. In doing so, we trade away the truth that we have been called to partner with God to bring about the restoration of all things for the lie that we have been called to defend and protect our God against all enemies foreign and domestic. I am not trying to be cute with that verbiage. It is a purposeful choice to draw the parallel between protecting our God and the pledge our servicemen and servicewomen take to protect our country. In the case of defending our country, who decides who the enemies are? Who gets to give the orders that defend against attack? The short answer: our leaders in the government—presidents, prime ministers, senators, representatives, generals, governors, chiefs—these people are trained, equipped, called to, and accountable for making these determinations and protecting the people. Without running too far down a rabbit trail, can we all agree that even though these leaders have been so tasked and equipped throughout history, they do not always get it right?

Mistakes have been made. Enemies have been wrongly labeled. People have been terminated and discarded.

Who decides who our spiritual enemies are? Who gets to determine that those who stand in opposition to our worldview, our religion, our understanding of the faith, deserve to be terminated or discarded? Is there a chain of command? Is there even a trained and equipped leader who is called to make such distinctions? I used to think so. I used to think it was the responsibility of the religious leaders to tell us who our spiritual enemies were. Maybe you have thought that, too. I believed they were called to help us protect the faith against all enemies foreign and domestic. Pastors, ministers, bishops, deacons, even the Pope—these were the people who were responsible for making those distinctions, right?

It didn't take long for one of those leaders to make a distinction with which I did not agree. Rock and roll is the enemy? Dancing is the enemy? Russians are the enemy? Homosexuals are the enemy? Atheists are the enemy? I have heard and seen all of these distinctions made from the pulpit in my lifetime. When my parents' generation was young, they experienced devout, spiritual leaders declaring different ethnicities as the enemy. Were any of those trained and equipped leaders right? Should those people ever have been labeled as my enemy? Should I really have defended my God against rock and roll or homosexuals?

Friends, I know we have highly intelligent, deeply rooted people who lead our faith. I believe in their calling. But at the end of the day, they are people—like you and me. No matter whom you have followed in your faith or whom you are following now, they are not perfect. They make mistakes. The truth is, there is no chain of command. In determining how to relate to people—especially those people we perceive as a threat, there is just God and us. The power to decide is ours. God gives it to us and invites us to use it in partnership with God. We cannot give this power away to a religious leader. Even if we think we have and follow the directions of someone else, we are fooling ourselves. We are choosing to align with leaders. The choice—the power—remains ours.

What does all that mean? It means I have no one else to blame for anyone being declared an enemy to my God or me.[6] I am the one who makes that distinction. Even if the idea does not originate within me, I have to choose to come into agreement with it. I, and I alone, have the power to decide from what God needs defense. I, and I alone, decide from whom my God and my faith must be protected. And if I cannot pass the responsibility off to someone else, then it seems only logical that I would ask God where I should spend my time defending. God, who are our spiritual enemies? Please point out those of whom you are afraid. Please show me the people who could cause the whole thing to crumble.

Let's be honest: how will God answer such a request? Is God afraid of anyone? We learned in the last chapter that God has no counterpart—no adversary. There has never been, there is not now, nor will there ever be an enemy to God who could cause the whole thing to crumble. Nothing knocks God off the throne. So if God is not at risk, then what is?

Now, my friends, we are getting to the heart of this lie. It is not God whom we defend and protect. It is ourselves. We may convince ourselves that we are standing up for what is right—that we are defending our God and our faith, but the reality is we are trying to assuage our own fear. When we encounter ideas, worldviews, beliefs, and doctrines that challenge our own, our most common response is fear. We are afraid that our faith, our God, our ideas can't stand up to the test. We are afraid that we have put our trust and our faith in the wrong thing. We are afraid that we may have gotten the whole thing wrong. We are afraid of not believing strongly enough—that somehow our lack of faith will be the end of us. We are afraid of doubt. We are afraid of uncertainty. We are afraid of being wrong. We are afraid of looking ridiculous. We are afraid of change.

That is a pretty big laundry list of fears, but trust me when I tell you that it is not an exhaustive list. We encounter people whose behavior or

---

[6] There is one through-the-looking-glass kind of exception here. If, through my action or inaction, I become an enemy to myself, I may not be capable of recognizing and labeling myself as such. Others may have to be involved in that discernment in an effort to protect me from me. What cannot be escaped, however, is my culpability. Even if I cannot discern myself as my own enemy, I am nevertheless responsible. Clear as mud? The Mad Hatter would be proud.

ideas cause us to be afraid, and when we are afraid, we seek to control. Much like cats, people cannot be controlled. Even if it appears that we can control others, it is an illusion. To control another human, one must essentially destroy the spirit and power that makes the other "human" in the first place. In doing so, oppressors necessarily deform their own humanity and lose both their own identity and the identity of those they sought to control. It is simply impossible for human beings to control another human being because the process of control removes humanity from both sides of the equation. The fabric of this existence is freedom. It is hardwired into our being by a God who loves so deeply that freedom is the only logical course. Our fear causes us to try to control people, and when we cannot control them (a foregone conclusion), we ultimately make the decision to separate the uncontrollable from its true identity. Accordingly, we terminate relationship, discard people, label enemies, and blind ourselves.

Okay, great … now what does all of that mean? How in the world does that help me in my day-to-day life? It means that I am not responsible for defending or protecting God from the bad ideas, doctrine, theology, morality, or behavior of other people. I couldn't do it even if I wanted to because I cannot control other people. It means that I do not have to worry about protecting my God against enemies, foreign and domestic, because in addition to lacking the authority to correctly recognize and ascertain who is an enemy, I also lack the ability to then control said enemy. In short, it is not my job to protect God. It never has been, and it never will be.

Let's make it practical. Days after Dr. Hawking's statement about science dispensing with the need for God went public, online message boards went wild in debate. Consider just a few responses culled from an article about Dr. Hawking's statement on webpronews.com.

RW posted

Well, Mr. Hawking can make all the atheist statements he wants to, however I am a Christian and have no doubts that not only

does GOD exist but HIS son Jesus Christ died on the cross for my
salvation. So who are you going to put your faith in?

NALA posts

RW, you are the reason people are getting more and more
against personal gods. You choose to make statements that go
beyond your own capacities. While Hawking has gone far, his
reason is grounded in scientific discoveries and reason. Your
utterance, though, is based on superstition and fear. That is not
a good thing.[7]

"You choose to make statements that go beyond your own capacities."
The writer may have simply been implying that RW had no verifiable
proof to make such statements about the existence of God, but the deeper
truth about our inability to control others remains. Dallas Willard is frequently credited as having said, "No one has ever been argued into the
Kingdom of God. We are loved there." Even if RW is ultimately proven
correct and one day NALA does come to believe in the existence of God,
do we really believe that this exchange was a positive force on that journey? Of course not! If anything, it is apparent that these two parties are
moving away from each other and entrenching in their ideological cor-
ners. There is no love or relationship being exchanged here. NALA even
calls the assertions about God based in fear and superstition. Does that
make us feel like this was a successful defense of God? Was the faith vic-
toriously protected?

If you have ever read any of the comments to an online article concerning a hot-button issue, then you will believe me when I tell you that
this thread contained countless posts of sometimes rational, sometimes
incoherent arguments from many different sides of the discussion. Page
after page of people standing up for what they feel is under attack. Some

---

7   Ibid.

of them stand up for Dr. Hawking, some for science and rational thought, some for Christianity, and some for other religions. Each defensive post represents a person who is convicted to stand firm where they are and declare, "This is what is right."

So what is right? Have you crafted your response to the Dr. Hawking controversy yet? What is it that you feel you are supposed to do with him and his God-disproving ideas? If it helps you to answer the question, imagine that you were in the room with Dr. Hawking and the newspaper writer conducting the interview. Imagine you are given the opportunity to directly respond to Dr. Hawking following his statement that there is no God. What do you do? What are you supposed to do?

Perhaps this particular discussion doesn't provoke you to defend or protect. Maybe you don't view the ponderings of a theoretical physicist on the godless nature of the universe as a threat or an attack. For some of us, the issue of God's existence is not a sensitive topic. That's okay—God knows there are a number of faith issues over which we will argue, fight, and even hurt others in order to stand up for what is right. Creationism, evolution, abortion, racism, capital punishment, intelligent design, homosexuality, gender-equality, capitalism—these are just a few of the significant issues upon which people of faith wage war every day. Unfortunately, we don't even stick to significant issues. Our hyper-offendable culture is so spoiling for a holy fight that we find ways to perceive spiritual battles where they do not even exist.

Case in point: our recurring need in the United States to counter-attack any person, organization, or idea that does not fully embrace the celebration of Christmas, as though not getting into the Christmas spirit is like kicking sand in the face of Jesus himself. The "War on Christmas" inspires the passion of Christians every year to stand up for the celebration of Jesus' birthday by boycotting retailers, demanding people say "Merry Christmas!" and not "Happy Holidays!" and passing city ordinances to protect the lawn nativity scene at City Hall.

So what does that have to do with arguing with Stephen Hawking? How are our religious battles over any of these issues related to one another? In a word, foolishness—and the foolishness is ours. It belongs to me, and it belongs to you. It belongs to any one of us who has at any time believed the lie that we were called to defend and protect God from attack. This foolishness is not a new phenomenon either. It belongs to any person—throughout history—who has believed that the highest calling in a moment of conflict or crisis was to stand up in defense of their religion, doctrine, theology, or idea. It belongs to all of us who have chosen an ideal over a person, a belief over a relationship, or being right over being loving.

Now, lock it in because this part is important. You are not crazy, you are not alone, and you are not wrong to have a desire to defend or protect the faith. And if, like me, you have yielded to those desires before and ended up in a spiritual argument or fight for one reason or another, you need to know that there is grace for every behavior under the sun. We are forgiven; we are still loved; it's not too late. Remember that God loves us as daughters and sons. While parents may not always approve of their child's behavior—and while parents may want more for their child—nothing the child does makes the parents love them less. We all swim in waters of endless grace.

No matter how bad and off-target our defense of the faith may be, our desire to protect, defend, and stand for what we believe is typically a noble desire. It is typically a desire to do and be about what is right and what is good. It is typically a desire to preserve that which we care deeply about. Such desires are based on good intentions. But as we all know, the road to hell—that is, the road away from God—is paved with good intentions. The problem is that we are called beyond good intentions. As people of faith, we are called to something else. We are called to love God and love others. We are not called to protect God. We are not called to defend God. We are called—repeatedly, consistently, and very clearly—to love God and to love others for God.

Topographical Obstruction

I want to invite you to imagine something with me. I want you to imagine a mountain—not a picturesque mountainscape—but an obstacle. I want you to imagine a single mountain that stands between two sides and separates them. Now I want you to consider that mountain to be one of those sticky issues or questions on which people are so divided. Imagine that mountain to be an issue that puts you on one side of the mountain and other people on the other side—one of those issues about which everyone seems to be so resolute and certain.

Can you see it? On either side of the mountain is a base camp of people who are certain they are on the "right" side of the mountain. Now, whatever the mountain issue is for you, let me tell you: that is nothing compared to the mountain that stood between the apostle Peter and the God-fearer Cornelius in the story found in the tenth chapter of Acts.

The story of Acts 10 begins as we are introduced to Cornelius, who the text calls a "God-fearer." God-fearer is a fascinating and somewhat confusing title for us to read these days, but the contemporary audience to the stories found in the Book of Acts would have understood that a God-fearer was a non-Jew trying to live a faithful life with and for the God of Abraham, Isaac, and Jacob. Essentially, Cornelius was an outsider (not born into the family of Israel) who was trying to live a faithful life anyway. N.T. Wright calls Cornelius a man "on the outside of Judaism but pressing his nose hard against the glass."[8] Right away, we are introduced to a mountain—something that separates Peter and Cornelius. Peter is a Jew; he is on the inside. In fact, Peter is a good Jew—born, bred, studied, keeping all the customs. Peter even followed a rabbi whom he believed to be the Messiah. Cornelius was no Jew. Good Jews knew that if they got too close or too involved with non-Jews, they would be considered unclean. They knew that they were to keep it in the family, so to speak—outsiders were dangerous and impure. The mountain, however,

8   N.T. Wright, *Acts for Everyone: Part One* (Louisville, KY: Westminster John Knox Press, 2008), 168.

gets bigger. In addition to being an outsider, Cornelius was a Roman centurion—a leader and an officer in the Roman army. Cornelius wasn't just an outsider; he was the enemy. Rome oppressed the Jews, killing them for living their lives before God instead of Caesar. Rome had the power—military, political, financial, and otherwise. Peter had grown up within a worldview that understood Rome was the enemy. Peter, as well as the rest of Jesus' disciples, thought the Messiah—a great military leader—would come to overthrow Rome with might and force. Instead, they watched as Roman soldiers tortured their rabbi and crucified him.

Are you beginning to get a sense for the size and complexity of the mountain that separated Cornelius and Peter? Culture, ethnicity, religion, purity, politics, economics, power—any one of these issues by itself would be enough to cause Peter to stand up to Rome and, by extension, Cornelius. There are numerous points—both philosophical and literal—at which Peter would be justified to say that Cornelius and his ilk had attacked Peter's God and feel compelled to defend and protect his faith from such enemies. This is one big-arse mountain.

This pairing of Peter and Cornelius is not accidental. As the story opens, we hear that, while praying one day, Cornelius receives a visit from an angel who tells him to send to Joppa for a man named Peter. Faithfully, Cornelius does just that. While his servants are on their way to Joppa to retrieve Peter, the story shifts to Peter in Joppa, sitting on the roof of the home where he is staying and waiting for lunch. As Peter waits, he has a dream where he sees a giant sheet lowered to the earth from the heavens. On the sheet is every manner of wild beast and unclean animal. A voice tells the dreaming and apparently hungry Peter to kill and eat anything on the sheet. An observant Jew, Peter refuses, noting that God's law forbids such behavior, and he would never do such an unclean thing. The voice corrects Peter, saying, "If God calls something permissible and clean, you must not call it forbidden and dirty!" This dream is repeated three times before Peter awakens to the arrival of Cornelius' servants. Peter invites the servants into the home to hear their request and then goes with them to Joppa. The story continues as Peter and the servants go to the home of Cornelius in Caesarea.

They arrived in Caesarea the next afternoon just before three o'clock. Cornelius had anticipated their arrival and had assembled his relatives and close friends to welcome them. When Peter and Cornelius met, Cornelius fell at Peter's feet in worship, but Peter helped him up, saying "Stand up, man! I am just a human being!"

Talking things over, they went on into the house, where Cornelius introduced Peter to everyone who had come.

Peter addressed them, "You know, we Jews consider it a breach of divine law to associate, much less share, hospitality with outsiders. But God has shown me something in recent days: I should no longer consider any human beneath me or unclean. That's why I made no objection when you invited me; rather, I came willingly. Now let me hear the story of why you invited me here.

Cornelius said, "Four days ago at about this time, mid-afternoon, I was home praying. Suddenly there was a man right in front of me, flooding the room with light. He said, 'Cornelius, your daily prayers and neighborly acts have brought you to God's attention. I want you to send to Joppa to get Simon, the one they call Peter. He's staying with Simon the Tanner down by the sea.'

"I wasted no time, did just as I was told, and you have generously accepted my invitation. So here we are, in the presence of God, ready to take in all that the LORD has given to tell us."

Peter exploded with good news: "It is clear to me now that God plays no favorites, that God accepts every person whatever his or her background, that God welcomes all who revere Him and do right. You already know that God sent a message to the people of Israel; it was a message of peace, peace through Jesus the Anointed—who is King of all people."

(ACTS 10:23–38)

Acts 10 closes with the Holy Spirit being poured out on Cornelius, his family, and all the Gentiles in his household as Peter continues to tell the story of Jesus. Peter concludes that the Gentiles have received the same Spirit of God that he and his Jewish brothers and sisters had received and asks those traveling with him, "Is there any reason why we should not baptize these people as fellow disciples?" This is Peter asking his Jewish brethren, "Aren't these people our brothers and sisters, too?" Everyone agrees, and Cornelius and his household—the outsiders, the enemies—are baptized into the family of God.

What happened to the mountain? Why didn't Peter feel compelled to defend his God against the Roman enemy? Shouldn't Peter have stood his ground and refused to even consider the point of view of a member of the same army that literally oppressed him, his family, his people—that tortured and crucified Jesus? Did Peter forget? Did he choose to ignore? Or was something else going on?

"If God calls something permissible and clean, you must not call it forbidden and dirty!" Three times Peter has this dream where he calls the animals on the sheet unclean—where he stands up for his God against that which is forbidden. Three times Peter is corrected and reminded that God calls those shots. Throughout this story, Peter seems to be coming to grips with the limitations that we have been discussing. Peter seems to learn that he does not have the capacity to correctly decide who is God's enemy—meaning those against whom he must defend God.

In Matthew 16, Peter professes that he will protect Jesus—standing firm and insisting he will never let anyone torture and kill Jesus. What does he get for his trouble? Jesus looks at him and says, "Get behind me, Satan! You are a stumbling block to me; you do not have in mind the concerns of God, but merely human concerns" (Matt. 16:21–28). As a side note, can we all just pause a minute and say, "Ouch!" for Peter? Seriously, the guy did what any one of us might have done in the same situation. His rabbi—his friend—is telling him and the rest of the disciples how he must go to Jerusalem to suffer under the elders and teachers of the law and be killed, and Peter responds with an understandable, "Not if I have anything to do with it!" For his loyalty, he receives the verbal slam of all time. Can't you just see the other eleven disciples' reaction with a collective "Doh!"

"Bet you didn't see that one coming did you, Peter?"

Perhaps John walked by, patted him on the back, and said, "Nice try, rabbi's pet."

Alas, I digress. This isn't the only time Peter tries to defend and protect Jesus. Consider John 18, when Judas brings Romans and officials from the high priest to arrest Jesus. Peter draws his sword in defense of Jesus and cuts off the ear of one of the posse. Jesus rebukes him again and tells him to put away his sword. By the time we get to Acts 10, Peter has been learning, for quite some time, the lesson that it is not his job to defend God.

"Get behind me, Satan."

(MATT. 16:23)

"Put your sword away."

(JOHN 18:11)

"If God calls something permissible and clean, you must not call it forbidden and dirty!"

(ACTS 10:15)

Peter is our poster child for coming out from under the lie that we are called to defend or protect God.[9] Peter learned in real time how to move away from the false responsibility of defending his faith against attack into the freedom of loving others. That mountain that separated Peter

---

[9]   If you will allow me, a brief digression for my kindred-spirit brother, Peter. I know it seems like Peter is quite the moron sometimes in these stories, but let's all take a look in the mirror. Peter is me. Peter is you. We is Peter. At least, let's all hope that we can grow into his shoes. If nothing else, we need to recognize that we would not have these stories of failure from which to learn had Peter himself not learned—and then told and retold—his own stories of failure to help and encourage others. Thank you, Pete!

and Cornelius cast quite a shadow, but gradually and through experience, Peter learned not to let that shadow define his reality. Peter learned not to let the base camps on either side of the mountain frame the conversation. Those camps ask questions like:

"How can you stand those people?"

"What are we going to do about them?"

"How can we win?"

"How can we make sure our way is sustained?"

Peter seems to ask different questions.

To Whom Am I Listening?

The first question Peter seems to have learned to ask is "To whom am I listening?" Whose voice am I following here? Is it my voice? Is it the voice of other people? By the time Peter gets to the story presented in Acts 10, he has learned that he needs to be listening to God. Peter has learned that he can't trust his own sources by themselves to reveal God's will; he needs to check them with God. In fact, Peter's dreams teach him that even his religion by itself can mislead him. If you will forgive the shameless integrated book plug, Peter confronts the reality of *faith lies*.

Let's be honest. Peter didn't just refuse the animals on the sheet on a whim. His religion—the laws of which were from the Scripture—taught him that those animals were unclean and were not to be eaten. The instructions Peter was following were from Torah! Have you ever found yourself in a place where you felt you were standing on biblical principle? That is exactly what Peter is doing when he refuses to take and eat. Peter essentially says, "I will not eat any of these animals because the Bible tells me not to." That is a totally reasonable response—some would even say it is a righteous response. Yet God invites Peter to something more. God invites Peter to see beyond the limits of the rules—to see beyond his religion, his upbringing, his culture.

Now, I want to be really clear on this point. God does not dismiss the law, and God does not contradict God. The Deuteronomic laws Peter was following by not eating unclean animals were given to the people of God by God. God is not saying, "My bad … got that one wrong." God is saying, "Let's not make the instructions that help you live into rules that blind us and oppress us." The Deuteronomic laws, which include what we call "the ten commandments," were just that—instructions. They were instructions on how to live life well from a God who not only wants that for all people but has the capacity to see and understand things people cannot. What happens to Peter happens throughout the scriptures. The instructions become laws. The instructions become idols, which means they become *the thing* instead of given by *the thing*. The instructions— rules, laws, commandments—become a replacement for God. People, like Peter, replace relationship with regulations.

Each time this happens in the biblical texts (as is the case in Acts 10), God invites people to come out from under faith lies. God does not change God's mind about the value of the instruction. Rather, God reminds the people that they have lost sight of the original intent. N.T. Wright sums up this seeming contradiction by relating it to a mother who is on one side of the street, calling out to her child to come to her by crossing the street. When the mother sees that a car is coming, she tells the child to stop. After the car has passed, she tells the child to come. The mother has not contradicted herself. The point was always to get the child to the mother—even when the mother told the child to stop.[10]

In this instance, God is not dismissing the religion or the law. God invites Peter to add to his understanding—essentially saying to Peter, "Let's add to our religion and our law. Let's take the story you know, the law you have learned, and let's add to it a new revelation." It's not one or the other. It's all of it—the story, the law, and the Spirit—existing in tension with each other. Peter learns that it is not enough to simply stand on biblical principle. Peter is reminded that his understanding of what

---

[10]   Wright, *Acts for Everyone*, 163.

biblical principle actually is must remain open and in communication with God.

Friends, I wish I could put this more delicately, but the reality is we need to keep this truth before us at all times. It is incredibly arrogant and dangerous to assume at any point that we have our God or our faith "figured out" and that we are now ready to stand firm for our interpretation. When we assume that our understanding of God, the Bible, faith, or even Jesus is complete, we stand in the most ignorant posture of our lives. All manner of evil and foolish behavior has been executed under the belief that somehow we have mastered what God wants and are ready to defend God's ideas. We can never stop receiving input from God. We can never put our fingers in our ears like a child and say, "No more. I got it." We, like Peter, have to stay open to new information. We have to remain open to the possibility that we have not yet experienced or understood all there is to experience or understand. We must keep asking ourselves, "To whom am I listening?"

How Should I Listen?

If the first question we learn to ask from the story of Peter and Cornelius is "To whom am I listening?", then I think the second question we learn to ask is, "How should I listen?" How do we actually pull it off? How do I make sure that I am receiving what God is saying? The simple answer seems to be *gradually and obediently.* I say simple because it is not complex. It is, however, by no means easy. Gradually and obediently?! Really? That sounds like slowly and with discipline ... boring and hard. These are not concepts that blend with our contemporary culture. But before you tune out and, like me, assume that you could never do something gradually and obediently, let's take a look at Peter and Cornelius and see what this really means.

The Lightning Bolt

As we mentioned before, Peter did not instantly understand that God was calling him to move beyond his religion. The stories of Peter show that he moves toward this understanding gradually and through a series of experiences. This wasn't even the first time Peter had received a divine invitation to take a step beyond his own understanding. Peter was the one whom Jesus invited out of the boat to walk on the water. Remember "Get behind me Satan!" and "Put your sword away!"? These are signposts of Peter's progressive apprehension—or gradually developing understanding. And friends, please remember these are just the greatest hits. These stories don't represent all of Peter's experiences. These are just the moments that were so important that they were recorded and remembered. Just like the rest of us, Peter had a lifetime of experiences leading him toward understanding.

Peter's unfolding understanding does not mean that there were never lightning-bolt moments. We all hopefully experience lightning-bolt moments in our lives where we feel as though we have instantly come to a new understanding or appreciation. Those moments have certainly happened to me. But I am learning that those lightning-bolt moments usually come after a series of experiences. They may seem like isolated moments at the time, but the truth is they are connected to previous experiences. While it may feel to us like an instant moment of lightning, more often than not we can look back and see a series of events that led us out into an open field in a thunderstorm, holding a lightning rod to the sky.

That is what happened to Peter. Throughout his time following Yeshua, he was making a journey toward the lightning-bolt moment he has at the home of Cornelius. Still not convinced? Let's look at what Peter's story records in the events leading up to the lightning strike.

- The Gospel accounts record Peter receiving correction from Yeshua on three different occasions for essentially trying to defend and protect God. (Matt. 16, John 13, Matt. 26/John 18)

- Probably more so than any other disciple, Peter finds ways to mess up and miss the point while following Yeshua. He eventually denies knowing Yeshua three times, as was predicted.

- Throughout his years following Yeshua—including being a witness to the crucifixion, resurrection, and ascension of Yeshua—Peter receives grace, love, forgiveness, and acceptance.

- While waiting on the rooftop for lunch in Joppa, Peter has the same dream three times telling him not to call unclean or profane that which God has made.

- Peter awakens and has to think about the dream. The text even says that it confuses him. (Acts 10:17)

- Three men are sent to retrieve Peter, and the text says the Holy Spirit has to encourage him to go with them to see Cornelius. (Acts 10:19–20)

- Peter goes to Caesarea to see Cornelius and listens to the story about why Cornelius has sent for him.

- Peter testifies about Yeshua to Cornelius and his household and, while doing so, witnesses the Spirit of God being poured out on them just as it had been poured out among the Jews weeks before. (Acts 2)

Then he gets it. After all of that, the lightning strikes, and Peter awakens to a new understanding that he is being invited to partner with God in extending to this household of outsiders the very same grace, love, forgiveness, and acceptance he himself had received. It had been years of experience. Peter had followed Yeshua around the Galilee and listened to every teaching—seizing opportunities to stick his foot in his mouth. He had missed the point of this very lightning bolt several times. But gradually, he is moved to a place where he can receive it. The totality of his journey lands him in the open field of Cornelius' home during a "Holy

Spirit" thunderstorm, and as he begins to testify about his rabbi, he raises a lightning rod to the sky and BAM! Lightning strikes.

Lightning strikes because Peter was willing to keep listening. Lightning strikes because Peter didn't close himself off and determine that he had learned all he needed to learn. Peter never wore a t-shirt that said, "All I needed to learn I learned in Hebrew school." He listened gradually.

Theologian Robert Wall wrote, "The process of getting on the same page with God is frequently confusing, profoundly dependent upon others and often takes considerable time." My rabbi, David McNitzky, says it this way, "Clarity comes in the living." If we want to understand something—if we really want to get something inside of us, we must be willing to live it out.

Obedience as Trust

Living out understanding takes time and includes our mistakes and misapplication. It is gradual. Because it is gradual, there will be times when questions go unanswered. Over the course of a journey, there will be times when we are asked to press on in the face of uncertainty. We will be challenged to take steps forward that may not make sense at the time. This is the second part of how we learn to listen from Peter—obediently.

Now, don't get all freaked out and start thinking about obedience the way we do when we housebreak our dogs. Obedience is not about rolled-up newspaper swats or bacon treats. Obedience is about trust. "How so?" you ask.

Great question...let me explain.

Obedience, by definition, is yielding or surrendering our will to the authority of another. In the case of our dogs, that obedience is typically based on fear or reward. Sometimes, we demonstrate our authority over our dogs with some sort of negative reinforcement—where they receive some sort of punishment for the behaviors we are trying to curtail. In these cases, the dogs surrender their will to our authority because they develop a fear of the negative consequence. They don't want to receive a swat from a rolled-up newspaper, so they surrender their desire to eat our house shoes to our superior authority that has determined we prefer our house shoes whole.

Still, that doesn't cover all of it. Sometimes dogs are motivated to surrender their will to our superior authority by rewards. We have a rescue dog named Annie Oakley. Before we received Annie, she apparently received a fair amount of abuse and negative reinforcement. Don't let the name fool you—Annie is not tough. Whatever she experienced out there on the mean streets of San Antonio has rendered her unable to deal with negative reinforcement. Any kind of correction makes Annie shut down completely. If Annie even thinks she may be in trouble for something she has done, she will disappear for days. She will cower, shivering, under a bed somewhere until she is convinced no harm awaits her. In this state she cannot learn, and she cannot grow.

Annie can only be trained by positive reinforcement. Annie has learned—albeit incredibly slowly—to surrender her will to our authority because we reward her when she does. She gets treats, encouragement, and affection for her good behavior, which, in turn, encourages further good behavior.

Okay, now that you are wondering why this spiritual book suddenly turned into a dog-training book, let's remember that the kind of obedience we are talking about has nothing to do with dogs. We are not dogs to God. We are God's beloved children. Aside from my developing experience of God and dogs, I know this to be true because of the biblical story of Job.

The Book of Job is one of the oldest stories in the Bible. In fact, many scholars believe that Job is the oldest book in the Bible, meaning it was the first in the oral tradition of the biblical stories to be written down. Scholarship also asserts that the story of Job was most likely a play that was performed among the Hebrew people for many years before it was written down. An extremely rich and complex narrative, the story of Job is among my favorite stories in the Bible because of the way that it pushes me beyond easy understandings of relationship to God and to others.

A very interesting thing happens in the opening of Job's story—

something we mentioned in our previous discussion about *Satan*. One day, the angels of the LORD are coming before the LORD to report on their activities. *Satan* is among them. God asks the *Satan* character what he has been up to, and *Satan* confesses that he has a bone to pick with God over this obedient human who God loves so much named Job. Now I am really condensing this important story here, but the *Satan* character then sets out to disprove Job's worthiness for God's love.

First, *Satan* suggests that Job is only obedient because of positive reinforcement. He challenges God to remove blessing from Job and asserts that the only reason Job is obedient is because God gives him treats, encouragement, and affection. God allows *Satan* to conduct this experiment (it doesn't work); Job remains faithful and obedient. Next, *Satan* suggests that Job must be maintaining his obedience because he is afraid of punishment. He challenges God to let him punish and inflict negative reinforcement (and we are not talking about a mere rolled-up newspaper swat here) on Job. Once again, God agrees to allow the experiment. Job is tortured in numerous ways ... and again, it ultimately does not work.

There is much more to learn and study about the story of Job, but the reason that we have looked at the beginning of the story is to note that the *Satan* character understands obedience like we understand our dogs. He assumes that Job, like a dog, surrenders his will to God's authority either because he wants something from God or because he is afraid of being punished by God. If that description of obedience to God is hitting a little close to home for you, rest assured that it is supposed to and that you are not alone. It is all too common for each of us to approach our relationship with God as though God is the Master and we are the dog. Our inclination to settle for such a hollow shell of a relationship with God is precisely why the story of Job is important—and I believe precisely why our forebears saw fit to tell, preserve, and pass this story on to us.

Job knows he is no dog. God knows that Job's love—his obedience—is not dictated by fear of punishment or the desire for reward. Job trusts God. Job sincerely believes that God knows what is best for Job, and therefore he surrenders his will to God's authority because he genuinely believes that if he follows God's will and not his own, things will go better for him.

If you know the whole story of Job, you know that Job eventually wavers. Eventually, Job cries out and questions God. He loses everything in *Satan's* little experiment. Death, destruction, disease, bankruptcy, pain, sorrow, agony—nothing goes well for him at all. At the absolute lowest of moments, Job finally caves and tells God that his trust is running thin. It's not working for him. In his extreme weakness, Job tells God that God is not acting like God. Job essentially says, *I have always trusted you, and you have always taken care of me. You have always protected and provided for me, and I have trusted you even when it made no sense at all. The only thing I have left to entrust to you is my death, so take it … kill me and get it over with.*

Here is the brilliant thing about Job: even though he ultimately caves and questions God's judgment, he remains in relationship with God. One of the rabbinical metaphors for understanding Job is that although he ends up throwing dishes at God, the fact that he stays in the kitchen for the argument is trust. Job doesn't abandon the relationship. Job refuses to act like a dog cowering from a newspaper swat or begging for a treat. Job stands in the relationship and argues with God. To Job, discomfort and death are preferable to disconnection. He would rather trust God through the deepest pain and the valley of death than disconnect from the relationship. That is obedience. Obedience is the deepest conviction—the most sincere belief—that surrendering our will to the authority of our good and loving God will be better than anything else—even to the point of death. Obedience freely trusts the authority of another over your own will.

To Job—and later to Peter—obedience meant trusting God even when it didn't make sense. Imagine being Peter on that journey from Joppa to Caesarea. With each step toward the home of Cornelius, I would be asking myself, *What the hell am I doing?! I am walking toward the home of a Roman centurion. This member of the army that crucified my rabbi wants me to come and tell them about the man they killed? Screw this guy!*

He is not even a Jew! What does he need me for? He has money, power, authority—the only thing he doesn't have is what I know from following Yeshua, and I'll be damned if I am going to give it to him! This doesn't make any sense. Why would God send me to this man?

The story in Acts doesn't record any of those thoughts... those are mine. Acts does tell us that Peter was confused when the journey began. Yet he goes anyway. Peter obeys. This is the same guy who walked—with Jesus—on water (if only for a moment). His experience of God has brought him to a point where—even if it doesn't make sense—he can trust. Peter trusts that God knows what is best—for Peter, for Cornelius, for everyone. Perhaps Peter did think thoughts like those I have listed above on the road to Caesarea. If he did, he may have also thought of Job—of obedience being about trust. Peter may have recalled his own experience and concluded, "Well, every other time I have thought I knew what was best, I was wrong. Maybe I should let God be God for this one, and I'll just be Peter."

Experiential understanding comes over time and through many encounters. It requires us to listen with patience and know that clarity will come in the living—gradually. Such patience will inevitably invite us beyond our capabilities and our comforts. Such listening will introduce us to experiences for which we have no plan and moments for which we have no explanation. We will be required to trust. We will be invited to obediently surrender our will to the authority of God and listen humbly for what comes next. How are we listening?

A Side of Freedom Fries, Please

I recently visited the 9/11 Memorial in New York City. That experience reacquainted me with the emotions and feelings of that day in a surprising way. My brain spent the next week or so spinning through one memory or another of that terrible day and the season of fear, anger, and nationalism that followed. Yesterday, I remembered "freedom fries" and it made me laugh—not in a finger-pointing kind of way but in a "What were we thinking?" way. Even still, it was good to find a memory of that time in the recesses of my mind that didn't make me want to cry. Do you remember "freedom fries"? Maybe for you it was "freedom toast" or "freedom bread."

In the months that followed that tragic day, our nation wanted to build a coalition of countries that would go after the perpetrators of this horrific offense. France wanted nothing to do with it. So, like a spurned fourteen-year-old dumped before the big dance, we decided to cut the French out of all of our photographs. A movement arose in which people would order "freedom fries" and "freedom toast" instead of ordering French fries and French toast—as if our adjective rejection was somehow hurting the French. Friends, I did this. I ordered freedom fries. I hope you can agree with me about how goofy that was. I don't know what the French would have thought of me ordering my freedom fries, but it is clear to me now that I found comfort in grasping for something I could control.

I was exercising a prejudice that made absolutely no sense. The French had not attacked us at all. Once more, the French hadn't even invented the French fry. My prejudice and behavior made no sense. As I scrambled to find meaning in the face of tragedy, I joined my voice to an illogical connection to bash the French. Well, not really, because they didn't care that I disassociated them from fried potatoes.

This is not unusual behavior for me. I frequently assign the wrong meaning to anything I can get my hands on. As the great Coen brothers' theologian Ulysses Everett McGill states in the movie *O Brother, Where Art Thou?*, "It's a fool that looks for logic in the chambers of the human heart."[11]

There is an apocryphal story about the great theologian C.S. Lewis as a child. The story goes that a young Lewis once declared to his father, "I have a prejudice against the French."

---

[11] Homer, Ethan Coen, and Joel Coen, *O Brother, Where Art Thou?* DVD, directed by Joel Coen and Ethan Coen (Burbank, CA: Buena Vista Home Entertainment, 2000).

Surprised by the declaration, his father said, "Really? And why is that?"

The perplexed child thought a moment and then retorted, "If I knew why, it wouldn't be a prejudice, would it?"

Whether or not that actually happened, I (unfortunately) really did order "freedom fries" for a time. I was not as reflective as the young Lewis supposedly was. I assigned meaning to French diplomacy in the weeks and months following 9/11 and determined they were traitors who deserved to be removed from our menus. I wish that was the only illogical meaning that I attached to the events surrounding 9/11, but the truth is there were others.[12]

How did I arrive at those conclusions? From where did they come? The short answer ... fear. When we human beings are afraid, we look to control. And in moments of extreme fear, we don't just try to control the thing that is causing our fear, we also try to control anything we can get our hands on—even food adjectives. I can look back and see now that during those terrible days, I was listening to fear—understandably so. In the face of such violence and evil, I did not possess the discipline or wisdom to be reflective and ask myself, *To whom are we listening?* or *How am I listening?* How could we possibly have the discipline to listen for God or attempt to gradually and obediently listen when confronted with such chaos? Instead, I behaved more like a wild and young Peter with a sword, cutting off whatever ear I could reach.

Are you beginning to understand the power of that picture? Peter jumps up and literally cuts an ear—the listening body part—off another guy, showing that he himself is not listening! That is symbolic irony, my friends. Peter is not alone, however. How about a young man who joins a movement to order "freedom fries" in an effort to control fear? Fear and

---

[12] How much more ludicrous do "freedom fries" seem now? Over the last several years, the French have suffered several attacks—killing hundreds of innocent people—at the hands of those claiming to be defending their God and their faith. This is just the kind of tragic irony with which Peter so frequently painted. I thought I was standing up for what was right. Man, did I ever blow it.

control are the opposite of freedom. I did the same thing that Peter did—just on a much goofier scale.

What Am I Hearing?

It's in the face of such ironic and sad behavior that I find the third question we learn to ask from Peter and Cornelius to be most helpful. That question: "What am I hearing?" Does what I am hearing sound like God? Is it consistent with what God has already revealed or said? Is it consistent with the overarching story of God?

Naturally, in order to answer these questions, we need to be familiar with what God sounds like. We will be unable to measure consistency with the overarching story if we do not know the overarching story. Learning that overarching story of God begins with the biblical stories. Peter knew those stories. In all likelihood, Peter knew the Torah (Genesis, Exodus, Leviticus, Numbers, Deuteronomy) from memory—much as any good rabbinic disciple of that time would have.

What does that mean? It means that as Peter walked on his journey to Caesarea trying to make sense of why God would send him to a Roman centurion, he had God's overarching story bouncing around inside of him. Peter knew that God had promised Abraham that "all the families of the Earth will be blessed through you"—not just the Jewish families but all the families (Gen. 12). Peter knew that the prophet Zechariah had declared that all the nations of the earth would celebrate the feast of Sukkot together for eternity—not just the Jewish nation but all nations (Zech. 14). Peter knew the story of Jonah—a prophet who was sent to a city full of pagans in Nineveh to urge them to repent and be in relationship with God (Jon. 1). Peter saw a pattern of God reaching toward people in relationship throughout the biblical story.

Peter also knew his own story—a story that included walking after Jesus as a disciple. While these passages were not in Peter's scriptures (they had not yet been written), he knew them nonetheless. Jesus had taught him that salvation would come through the Jewish people—not just for the Jews but for the entire world (John 4). Peter had been given a new commandment by Jesus to "love one another" that the world would know Peter was a follower of Jesus by his love (John 13).

It is impossible to gain familiarity with the overarching story without the biblical stories. Yet, knowing the overarching story does not simply mean knowing the stories of the Bible. The biblical narrative is not the totality of God's story. The story did not end in the third century when the biblical canon was closed. God still moves. God still speaks. God still intercedes in our lives. The story continues.

To know the overarching story of God requires that we know the stories of the Bible, but it also requires that we know other stories…the stories of other people…stories other than our own. Peter knew the stories of many other people who had encountered God. As a disciple, he had watched in person as hundreds—if not thousands—of people brought their stories to his rabbi, Jesus. In Acts 10, we get to observe as Peter learns the story of a God-fearing Roman centurion named Cornelius. We watch as Peter connects the dots and sees the overarching story. We witness Peter recognizing that the divine desire has always been to transcend and include, seeing past the mountain that separates and moving into loving relationship.

As Peter asks, "What am I hearing?", he brings God's story into focus and in doing so, is able to make sense out of the story that is happening before him and to him. That's the thing about knowing other stories: they give our story context. When we know God's cosmic story and consider the stories of those around us, our stories make a whole lot more sense. When our story exists in isolation—as if it is the only story that matters, we have no bearing, no direction, and we are easily lost.

To whom am I listening?

How do I listen?

What am I hearing?

These are the questions I learn to ask from the story of Peter and Cornelius. Their story provides context for my story as I try to grow away from fear and control and toward relationship and freedom. These questions are not easy to ask. They don't come to us naturally when we are anxious. They will not magically roll off the tongue when we feel our God or our faith is under attack. Learning to ask these questions is a discipline. It takes practice.

I have found that one of the most effective ways to practice these questions is to try them in situations that don't really affect me directly. Say, for example, when a noted theoretical physicist releases an interview in a magazine claiming that there is no God.

Stephen Hawking's comments really do not have a direct impact on my life because—at present—I am not even remotely in relationship to Stephen Hawking—or even anyone who knew him for that matter. So as reactions begin to grow inside of me to what could be perceived as an attack on God, I am offered an opportunity to slow down and practice. In such moments, I am being given an opportunity to ask questions and remember.

Do I need to protect God from the teachings of Stephen Hawking?

Do I need to defend my faith to anyone who agrees with him that there is no God?

What about Dr. Hawking's comments makes me anxious or afraid?

If I am anxious or afraid, to whom am I listening?

Am I listening to those truths that are revealed gradually and through obedience?

What am I hearing?

Are the voices that rise up inside of me consistent with the compassion, love, and relentless pursuit of relationship that God has demonstrated throughout human history ... or even in my life?

If I can practice and learn to ask these questions during the moments of my life that only seem anxious, I am better prepared for those moments that do directly affect me. If I can walk this discipline out in an imagined relationship—which is the only kind of relationship I could have ever had with Stephen Hawking—I am training for the very real and often conflicted relationships of my life. While the absence of relationship between Dr. Hawking and myself precluded the existence of a mountain separating us, there are mountains in my life that separate me from people I actually know.

Tolerate, Climb, or Perch

You remember those mountains we imagined at the beginning of this chapter? Whatever the issue was for you, bring it back to the front of your mind. When I really think about the mountain issues that stand between me and other people, I can get easily overwhelmed. Often, I give up and accept the mountain as the cost of doing business—it's just the way things are. Who am I to change it? Have you ever done that? Have you ever just tolerated the mountain?

Let me be clear: this isn't about tolerance. Tolerance is not what Cornelius wanted. He was on one side of the mountain, and he wanted a way to other side. He wanted relationship. He was looking for a way into the family. He didn't want to be tolerated, nor did he want the mountain that isolated him to be tolerated. He wanted to be welcomed, forgiven, healed, transformed, and adopted. When the mountain looms largest and obscures the people, we must remember that there are real relationships—real people—at stake. Tolerance is too small of an idea.

Even when I am operating at my best and making an effort, I just end up exhausted trying to climb the mountain in order to get to the people. Sometimes I find myself on the top of the mountain, running back and forth over the summit—depending on the people I am around. If I am in a group of people who think one way, I stay on their side of the mountain—acting like them, sounding like them. The next day, I could find myself surrounded by people who are from the opposite base camp, and—ever the chameleon—I will blend in with that group too. I will just wear myself out, running back and forth over the top of the mountain—from one side to the other—depending on the voices that surround me.

If I find myself tolerating the mountain or wearing myself out climbing the mountain, I must remember to ask, "To whom am I listening?" Am I listening to the mountain? Am I listening to the base camps that populate the differing sides of the mountain? Who is setting the tone here?

Sometimes the mountain seems so dang big or complex that I just can't wrap my mind around it. I can't figure it out or think my way over the mountain. I might really want a solution, but I just can't seem to think my way through it. In such times, I need to ask myself, "How am I listening?" Am I remaining obedient to what I already know to be true? Am I continuing to grow and learn gradually, or am I listening only for the quick and instant solution? I have to remember to move forward in obedience even when it doesn't make sense and allow for understanding to come gradually.

If I am honest with myself, the reason the mountain can seem so complex and confounding sometimes is because I have somehow closed myself off. Somewhere along the line in the conflict, I determine that I have all the information I need, and I shut the door on new input and information. I find a perch somewhere on the mountain, and I plop myself down to stay. I can get way too comfortable in one place on the mountain—be it in a base camp or on the peak. I get settled and comfortable with the view that I have. I become entrenched in one isolated story and one isolated perspective when what I really need is to hear other voices. I need to know other stories. I have to ask, "What am I hearing?"

Tolerating the mountain—to whom am I listening?

Climbing the mountain—how am I listening?

Enjoying the view from my perch—what am I hearing?

This is what I have learned from Peter and Cornelius. This is what I have learned from repeatedly and epically failing to fight for relationship in the middle of conflict. This is what I am reminded of when I read posts or listen to arguments from faithful people as they respond in fear and anger to whatever person, group, or issue they feel is threatening their God and their faith.

God does not call me to protect God or my faith from the theories of Dr. Hawking. Even if I had been given an opportunity to actually be in relationship with Dr. Hawking, I still would not have been called to straighten him out or correct his theories of the universe—as if that could have ever happened.

We are called to love—to size up any mountain that appears to stand between us and another and move it—not to tolerate it, not to climb it, not to rest upon it—but to move it. We are called, instructed, and equipped to love—that's it, nothing more, nothing less. We must recognize that we are safe and loved children of God and so is whoever is on the other side of the mountain—even if they don't know it. Whoever they are and however they may believe or behave, they are our brothers and sisters. They are worthy of our time and our love.

I bet you can bring to mind a relationship, a situation, a pain, or an issue right now that seems like an impossible mountain to move. We can all summon up a viewpoint on which we would bet the farm—an idea or belief that we would be willing to fight for unto the death. We can imagine no reason or eventuality that would ever cause us to waver or surrender the ground upon which we stand so firm. As the mountain rises up, we feel we must be true. We must defend our idea, our belief, our faith, our God. After all, if we surrender, what will happen to us? We've built our lives around this mountain.

Hear these words. Read them out loud: **"Put down your sword. Return it to its sheath."**

The mountains that stand between you and another person or people group are a barrier, and the truth is, those mountains should not be there—no matter how they got there. As people of the God of Abraham, Isaac, and Jacob, we are called to move mountains. As hard as that may seem, that is exactly what God invites us to do—to remove those barriers that stand between us and other people. Within each one of us dwells the divine creative power to repair—to bring restoration and wholeness.

Each fractured relationship and broken person is an opportunity to breathe love and speak life—to introduce *shalom* where chaos lies—and move mountains. Don't get me wrong: I find that just as overwhelming as you do.

But here's the good news: we don't do it alone. We have the stories—like that of Peter and Cornelius—to guide us. We have each other to strengthen and encourage us. And we have a partner in the One who made the mountains. The One who said, "With a mere kernel of faith the size of a mustard seed, you can tell this mountain to move" ... and it will move.

LIE 5

THERE IS ONE RIGHT WAY
TO BELIEVE AND ONE RIGHT
WAY TO BEHAVE

We worshipped Jesus instead of following him on his same path. We made
Jesus into a mere religion instead of a journey toward union with God
and everything else. This shift made us into a religion of 'belonging and
believing' instead of a religion of transformation.[1]

— Richard Rohr

If you're not sure what this lie is trying to get at, let me ask you a
few questions. Are Orthodox Jews more right than Reform Jews?
Is Christianity more right than Judaism? Is Catholicism more right
than Protestantism? Is one Protestant denomination more right than
the rest? Is baptism by immersion more correct than baptism by sprin-
kling? Does a Greek Orthodox worship service provide access to the

---

[1] Richard Rohr, *Jesus as Paradox*, Richard Rohr's Daily Meditation, accessed July 29, 2014,
    http://myemail.constantcontact.com/Richard-Rohr-s-Meditation–Jesus-as-Paradox.
    html?soid=1103098668616&aid=oce_J7-8kkI

divine that a Baptist worship service does not? Is there one correct way to observe communion? Are certain methods of prayer more right and true than others?

By this point in this journey, you are much too savvy to answer yes to any of those questions because you know it's a setup. You know that the idea we are going to debunk in this chapter is the lie of "one right way." Nevertheless, I am guessing that thinking through those questions and not being able to give a resolute answer might make you uncomfortable. We can probably all think of people who could answer those questions with resounding certainty. We may even be those people. I certainly have Orthodox Jewish friends who believe that their embrace of the Jewish faith is truer than that of their Reform brothers and sisters. Likewise, I have Catholic friends who are convinced that all Protestants must return to the Mother Church and Protestant friends who sit in judgment of the Catholic Church. In my hometown, it is easy to find someone who "knows" a certain mode of baptism is the only true baptism—or that a specific style of worship is God's preferred style.

All of these questions and thoughts can be summed up with two words: *orthodoxy*—correct belief and *orthopraxy*—correct behavior and practice. We're all familiar with the *ortho* part of these words, right? It is a Greek prefix that simply means "right, correct, or straight." We probably use it most commonly when talking about orthopedics—the study of the musculoskeletal system where doctors concern themselves with keeping our bodies "right, correct, or straight" or orthodontics—the study of improper bites due to tooth and jaw irregularities. Orthodontists help us get our teeth and our jaws "right, correct, and straight."

Following that line of thinking may make us wonder if there are orthodoxologists and orthopraxologists out there concerning themselves with keeping the beliefs and the practices of our faiths "right, correct, and straight." But we don't wonder long because we know the answer, don't we? Yes ... they're out there. They are everywhere. They are in every church, synagogue, and mosque. They are in the schools, offices, and boardrooms of our lives. Most likely they are even in our homes—looking back at us in the mirror. They are we … we are they.

Whether we admit it or not, we answer or avoid the kinds of questions drummed up by orthodoxy and orthopraxy everyday. What do we believe? How do we behave? The nightly news always contains stories of some group of people somewhere fighting or defending a religious or spiritual principle. Those people—just like most of us—have arrived at an interpretive decision. They have decided that the "right, correct, and straight" version of their faith requires them to believe something, do something, defend something, refuse something, and in the most tragic but all-too-common expression, to attack something.

Now, I get it. Most of us reading this book have not made the evening news because of our stance on orthodoxy or orthopraxy. Yet, every single one of us is affected by this unending and ubiquitous argument. Pick a topic—any topic: creation, evolution, abortion, birth control, homosexuality, global warming, genetic manipulation, stem cell research, capital punishment, or corporal punishment. And friends, let's be honest—those are just a few of the media-rich topics that fill our newscasts and public debate. There are much more mundane and everyday-life topics that don't always make the news but cause us to question which way is the "right" way—things like sex, drinking, drug use, dancing, and movie ratings. On top of all that, many of us are also confronted with the overtly and specifically religious questions about what clothing is appropriate, what the correct gender roles are, what food is okay to eat, what words are too bad to speak, and what constitutes working on the Sabbath.

Are you starting to grasp the prevalence of the *ortho* conversation? It is impossible to escape these questions. We use these issues to divide up the world. We group ourselves formally in religions, political parties, neighborhoods, churches, and schools based on decisions of orthodoxy and orthopraxy. We want to be around those who believe and behave like we do—those who will affirm for us that we are "right, correct, and straight" in our thinking and activity. Even in informal groupings with our friends and social connections, we align ourselves with people whose "right way" looks like ours. And don't think that by rejecting religion altogether we can somehow remain above the fray. The rejection of religion is still an interpretive choice of orthodoxy and orthopraxy. Rejecting religion is yet another method of defining our "right way." We all decide where our plumb line or our true north is, and we follow it as best we can.

Many of us rely on other people—both the living and the dead—to help us determine where the "right way" is. Some of us look to the Scripture, the stories of those who have gone before us, and the wisdom of the ancients. Some Americans look to the laws of our land, the Constitution, and the history of our government to define what is "right, correct, and straight." Those labeled as mystics seem to rely on things like prayer, revelation, and the direction of the Spirit to better understand a path that is true. Some of us reject it all and just follow our gut—what feels right. So which is it? Who is right? What is the best way to determine what is orthodoxy and orthopraxy? How do we know what is the right thing to believe and the right way to behave?

Before we struggle to answer that question, let me suggest that our problem may be that we misunderstand orthodoxy and orthopraxy—that we have completely missed the point of *ortho* altogether. What if *ortho* didn't mean that "one right way" exists? What if, instead, *ortho* meant right ways—plural?

Rather than seeking to grasp the one way that is "right, correct, and straight," what if *ortho* was simply a record of those things that had been discovered to work or to be helpful? What if *ortho* was a growing and evolving list of those things that had been tried and found to be "right, correct, and straight?" If that were the case, then orthodoxy would not be the right way to believe. It would be a collection of tried and proven beliefs that guide us toward being fully alive. Orthopraxy would not be the right way to behave. It would be a logbook of practices that people have found encouraging and useful in their pursuit of a deeper relationship with God and each other. And these logbooks and lists—of ideas, beliefs, and practices that people have learned are helpful—would evolve. They would have to, wouldn't they? Time marches on, and people continue to practice and experience faith. People continue to live and learn and therefore would continually be adding to the logbooks or amending the lists.

It can't be that easy, can it? The lie of "one right way" can't simply be boiled down to our misunderstanding of the Greek prefix *ortho* can it? Not really. I wish it were that easy. But I have this sinking feeling in my gut that misapplying *ortho*—trying to make it mean "one right way"—is merely a symptom of a deeper problem. Something inside of me knows that is just a cover—a word behind which I can hide my true motivations.

Wow! That sounded sinister, didn't it? It makes you wonder what my true motivations may be. What would be driving me to such lengths? What could possibly cause me to misapply the word *ortho* in an effort to make myself and others believe that "one right way" exists—that it is definable, attainable, and worthy of our pursuit?

You know the answer, don't you? One little four-letter word that drives so much of our world—the word upon which all of the lies we are tackling find their root.

Fear.

The emotion of fear and our desire to not be afraid generates much of the control that surrounds faith and religion. Think about that for a moment. When we are afraid, our most natural response is to seek to control or remove that which we fear. If we can control it or remove it, then we can stop being afraid. Fear drives us to do all manner of inconsistent things. It literally causes our brains and our bodies to function differently. As we discussed in the first chapter, some of the more typical responses to fear include fight, flight, and freeze. We will fight that which we believe is causing our fear. God forbid that we feel cornered by something. We can be very dangerous to ourselves and to others when we are afraid, and our efforts to seek control come through fighting. Sometimes, we flee. We run away or hide from whatever it is we have determined is causing us to fear. Lastly, we can freeze. In a moment of terror, we shut down. We don't know what to do, so we don't do anything.

If we think we are in danger—or something we care about is in danger, we will respond by trying to control the situation or person that we believe is causing our fear. Even if our response is to flee or freeze, those are still efforts to control the situation by getting away from it or ignoring it altogether.

I understand this. I can see it in my behavior—a lot. I can trace almost all of my dumbest behaviors to fear. The church, religion—they are no different. Throughout the history of the faithful, our dumbest behaviors—the treachery, murder, destruction, and heartbreak caused in the name of God—can be traced back to our fear. And here is the kicker: those fears we discussed in the last chapter—the ones that cause us to believe that our God, our faith, or our religion is in danger unless we do something about it—are learned.

Let that one sink in. We are not born with a natural fear of that which attacks our God, our faith, or our religion. That is a learned fear. We learn it through our own experiences or by the watching or learning through other peoples' experiences. It's not born in us: it's learned.

So what are we afraid of that relates to orthodoxy and orthopraxy? Quite simply, we are afraid of being wrong. Don't misunderstand me. I do not mean to trivialize what is at work here. We view our commitment to God, to our faith, to our religion, to our denomination as central to life. Those commitments, whatever they may be, are wrapped up in the meaning of our existence—our purpose. The last thing we would ever want to do is be wrong about God. We want to make sure that we have the right beliefs about God and that we are practicing our faith in the right way. Why wouldn't we? This stuff is important. We have invested everything we have into trying to get God and our faith lives "right, correct, and straight." We want our *doxy* and our *praxis* to have *ortho*.

Crushing Certainty

Author Lawrence Wright—explaining why he has done extensive research across different religious traditions—stated, "I was interested in intelligent and skeptical people who are drawn into a belief system and wind up acting on those beliefs in ways they never thought they would." While I can certainly identify with Wright's driving interest, I have to confess that I have acted in ways I never thought I would because of my belief system—or more specifically, the lies of my faith. Yet, here is the gut punch. In describing the commonality among those whom he studied, Wright states, "They're oftentimes good-hearted people—idealistic—but full of a kind of crushing certainty that eliminates doubt."[2]

I feel like Wright nailed it on that conclusion—seriously, he stuck the landing—"a crushing certainty that eliminates doubt." That stings a bit, doesn't it?

I know he's right. I have lived that way. I have crushed things with my certainty. Ideas, hopes, conversations, arguments, even people—they have all been subject to the crushing certainty of my orthodoxy and orthopraxy before. I have ignored nuance. I have refused to see shades of gray and instead believed certain areas or issues to be only black or white. I have hidden under the lie of Chapter 3—the lie of dualism—that everything has a good side and a bad side, a right way and a wrong way. Wright is describing me. I sure hope I have been "good-hearted and idealistic" because I have walked in crushing certainty and eliminated doubt.

There have been plenty of times when my fear of believing the wrong thing, my desire to feel the supposed safety of being certain, has caused me to avoid doubt at all costs and behave as though I knew I was absolutely right. None of us want to give our lives to the wrong thing. We do not want to get to the end and find out that we did it all wrong. Such thoughts fill us with fear.

And what have we learned that we humans do when we are filled with fear? We seek to control. So, give us some time—let's say a few thousand years, and every time we face the fear that we might not have God, or faith, or spirituality, or religion figured out right—we do something about it. Sometimes, we do good things, like move past the fear and learn from our mistakes. We continue to add to our ever-changing, ever-growing understanding of God and our relationship with God and each other. We

---

[2] Alex Gibney and Lawrence Wright, *Going Clear: Scientology and the Prison of Belief*, Directed by Alex Gibney (Los Angeles, CA: HBO Documentary Films, 2015).

begin archives of beliefs and practices that seem to be helpful and formative. We write down those ideas and behaviors that move us toward relationship and freedom. We develop orthodoxy and orthopraxy—not as the "one right way"—but as a documentation of hard-earned wisdom gained through experience, pain, and growth.

Still, other times we let fear govern our actions and our thoughts. Instead of moving past our fear, we steer into it and look for ways to control it. If our fears have to do with getting God wrong, or getting faith wrong, or even worse—someone else getting God or faith wrong— then we build constructs of control. Rules, regulations, expectations, standards, disciplines—things that can be cataloged and measured. We codify and regulate what a relationship with God should look like. We say, "Here is what you should believe about God, and this is how you should behave." As mentioned before, we misunderstand orthodoxy to be the "one right way" to believe and orthopraxy as the "one right way" to practice our faith.

Although the writer of Hebrews defines faith as "the assurance of things hoped for and the conviction of things not seen," we tend to prefer things we can know and things we can see. In the face of fear, we often prefer the assurance and conviction of our faith to rest on empirical data or measurable facts. We are especially fond of empirical data and measurable facts. We like to know that we are right and have proof to back it up. Reports, statistics, eyewitness accounts—all dedicated to helping us feel we are making the right choice when we choose to have faith, to believe, to base our lives upon something. Ever striving for security, we build constructs around our faith that give them the illusion of measurement.

What does that even mean—the illusion of measurement? It means we want to know and believe that we are giving our life to the "right" thing. The last thing we would want is to be duped into professing our faith in the "wrong" thing. We want to be sure that we are giving our heart, our soul, and our strength to the true God—the true religion—the true faith. Accordingly, we construct ways to measure what is true. We determine standards, set bars, and make rules in order to provide a basis for comparison—a basis for measurement. We find comfort in the ability to measure and compare because it feels like the safety of control in a chaotic and uncertain world.

If I can find a "right" way, I can measure my actions or efforts against that guide and judge the results. I succeeded. I failed. I was so close. I missed it by "that much," so here are the things I need to work on. We determine all of that by measurement and comparison. Once more, we find measuring and judging the success and failure of others against the "right" way even more fascinating. It is incredibly satisfying to establish a norm or an accepted standard that I can keep or achieve and then sit comfortably and included while determining who is not able to achieve it or keep up the standard.

In his book *Against Football: One Fan's Reluctant Manifesto*, Steve Almond writes about the human propensity to set such standards as a way of distancing ourselves from the realities we create and accept. Dealing with his ability to deflect any personal responsibility he felt as a paying fan of football for the traumatic brain injuries incurred by the players, Almond writes,

> I assumed, in other words, a posture of ironic distance, which is what we Americans do to avoid the corruption of our spiritual arrangements. Ironic distance allows us to separate ourselves from the big, complicated moral systems around us (political, religious, familial), to sit in judgment of others rather than ourselves. It's the reason, as we zoom into the twilight years of our imperial reign, that Reality TV has become our designated guilty pleasure.
>
> But here's the thing: You can run from your own subtext for only so long. Those spray-tanned lunatics we happily revile are merely turned-out versions of our private selves, the whores we hide from public view.[3]

---

[3] Steve Almond, *Against Football: One Fan's Reluctant Manifesto* (Brooklyn, NY: Melville House Publishing, 2014), 4-5.

Let me first respond to that quote by saying, "Son of a motherless goat!"[4] If you don't feel the sting of Almond's conclusion, you need to go back and read it again. That should hit home. Whether or not you are a football fan, we should all see ourselves in that quote. We all have areas where we "run from our own subtext," judging others and denying the existence of the whorish self that "we hide from public view." I know that sucks to think about, but remember that you are not alone. We all do this—and when I say all, I don't mean football fans, or Americans, or even those of us who are alive at present. I mean all of humanity—since the beginning. Can you imagine what a life would look like if it did not fall prey to the "illusion of measurement" or "ironic distance?" Can you picture a life lived without fear—the fear of believing the wrong thing, the fear of acting the wrong way? Hold that thought.

Whether we realize it or not, we all struggle with fear. We all engage the illusion of measurement and assume postures of ironic distance. The thoughts, questions, conversations, and decisions about orthodoxy and orthopraxy that fill our lives cause us to pursue the false safety of control and separation. It is a lifestyle of spinning plates on the tips of sticks—never-ending, stressful, exhausting. Trying to determine "right way" for every belief and situation is an overwhelming task in and of itself. But once we feel we have determined the rules and regulations, we set about the endless work trying to keep everything in our world in line. Trying to keep our lives parallel to any plumb line takes a lot of energy—and what if the plumb line keeps changing? Wait, what was that last sentence? Our plumb line changes? How could that be? Shouldn't our orthodoxy and orthopraxy get set and be still? What would cause it to change?

This is another one of those questions to which you already know

---

4   Steve Martin, Lorne Michaels, and Randy Newman, ¡Three Amigos! DVD, directed by John Landis (Los Angeles, CA: HBO Home Video, 1995).

      That one was for all you ¡Three Amigos! fans out there. You know who you are—and now you know that I care. I can't just rip these quotes off. Every time I place a jewel like that in this book, I have to go do the citation work—looking stuff up and making sure the proper credit is given. So now you know. It's not easy, but I give because I love.

the answer. The answer is life. Life causes our plumb lines to change. Life alters our perception of where true north really is. Life sizes up our walls of orthodoxy and orthopraxy—sometimes giving them a gentle nudge or realignment and sometimes completely leveling them. Right at the moment I usually think I have figured out what is "right, correct, and straight," a situation arises in my life that makes me realize I don't have it figured out at all. In essence, I awaken to a new question, a different perspective, or a level of understanding that I did not have before. *Awaken* is an important word; it's an important concept for us to remember when dealing with the lie of "one right way." Make a mental note of that—highlight it, underline it, whatever works for you. What if, instead of believing there is "one right way" to learn and apply, we viewed our faith in terms of a continually expanding consciousness to which we *awaken*?

The Never-Ending Awakening

There is, perhaps, no greater example I could provide for how life has caused my orthodoxy and orthopraxy—my understanding of what is "right, correct, and straight"—to change than the journey of parenthood. For those of you who do not have children, I am certain you have witnessed this journey nonetheless. In spite of the sleep deprivation it typically generates, parenthood leads to many, many awakenings.

Everyone tells you how much your world is going to change when you have your first child. My wife and I never had the experience of a first child as her first pregnancy was with twins. We went from no child to children—from zero to two. We never even had a chance to run a 2-on-1 zone defense. From the moment our sons were born, it was 1-on-1 defense. As much as your family and friends try to prepare you for the shift that having children forces on your life, the truth is you just can't understand it until you live it. Things that you used to think were important disappear from your life completely. Your values change—mostly because your children become the most important value. If you are the primary caregiver for a small child, you learn to value things like sleep, stillness, quiet, and peace.

The continuum of change does not stop after the birth of a child, however. It just keeps going. After having two sons for four years, my wife and I were expecting a baby girl. Once again, every "father of a daughter" in my life tried to prepare me for how my world was about to change—including my own father. I tried to dismiss most of these warnings as sentimental junk. I was raised with sisters: they didn't seem that different to me. I already had two sons—this was just going to be one baby girl. Surely, I am prepared for this, right? Wrong.

Just as every "father of a daughter" had predicted, our daughter changed everything. Once again, my values—my sense of what is important, what is "right, correct, and straight"—were subject to upheaval. Just as our sons had done, our daughter changed me. My perspective shifted. My understanding deepened. My worldview increased to include room for this new, mysterious and beautiful little girl.

Before we all disappear into schmaltzy bliss together, let me add a little wrinkle to this story. Our best friends were pregnant with their first child when we were pregnant with our third. They, too, were having a baby girl. Their daughter, Grace, was born a few weeks after our daughter, Abigail. Abigail's birth was pretty standard (not to diminish the pain and agony endured by my wife), but there were no major complications, and Abigail was perfectly healthy.

Grace's birth was not standard. There were problems. In fact, the problems were so severe that mother and daughter were immediately separated moments after birth so that Grace could be rushed to a different hospital that had the means to care for her. Can you imagine that? My friend—Grace's father—had to get into an ambulance with his minutes-old daughter and leave his wife behind. I don't even want to think about what that was like, let alone what Grace's mother had to endure moments after giving birth. She was left alone. She was left not knowing what was happening or what was wrong with her daughter.

The story of Grace does not get much simpler from there. She is alive and well today, to be sure. We all love Grace and bless God for what she brings to our lives, but it is not easy. Grace is a special-needs child. She is developmentally disabled and requires round-the-clock supervision. Taking care of Grace is more than her parents can manage on their own— it's just not humanly possible.

I won't go into too much detail here about Grace because I know her story is being written. Her amazing parents—surrounded by their family—will tell the story of Grace and all that she has brought to their lives. What I can affirm for you here is that Grace changed everything. If I thought my world was turned upside down by Abigail, that was a walk in the park compared to the worldview expansion brought on by Grace. Our friends' lives shifted. Their values moved. Their understanding of what is "right, correct, and straight" changed, and there was no going back. In fact, the change was so drastically different that, at first, it strained our friendship. Stacy and I didn't understand—we couldn't relate. The day Grace was born caused such a radical realignment of our friends' lives that our relationship with them had neither the groundwork nor the tools to keep up. To be completely honest, for the first year or so of Grace's life, I was a terrible friend.

Don't get me wrong. I kept up appearances. I made sure to inquire about how everyone was doing, asking how we could pray for them, how we could help them. I made sure that all the boxes of propriety were checked. I clung to my understanding of what was "right, correct, and straight" in our relationship. What I didn't do was make room in my life for new information. I didn't open myself up to the shift they were experiencing. My friends' worldview and value system was under siege, and I made sure to keep my distance.

It wasn't until Grace was almost two years old that something changed in me. My world was falling apart. I had been fired from one job and was about to be fired from another. One of my sons had faced some severe medical issues. I was wrestling with my calling, and I was losing. I needed help.

My circumstances brought me to a place of humility—a place where

I recognized that there was no way out on my own. If I was coming out of the hole I was in, it was going to be on the strength of others. My worldview, my perspective, my values—they were all in shambles. The systems and rules I had put in place to keep me locked in on what was "right, correct, and straight" had failed me. They flat out didn't work. My orthodoxy had not protected my son from his health problems. My orthopraxy had not prevented my career failure and impending financial ruin. Even the God in whom I believed had failed me.

Lots of people found me in that hole. Wise and learned elders looked into that hole and told me smart things about my situation. Generous and caring people looked into that hole and lowered provisions and gifts. Spiritual and serious people stood over the hole and prayed for me. I am grateful for all of these people. They made my time in the pit survivable. They kept me alive. They made sure I did not surrender to the dark night of my soul.

Still, there is an important distinction to be made. There were only a handful of people who came upon me during this time—who saw me in the pit—and decided to climb down to me. These were people in my life whose response to seeing me in the hole was to get in the hole with me. Most of them—my wife, for example—were bound by familial covenant to go where I go. If I was in the pit, then she was in the pit. That's just the way it is. You know who those people are in your life, right? They're the kind of people who are going to be with you through thick and thin. Bless God for those people: they are your family.

None of that really surprised me. The smart people in my life told me smart things. The generous people in my life were generous with me. The prayerful people in my life prayed for me. My family—those with whom I "do life"—stayed with me, proving that I was not alone. What surprised me was Grace's dad. My friend—whose life had been turned upside down with the arrival of his special-needs daughter—showed up. In spite of the "ironic distance" I had kept between us ... in spite of my inability to be a good friend when he most needed one ... in spite of our deteriorating relationship, he showed up. He jumped in the pit, told me he had been there before, and he knew the way out.

I want to be clear here. Some of what put me in that pit in the first place was my relationship with this guy. To him, that didn't seem to matter. He had an understanding I did not yet have. His grasp of "right, correct, and straight" had been altered by his life and experience. However it changed him, it enabled him to lead me out of that pit. That is why I started this story by saying "our best friends" and not "our old friends."

I changed—sometimes instantly and easily, sometimes slowly and painfully, usually awkwardly and clumsily. I learned, little by little, what it meant for my friend to be the parent of a special-needs daughter. I am still learning from Grace and her parents. Everything I experience with them changes my perspective a little more. Our deepening friendship with Grace's parents has caused our entire family to awaken to the world of special-needs people. Every burden they are willing to share with us causes us to realign our perspectives, our beliefs, our ideas about what is "right, correct, and straight."

Friends, that is just one example from one relationship. We could all fill volumes with the ways different relationships in our lives have shaped us and changed us. If we started writing all the ways our relationships with other human beings have altered our orthodoxy and orthopraxy— changed the way we understand what is "right," we would never stop writing. Therein lies the hint toward the truth: relationship.

When we find ourselves choosing "right beliefs" or "right behavior" over right relationships, we are destined for a crash. If we look at our lives and see that we are using orthodoxy and orthopraxy to separate and divide us from other people rather than unite and include, we are heading for a pit. We must remain diligently open to relationships—awkward, clumsy, uncomfortable relationships. People change us. People cause us to consider things we would not consider on our own. People carry their perspectives and their experiences around with them and invite us inside. If you want a surefire way to make sure that you lock your orthodoxy and your orthopraxy down and keep it from ever changing, then cut yourself off from people—don't let anyone inside your heart. It's the only way.

The Myth of the Singular Precedent

At this point, you may be experiencing some pushback. You may be thinking something along the lines of … *Whatever, Darrell. Just because life and other people cause us to change doesn't mean we should. Aren't we supposed to be strong? Aren't we supposed to drive toward the standard? Our society today is just evidence of our continuing moral decay. We have lost our way. We should try to be more like the people in the biblical stories. We should be more like Paul or the disciples. We should return to the ways of the early church. Aren't these the standards we should espouse and to which we should hold ourselves accountable?*

My answer to such questions: "Which one?" Which standard in the past is the right one? Which of the "good old days" are the real "good old days" to which we should return and hold fast? Let's talk turkey, folks (that is a Southern colloquialism for getting down to brass tacks … which is a colloquialism for cutting the bull … which is … you know I could go on a while with this, right?). Let me give it to you straight.

The singular precedent—that one benchmark of excellence somewhere in the past that does not exist in the way that we think it does. If we think we need to return to the ways of the "early church" or the "first-century faith," we have an impossible task ahead of us. Even if we could convince Doc Brown to throw us in the time machine and take us back, we would find that there simply was not one "early church."[5] There were several. At the time when Jesus and the disciples were walking around the Sea of Galilee, there were at least eleven different sects of Judaism. Following the resurrection and ascension of Jesus, the missionary efforts of Paul and the disciples spread the story of the Messiah around the

---

5   Great Scott! If you don't know who Doc Brown is, it's time to put this book down, get to your nearest computer, mobile device, or television, and watch three *heavy* movies.
     Bob Gale and Robert Zemeckis, *Back to the Future* DVD, directed by Robert Zemeckis (Universal City, CA: Universal, 2002).

region, but that story didn't manifest itself in a singular expression. Duke University professor Dr. Lester Ruth says it this way: "We really shouldn't speak about worship of the 'Early Church'; we should speak about worship of the 'Early Churches.' What you're looking at in the first century is a rapidly expanding missionary movement—crossing a variety of people groups and geographic regions and cultures—and that's just a formula for diversity, not uniformity."[6]

None of this should seem strange to Christians, who now have over 30,000 distinct denominations around the world. There has never been one universally recognized "right way" of living, expressing, or understanding the faith.

Case in point—baptism—something that some Christian denominations can get really bent out of shape over. People have been arguing about baptism for a long time. Who can be baptized? When do we baptize? How do we baptize? Can we rebaptize? What does baptism do? Today, there is surprisingly little agreement on the answers to any of these questions. So who has it right? Who has the orthodoxy and orthopraxy when it comes to baptism? Who is holding on to what is "right, correct, and straight?"

Worship and liturgical scholar John D. Witvliet of the Calvin Institute for Worship points out that archeologists have unearthed first century baptismal fonts in varying locations that demonstrate differing understandings of baptism.

> There are early baptismal fonts that look like washbasins—and that makes sense as the waters of baptism, in part, convey meaning to us as a symbol of cleaning ... some early church fonts look instead like tombs. They are cut out of the ground and that makes sense, too, if in Scripture, we remember the powerful imagery of how baptism is for us a chance to identify with Christ's death and resurrection.... There are even some early church fonts that resemble wombs ... the texts associated with

---

6   Lester Ruth, quoted in "Part 2: The Body" of *A History of Christian Worship: Ancient Ways, Future Paths*, DVD, directed by Tom Dallis (Worcester, PA: Ensign Media, 2010).

these fonts very clearly suggests the image of a womb—and that makes sense, too. There are New Testament texts that speak about the waters of rebirth. So, water for washing, for drowning and for birthing, and fonts that correspond with each of these scriptural images—it's really remarkable to see the early churches' imagination at work.[7]

I have to admit that allowing imagination room to work seems much more interesting to me than isolating one "right way" to baptize.

I was baptized in a particular way—water was sprinkled on my head three times—in the washbasin sense mentioned above. That has meaning for me. I can connect to the fact that I am cleansed in the waters of baptism. I can trace the connection of my baptism to the Jewish mikvah or ritual cleansing—the tradition from which Christian baptism springs. At the same time, the idea of descending down into a tomblike pool and being resurrected from beneath the waters sounds pretty awesome to me. Likewise, the picture of being born again out of a womblike baptismal font seems incredibly consistent with the story of God. So, which is it? Which way is the right way to baptize? Which way is the orthodox way?

The Context of Faith

The basic problem of misunderstanding orthodoxy and orthopraxy as the pursuit and preservation of "one right way" is that it sets the context of our faith as rules. At this point, you're thinking, *Ummmm... duh, Darrell. Faith is about rules.* I assure you, I understand that narrative. It is the narrative that sees faith as a contract between God and us. That contract stipulates what it is that is expected of us—the codes and rules that we are supposed to follow. If we follow those rules and keep up our end of the bargain, then we will be blessed—with a better life now and with a heavenly afterlife. If we fail to follow the rules and honor our

---

7   John D. Witvliet, quoted in "Part 2: The Body" of *A History of Christian Worship: Ancient Ways, Future Paths*, DVD, directed by Tom Dallis (Worcester, PA: Ensign Media, 2010).

contractual agreements, then we can expect punishment and a torturous, hellish afterlife.

I realize that is a boiled-down description and that most of the faithful would not choose such a description for faith, but when we elevate rules, that is exactly what faith becomes. Orthodoxy and orthopraxy become the rules by which we are all measured and judged as being faithful or unfaithful—as being worthy or unworthy—as being heaven-bound or cursed to hell. If this seems too harsh of a light to shine on your faith, I challenge you to ask yourself how it is you define the different faiths or denominations to which you have been exposed. Most of us—if we are honest—classify and group the different faiths and denominations in our world based on what those faiths believe to be *ortho*—what they believe to be the "one right way." We learn what their rules are and use those rules to define their faith. For example:

> "Southern Baptists can't drink alcohol or smoke or (until very recently) dance."
> "Jews can't eat pork or shellfish."
> "Mormons can't drink caffeine."
> "Catholics have to go to confession."
> "Muslims have to pray five times a day."
> "The Church of Christ doesn't allow musical instruments in worship."

None of these statements are completely true in the sense that they accurately describe what is going on in each of those faiths, but they are exactly the kind of divisions we make in our spiritual world when we define the context of faith as rules.

The effects of this warped context are ubiquitous and ancient. This is not a new or localized phenomenon—it's everywhere, and it has been for a long time. Perceiving faith as being about rules—as being about "one right way"—shapes our world. Contextualizing faith with rules necessarily requires us to build and sustain extensive systems of measurements and judgment.

But we don't stop with just the rules. We must also have scholars and experts in understanding and keeping the rules—writing and arguing through codes and discipline. We have pastors and priests to sit in judgment as to how well the rules are being followed, deciding whether we are worthy to engage the sacraments or receive the blessing. We require systems of enforcement, punishment, and repentance that try to bring order to our behavior when we fail to follow the rules.

As bad as that may sound, the reduction of our faith to an infrastructure of measurement, judgment, and punishment is not the worst effect rules have on us when we see them as the context for our relationship with God. The truth is when we make our faith about *ortho*—about knowing and keeping the rules—we make God smaller. In my opinion, we make God so small that the result is not God at all—it is an idol. I readily admit that if all God has to offer me is a list of rules—things that I must do and must not do in order to be blessed—then God becomes the hall monitor of creation. With all deference to those of you who dutifully served in the position of hall monitor in your schools growing up, nobody wants to hang out with the hall monitor—at least, not while they're in the hall.

None of this is to say that rules, laws, commandments are inherently bad ... quite to the contrary. Rules, like hall monitors, are important. They can help to bring order and create healthy boundaries. When our orthodoxy and orthopraxy are seen as the accumulated wisdom of the faithful living out their relationship with God and each other—those beliefs and practices the faithful have tried and determined to be helpful—then rules can seek to protect and preserve. Such a perspective is not about control and judgment; it is about relationship and edification.

The Filing System

We learn from our Hebraic brothers and sisters that the Hebrew Bible contains 613 *mitzvot* or instructions—rules and guidelines by which to live. 613! That is a lot of rules. If we look at them as lines not to cross for fear of punishment—or even lines to stay within if we want God to like us—then we are going to be overwhelmed. We'll never win. We'll never be able to remember and keep all the rules.

What if that's not what they are? What if the 613 *mitzvot* are something else entirely? What if, instead of being rules, the 613 *mitzvot* were insight into how to live life better? To be more fully alive? Such thinking follows the idea Jesus referenced when speaking on the "rules" of keeping the Sabbath. "The sabbath was made for humankind, and not humankind for the sabbath" (Mark 2:27). Those 613 *mitzvot* were written down by the faithful because the faithful believed them to be helpful and instructive in their developing relationship with God and each other. The *mitzvot* exist for the people. The people do not exist for the *mitzvot*.

That makes sense, doesn't it? It is basic logic when we stop to think about it. Nevertheless, we must be honest that when we boil our faith down to a collection of "can dos" and "can't dos," we turn that logic on its head. We elevate the rule or the law as if it were the point. We make rules the context within which our faith exists. It's an easy—and sometimes all too comfortable—mistake to make. The Hebrew Bible alone gives us 613 *mitzvot,* for crying out loud! That, in and of itself, is enough to be confusing.

Yet, if the context for those 613 *mitzvot* is relationship instead of rules, things begin to change. Hold that thought for a moment.

I have learned from my Hebraic teachers that those 613 *mitzvot* are more correctly understood to be part of a larger filing system. The idea is that each of the 613 *instructions* can be filed under one of what most of us call the "Ten Commandments."

I apologize for this oncoming rabbit trail, but it is unavoidable—so a brief moment of digression, if you please. Nowhere in the biblical text are the "Ten Commandments" referred to as the "Ten Commandments." That is one of those titles that biblical interpreters and scholars added in to help break up the biblical text and make it easier to organize—much like chapter and verse numbers. God bless these people for trying to help us navigate our way through the Bible; their intentions were honorable. I am sure they never imagined that we would become more familiar with the subheadings than with the content of the Bible—but we did. We know the titles. And by the way—with apologies to Cecil B. DeMille—*The Ten Commandments* is a horrible title.[8] Calling these instructions the "Ten Commandments" is the kind of thing that starts us down the path of elevating the rules above the relationship. How many court battles have been fought, how many lives have been hurt, how many millions have been spent in the United States alone fighting for the right to have or not have the "Ten Commandments" enshrined in our courtrooms, classrooms, and civic spaces? It is an incredibly ridiculous and sad irony that we would use the relationship instructions contained in the "Ten Commandments" to destroy relationship—but we do. We declare that our faith is about rules and that those rules must be kept sacrosanct and holy—they must be displayed and honored. All the while, we are unaware that the Bible itself does not even call those instructions the "Ten Commandments," and the overarching narrative contained in the biblical texts certainly does not call us to elevate rules above relationship.

Instructions is a much better word because that is exactly what they are—instructions revealed to a people who were searching for ways to better understand who God was and who they were called to be. At the time, those instructions were incredibly progressive and revelatory. They were the kinds of ideas that helped people see that this God—the God of Abraham, Isaac, and Jacob—was different. This God was the one God— the only God. This God valued people and relationship and wanted the people to do likewise. These instructions were basic principles about how to view God and each other.

Given the basic nature of these principles and instructions, it would make sense then that some of our Hebraic brothers and sisters see each of the 613 *mitzvot* found in the Hebrew Bible as being tied to one of those basic principles about how to view God and each other. Thus, we return to the aforementioned filing system. The 613 *mitzvot* can all be filed under

---

[8]   Dorothy Clarke Wilson, J.H. Ingraham, and A.E. Southon, *The Ten Commandments* DVD, directed by Cecil B. DeMille (Los Angeles, CA: Paramount Home Video, 1999).

one of the ten principal instructions (formerly known as commandments) and that's not all, folks! Those ten principal instructions can all be filed under one of two even more basic ideas—love God, love others.

This is one of those moments that I so wish books had sound effects. This would be the perfect time for the sound of a lonely, empty wind to blow as we all ponder the fact that everything in the biblical narrative flows from the relational instructive to love God and love other people. Maybe you would prefer a less subtle sound effect—like a mic drop. Love God, love others ... boom! ... the mic hits the floor ... nothing else to say.[9] From 613 to 10 to 2. It can't be that simple, can it? Try this on for size.

> When the Pharisees heard that Jesus had silenced the Sadducees, they gathered together, and one of them, a lawyer, asked Jesus a question to test him. "Teacher, which commandment in the law is the greatest?" Jesus said to him, "'You shall love the Lord your God with all your heart, and with all your soul, and with all your mind.' This is the greatest and first commandment. And the second is like it: 'You shall love your neighbor as yourself.' On these two commandments hang all the law and the prophets."
>
> (MATT. 22:34–40)

So, if we think this Jesus guy has a clue to what he is talking about, he seems to be saying the context for faith is one of love and relationship, not rules and control. The great thing about the answer Jesus gives is that he didn't just pull it out of thin air. He was quoting the Hebrew scriptures—Deuteronomy and Leviticus, to be exact—which, incidentally, are the two books containing most of the 613 *mitzvot*.

Jesus was quoting what our Hebraic brothers and sisters call the *Shema*. We find most of what is known as the *Shema* in Deuteronomy 6:4–9. It is called the *Shema* because it begins in Hebrew with *Shema*

---

9   That might be the worst sentence typed in this book so far. Sound effects just cannot be explained with the written word. Bless the LORD for sound effects technicians and Foley artists—the work they do is important!

Israel, Adonai Eloheinu, Adonai Echad... or "Hear, O Israel, the LORD our God, the LORD alone." The *Shema* continues:

> You shall love the LORD your God with all your heart, with all your soul, and with all your strength. Keep these words that I am commanding you today in your heart. Recite them to your children and talk about them when you are at home and when you are away, when you lie down and when you rise. Bind them as a sign on your hand, fix them as an emblem on your forehead, and write them on the doorposts of your house and on your gates.
>
> (DEUT. 6:4–9)

Add to that the instruction of Leviticus 19:18, "You shall love your neighbor as you love yourself," and you have Jesus' answer to the question of which commandment was the most important.

The lawyer who questioned Jesus (which, by the way, was not a lawyer like we think of today but essentially a scholar and teacher of the 613 *mitzvot*) may have been trying to catch Jesus in a wrong answer, but his question was still asking, "What is the context? How are we to understand this faith? How do you say I should understand this religion?" Jesus' answer was love not rules—relationship not control. Love God with everything you have and love each other as you love yourself. Jesus seems to be teaching that if we pull one of the 613 *mitzvot* out by itself without the context of love, it won't make any sense. It's not that Jesus refutes or dismisses the 613 *mitzvot* or the 10 *instructions*, it's that he asks where they came from—what inspired them?

Do the instructions, rules, and guidelines exist for us or do we exist for them? Were they intended to be a guide to a growing, progressive relationship with the divine that would, in turn, reshape how we related to one another, or were they intended to be the rules that we have to obey in order to be "in"?

Richard Rohr wrote, "This tendency in religion to 'absolutize' things comes from a deep psychological need for some solid ground to stand on, and I understand that. But what the prophets keep saying is, 'God is the only absolute!' Don't make the fingers pointing to the moon into the moon itself, as it were."[10]

Are the rules, the instructions, the commandments the moon or are they the finger that points to the moon?

That question is the question the Shema tells us to ask—it's the same question Jesus repeatedly challenges his followers and accusers to ask. It's the same question we must ask of our denominational doctrines, our books of discipline, our rules of the faith. It is the x-ray under which all of our orthodoxy and all of our orthopraxy must be examined. What is at the center? If we peel away all the layers from our "right beliefs" and "right practices," do we find helpful guides for progressive and growing relationship? If we hold our orthodoxy and orthopraxy up to the light, do we find instruction that can be filed under the principles of loving God or loving others?

For those of us who find orthodoxy and orthopraxy to be a terrifyingly amorphous abyss, this question makes it really simple. Does this instruction—this guideline, this rule—help me to develop my relationship with God or with another human being? If the answer is no, then we must have the courage to lay such ideas down and leave them behind. In doing so, I believe we can discover a freedom that comes from taking ourselves out of the seats of judgment—from leaving behind the illusions of measurement and ironic distance.

You may wonder what that looks like in a practical sense. I wonder that, too. I am still learning. I can only testify to what has worked for me—that which I have found to be *ortho.* What helps to keep me "right, correct, and straight" is believing that all the people I encounter matter to God—not just the ones with whom I agree and have a similar experience. My behavior and experience are undeniably realigned by the knowledge that it is not my beliefs or my practices that make me worthy of love. It

---

[10] Richard Rohr, *Prophets: Self Critical Thinking*, Richard Rohr's Daily Meditation, accessed February 17, 2015, http://myemail.constantcontact.com/Richard-Rohr-s-Meditation–Archetypal-Religion.html?soid=1103098668616&aid=JJ-SgyYu2H0

is my identity. It is your identity. We are all born into this world with an inherent identity that cannot be changed. We are all daughters and sons of God.

Such thinking opens me up to other people and allows me to pursue relationships, making sure that I don't just surround myself with people who agree with everything I already think. This is the simple and singular advice on how to come out from under the lie of one "right way"; invest in some relationships with people whose experiences and thinking are completely different from your own.

They're really not that hard to find. We won't have to look far to find someone whose orthodoxy and orthopraxy is strange to us. Get to know them. Listen to their stories and learn why they think and move the way they do—not for the purpose of changing them—but for the purposes of learning, love, and light. In pursuing such relationships, we learn of the world outside of ourselves. We love the people in front of us regardless of the similarity of our orthodoxy and orthopraxy. And we live into the light of the truth that there is no such thing as "one right way." In fact, there never has been.

Hear O Israel; the LORD *is our God, the* LORD *alone. Love the* LORD *your God with all your heart, all your soul, and all your strength; and love your neighbor as yourself.*

Please, God, let it be so.

LIE 6

FAITH IS A PRIVATE MATTER

In fact, people use drugs, legal and illegal, because their lives are intolerably painful or dull. They hate their work and find no rest in their leisure. They are estranged from their families and their neighbors. It should tell us something that in healthy societies drug use is celebrative, convivial, and occasional, whereas among us it is lonely, shameful, and addictive. We need drugs, apparently, because we have lost each other.[1]

— Wendell Berry

The closer we get to the end of this journey, the more apparent it should be that each of these lies is related. You are probably starting to notice that these lies are not isolated ideas that stand on their own but rather an undesirable tapestry interwoven in our lives. Coming out from under any one of these lies should reveal other shaky foundations that need to crumble and fall. In a sense, once the light of truth begins to shine forth, darkness cannot hide. Light works that way—it just kind of gets all over everything.

That being the case, we should see how coming out from under the bad ideas of believing we have a duty to defend God and that there is only

---

[1] Wendell Berry, *The Art of the Commonplace: The Agrarian Essays of Wendell Berry* (Berkley, CA: Counterpoint Press, 2002), 61.

one right way to believe or behave turn our inward-looking faith outward. As the context of love takes hold in our faith, we are directed away from building and maintaining our own kingdoms and turned toward loving other people. It is at this crossroads where that light spills out onto another area of shadowy, incorrect thinking: a lie that tells us that our faith is a private matter—existing only between you and the divinity in which you choose to believe or not believe.

Much like divulging whom we voted for in the last election, many of us have embraced the incorrect idea that our spiritual lives are strictly personal—part of an internal dialogue between our heart and the source to which we hold. This, like so many of the lies we face, is a lie of incomplete thinking—a half-truth. Faith is most certainly personal. We are not wrong to think that we have an internal dialogue with the divine. We are not crazy when we recognize that the God of the universe knows us and loves us personally. We are right to recognize that the same transcendent power and ultimate authority that spins the cosmos also chooses to pursue relationship with us—to actually dwell among and within us. Faith is intimately and awesomely personal. But personal is not synonymous with private. In no way is our faith a private matter.

What you do, what you believe, how you practice your faith, how you live your life affects others. None of us is an island unto ourselves.[2] Each of our lives intersects the lives of others, and that is not a coincidence. It is how the whole thing is set up! But wait, I am starting to get worked up. Let's slow this thing down a bit and explore before I get all wound up and start beating you over the head with conclusions.

By this point in the journey, we know that it is helpful to understand

---

[2] John Donne, *Devotions Upon Emergent Occasions and Death's Duel* (New York: Knopf Doubleday Publishing, 1999), 63.

From Donne's *XVII Meditation*: "No man is an island, entire of itself; every man is a piece of the continent, a part of the main. If a clod be washed away by the sea, Europe is the less, as well as if a promontory were, as well as if a manor of thy friend's or of thine own were: any man's death diminishes me, because I am involved in mankind, and therefore never send to know for whom the bells tolls; it tolls for thee."

and deconstruct the lie in order to better understand the truth. So, let's understand this lie. What is it exactly and where does it come from?

A Personal Relationship

Before you begin to worry that your personal relationship with Jesus is going to come under attack here, let me assure you that we are all safe. Your personal relationship with Jesus or God is not going to come under attack. No one is going to try to take it away from you. As we have frequently experienced on this journey, the lies we allow ourselves to live under are, more often than not, just incomplete ideas. It's not that they need to be eradicated or removed altogether but that they need expansion—they need something added. That is the case here. It's not that we don't have a personal relationship with God or Jesus or the divine, it's that there is truly more to our relationship than just a private exchange.

In the novel *Blue Like Jazz*, the narrator and central character—struggling with modern spirituality—states, "When I walked into the Christian section of a bookstore, the message was clear: faith is something you do alone."[3] Friends, that is the lie—and if we are honest, we can see the bad idea that "faith is something you do alone" all around us. Whether we have recognized it or not, we have been experiencing a trend toward faith becoming more and more of a personal and private matter in our society for quite some time. Before any of us reading this were even born, our cultural pendulum began to swing away from the perception of faith as a communal endeavor toward seeing faith as something private—between only us and our God.

In his 1985 work, *Habits of the Heart*, Dr. Robert Bellah attributed this pendulum swing to the explosion and dominance of scientific thought in the public sphere, beginning in the late nineteenth century. That should make sense to us today as "scientific thought"—meaning that which we can test and empirically prove—continues to define so much of

---

[3]   Donald Miller, *Blue Like Jazz: Nonreligious Thoughts on Christian Spirituality* (Nashville, Tenn: Thomas Nelson, Inc., 2003), 175.

our reality. This gets a little deep but stay with me here. Bellah wants us to recognize that as our society became scientifically enlightened and we learned to define our existence by all the things that science and empirical data can measure, test, and prove, our faith migrated toward that which could not be measured or empirically proven—"feeling and sentiment." In his article "A Personal Relationship with Jesus?", theologian John Suk summarizes Bellah's assertion by writing, "By this account, the triumph of science meant that faith had to make a strategic retreat to private experience or morality."[4]

Okay, I realize that after reading and possibly rereading that last paragraph a few times, you may be cursing at me and wondering what in the wide, wide world of sports all of that has to do with anything.[5] Simply put, it is this: the notion that we are called to have a personal and private relationship with God or Jesus comes neither from the Bible nor the long history of faith. It is a recent development that is a cultural reaction to the scientific awakening. The last 200 years of scientific development—and the subsequent mistake of often viewing science and faith as competitors to one another—caused our faith to retreat from the communal sphere where it belongs to the private sphere. It's as if our communal consciousness concluded that anywhere science and empirical thought exist is a place where faith is no longer welcome, so faith must, therefore, only be about our private feelings and our personal experience.

There is another lie at work here—the lie that faith and science are opposites or are somehow mutually exclusive. It's a little lie with a huge impact, and causing our faith to be reduced to the personal and private is just one small effect this lie has had on us. We will get to this lie, I promise. But for now we must focus on the lie at hand—the lie that our faith

---

[4]   Dr. John Suk, "A Personal Relationship with Jesus?" Perspectives: A Journal of Reformed Thought, accessed July 2, 2014, http://perspectivesjournal.org/blog/2005/11/16/a-personal-relationship-with-jesus/

[5]   Andrew Bergman, Mel Brooks, Richard Pryor, Norman Steinberg, and Alan Uger, Blazing Saddles, DVD, directed by Mel Brooks (Burbank, CA: Warner Home Video, 1997). God bless Mel Brooks.

is a personal and private matter—that our relationship with God is just between God and us.

If we have understood nothing else in this chapter up to this point, let us pause and stare at this truth until it sinks in. Our faith was never meant to be something we do alone. Both the stories of the Bible and the over-arching story of the history of the faithful confirm that faith is communal. The idea that our faith is personal and private represents a recent and continuing cultural reaction to our scientific awakening and our struggle to reconcile science and faith. When we steer into this skid and allow faith to retreat only to the personal and private, faith then becomes that which divides us rather than that which unites and ties us together. The context of such a faith is not love and relationship but rules, boundaries, orthodoxies, and orthopraxis. The results of such faith include division, isolation, loneliness, resentment, bitterness, hatred, and bigotry as we turn more and more inward and fear that which is different from us. Is that a bleak enough picture to get your attention? I hope so.

How about a bigger picture? Hold on to your personal relationship with the divine. It is not in any danger. Just don't grasp it so tightly in your clinched fist. Let it sit in your open palm. It will remain there. No one will steal it away. And if we hold it openly, we can receive more. Our personal faith can be added to; it can become more than it is now.

We Come from Community

"Then God said, 'Let us make humankind in our image, according to our likeness....'"

(GEN 1:26)

Verse 26 of the creation poem found in the first chapter of Genesis has God saying to God's self, "Let US make humankind in OUR image, according to OUR likeness...." That is supremely weird. Who is God talking to? Don't worry, I am not getting literal on you here. The poem in Genesis 1 doesn't exist to provide us with empirical data on the creation of the cosmos. This poem—as poems generally do—points toward bigger ideas. One of those ideas is that God is not a created, singularly contained being—God is better understood as a relationship—and we come from that relationship.

Now before we spin off into the mind trip of the One God and the Christian doctrine of the Trinity (Father, Son, Holy Spirit), let's pump the brakes here. The Trinity is well worth exploring—and there are plenty of writings that do just that. What we need to recognize here is that there is nothing really radical being said. The use of plural pronouns (us, our) in verse 26 should point us toward the easy revelation that God is different from singular, contained human beings. That's not that radical, is it? If I said to you, "God is bigger than or beyond humanity," you would most likely look at me with compassion and say, "No kidding."

However each of us may understand God, we should all be able to confess that God—the ultimate reality, the Most High, the LORD of Hosts—is not a man … or a woman. In fact, when we talk about God as the Creator, we are necessarily implying that God is not created. Theologian Roger E. Olson notes the distinction by saying that God is "uncreated, self-existent" while human beings are "created and dependent."[6] According to the Scripture, God is not made in our image—we are made in the image of God (Gen 1:27).

Now, don't get lost here—it's rather simple. However we may define or perceive God, the truth is that God is beyond an accurate definition. To be sure, God may, at times in our limited perspectives, seem to fit into different definitions or allow us to garner meaning by existing within our definitions, but God can never be limited to any understanding we have of being or reality. God is beyond.

We humans anthropomorphize God. That means we describe and understand God in humanizing terms. We ascribe human descriptors and traits to God, and God certainly lets us anthropomorphize God. I

---

[6] Roger E. Olson, *My evangelical Arminian theological musings*, "Is God 'A Being' or 'Being Itself?'" accessed August 4, 2015, http://www.patheos.com/blogs/rogereolson/2015/05/is-god-a-being-or-being-itself/

would even say God encourages us to anthropomorphize and even joins in the act because it helps us to relate—to think and talk about God. And remember, that is the point—relating! But the truth is God is beyond the form and constraints of our human descriptions—we know that. We don't always talk like that, but we know that our finite language can only go so far in striving to describe the infinite. We have limits. We have edges. There are times and spaces where we stop. God does not have limits or edges. There are no times and spaces where God stops. Is your mind cramping yet? Mine is.

I know the waves get big and the waters get deep out here where we are swimming, but it helps us to remember that God is not like us. The ancient writers of the Hebraic creation poem thought the best way to push understanding and point to that truth was to remind hearers and readers of that poem that God is better understood as a relationship—a community. *"Let us make humankind in our image, according to our likeness...."*

Christians define that community through the doctrine of the Trinity—the understanding that God has been and can be expressed as the Father, the Son (Jesus), and the Holy Spirit. Again, I don't want us to get lost in the doctrine of the Trinity because it will not help us to do so here. What is helpful to note is that most of the faiths and spiritual systems of humans have understood and continue to understand God as something beyond our limits of understanding.

Two terms are helpful in understanding this relationship that we call God. The first is *perichoresis* and the second is *tzimtzum*. Say what? You may be wondering if we have gotten to the point in the book where I just start making up words.

I must confess that if you had met me five years ago and given me a million guesses at what two words best describe the communal relationship of God, I would never have come up with *tzimtzum* and *perichoresis*. Those are some goofy-looking words that we simply do not hear or say in real life. But I assure you that these words are real. In fact, they are really old words. They are words that the faithful have used for thousands of years to describe this mind-boggling relationship from which all things—including us—flow.

Let's start with *perichoresis*—an ancient Greek compound word first used by early Christian church father Gregory Nazianzen in the fourth century.[7] *Peri* means "around" while *chorein* can be understood as "to contain" or "to make room for." Theologians use big synonyms like "inter-penetration" and "commingling" to explain *perichoresis*. The most helpful definition I have heard is that of "a spinning dance." Move past all the scholarly stuff and try to take that in. God is a spinning dance of relationship. Yum.

That spinning dance has been a primary understanding for Christians, defining the relationship between the Father, Son, and Holy Spirit for over fifteen hundred years. It is, I think, a helpful idea that sees God as being the encompassing relational dance in which the Father is with and points us toward the Son and the Spirit, the Son is with and points us toward the Father and the Spirit, and the Spirit is with and points us toward the Father and the Son. In this loving relationship, each "contains" the other and each "makes room for" the other—and if that's not enough to blow your mind, the whole thing spins "around." Around what? That is a great question! Here is Jesus' answer, according to John's Gospel:

> Father, may they all be one as You are in Me and I am in You; may they be in Us, for by this unity, the world will believe that You sent Me.
>
> All the glory You have given to Me, I pass on to them. May that glory unify them and make them one as We are one, I in them and You in Me, that they may be refined so that all will know that You sent Me, and You love them in the same way You love Me.
>
> Father, I long for the time when those You have given Me can join Me in My place so they may witness My glory, which comes from You. You have loved Me before the foundations of

---

[7]   Oliver D. Crisp, "Problems with Perichoresis" *Tyndale Bulletin* (56.1: 2005) 122.

the cosmos were laid. Father, You are just; though this corrupt world order does not know You, I do. These followers know that You have sent Me—I have told them about Your nature; and I will continue to speak of Your name in order that Your love, which was poured out on Me, will be in them. And I will also be in them.

(JOHN 17:21–26 VOICE)

The *perichoresis* spins around you! It spins around me! The loving, glorifying, interconnected relationship of God "makes room for" us.

Tzimtzum—meaning "contraction" or "constriction" in Hebrew— also aligns with the idea of God "making room" for relationship. You may have heard of Rob and Kristen Bell's book, *The Zimzum of Love* (which, coincidentally, is how you pronounce *tzimtzum*—zimzum.) The Bells do a wonderful job of defining *tzimzum* and showing how it should inform our relationships.

> *Zimzum* is a Hebrew word used in the rabbinic tradition to talk about the creation of the world—not in a scientific way but more like something somewhere between poetry and metaphysical speculation. Followers of this tradition began with the assumption that before there was anything, there was only God. The divine, they believed, was all that was. For something to exist other than God, then, God had to create space that wasn't God…. Their contention was that for something to exist that wasn't God, God had to contract or withdraw from a certain space so that something else, something other than God, could exist and thrive in that space. And the word they used for this divine contraction is zimzum.[8]

Are you making the connection? *Tzimtzum* holds that the primary act of the divine was to create space—to make room—for another to thrive. That is an action of relationship. That is an action of community.

---

[8]   Rob Bell and Kristen Bell, *The Zimzum of Love: A New Way of Understanding Marriage* (New York: Harper Collins Publishers, 2014), 18.

The great theological and philosophical rock star Dallas Willard said it this way, "The aim of God in history is the creation of an all-inclusive community of loving persons, with Himself included in that community as its prime sustainer and most glorious inhabitant."[9]

>We are not alone.
>We are not supposed to be alone.
>God made room for us.
>Our existence finds its birth in the contraction of another.
>God *tzimtzum*'ed so that we could be in relationship with God and each other.
>God exists in a communal perichoretic dance—spinning around us in relationship.
>We come from relationship.
>We come from community.

We Need Community

If we come from community, it stands to reason that we would likewise be designed to exist in community. God does not exist in perichoretical community so that we can exist in isolation. God did not *tzimtzum* so that we could be apart from God and each other. We are children of a relational parent. Relationship and community are in our DNA. We need community.

Pastor and author John Ortberg points out, "Adam's fellowship with God was perfect, and God Himself declared Adam needed other humans."[10] This, again, is referring to the creation poems of Genesis—specifically, the poem found in the second chapter. In that poem, after God creates Adam and places him in the garden, God says, "It is not good

---

9   Dallas Willard, as quoted by Richard Foster in *Celebration of Discipline* (New York: Harper Collins Publishers, 1998), 154.

10 *Every Good and Perfect Gift: Devotional Thoughts on the Gift of the Savior*, under "13: Growth," (Uhrichsville, OH: Barbour Books, 2014), 69.

for the man to be alone, so I will create a companion for him, a perfectly suited partner" (Gen. 2:18 VCE).

It is not good for the man to be alone. Don't miss the significance of that statement. I realize this is an incredible opportunity for all women to shout "Amen!" as you are all well aware of the many bad ideas men can generate when they are left alone, but that is not the point—at least, it is not the whole point. Up until now in the creation poems, everything that God has created has been "good." Don't miss that. In the first poem of Genesis 1, God creates the heavens above and the earth below, and they are good. God creates the dry land and the seas, and they are good. God creates the plants, vegetation, and trees of the earth, and they are good. God creates living creatures in the waters, on the land, in the skies, and they are all good. We move into the second poem found in Genesis 2, and God has created a garden in the east called "Eden—a place of utter delight" (Gen. 2:8 VCE), and everything in it was good. Then, the first thing that is not good shows up—"It is *not good* for man to be alone..." (Gen 2:18).

Once again, right out of the gates—in the poems that are meant to speak to us about who we are and who God is—we have an emphatic statement about relationship. It is not good for us to be alone. We are built for community. Hopefully, at some level, we all understand that. It's not that we can't benefit from times of solitude but rather that our lives are meant to be in relation to one another. The writers of the creation poems in Genesis understood this truth and made sure that the obvious was stated. It is not good for man to be alone.

Rabbi Jonathan Sacks writes about the importance of what happens next in the Genesis poem.

> Having created man, God sees him isolated, without an other, and says, 'It is not good for the man to be alone' (Gen 2:18)—the first occurrence of the words *not good* in the Bible. Dwelling alone is not a blessing but a curse. God then, while the man is sleeping, makes the first woman.
> Waking and seeing her, the man utters the first poem in the Bible:

Now I have found
  bone of my bone,
  flesh of my flesh.
  She shall be called 'woman' *[Ishah]*
  for she was taken from man *[Ish]*

(GEN. 2:23)

At the first reading, this sounds as if man is claiming ontological priority. First there was man; only afterwards was there woman. Man comes from God and woman comes from man. That is how classic Christian theologians read the text. But the Hebrew contains a nuance missed in translation. Biblical Hebrew contains two words for 'man,' *adam* and *ish*. Adam is the species. It means, roughly, *Homo sapiens*. *Ish* is the individual, the person. Until this point, the Bible has consistently used the word *adam*. This is the first occurrence of the word *ish*, and it comes after the word *ishah*, woman.

The Bible is here signaling a momentous proposition. Adam has to pronounce his wife's name before he can pronounce his own. I have to say 'you' before I can say 'I.' *I have to acknowledge the other before I can truly understand myself.* Not only can I not live alone, I cannot think, know, understand alone.[11]

What a profound truth! Hidden within the poetic Hebrew of the creation poem is a profound truth about our need for community and relationship. In order to know ourselves, we must first relate to another. We are inexorably connected. We need each other in order to be fully alive and fully aware. We have to learn about another, relate to another, listen to another in order to know ourselves.

One of my daughter's favorite movies is a dog movie called *Because of Winn Dixie*. In that movie, the lead character—a lonely little girl moved to a new town by her father—befriends an old blind woman on the outskirts

---

[11] Jonathan Sacks, *Future Tense: Jews, Judaism, and Israel in the Twenty-First Century* (New York: Random House, Inc., 2009), 186.

of town who also finds herself isolated from people. When these two first meet and the little girl begins to share some of her story with the old woman, she narrates her thoughts, saying, "I could feel her listening to me with all her heart... and it felt good." That really nails it for me. I know when I am connected to people that way. I know when they are listening to me with all their heart, and it does feel good.

I think it feels good because it helps to fill a need that I have—that we all have. *Need* seems to be the right word. We need to share our stories. We need to give and receive love. We need relationship with each other. We need community. We need the things we get from community— things we cannot get elsewhere. These things include love, listening, and belonging, but there is even more to it than that.

- We need community to center us outside of ourselves.

  The spiritual path is not a solo endeavor. In fact, the very notion of a self who is trying to free her/himself is a delusion. We are in it together, and the company of spiritual friends helps us realize our interconnectedness.[12]

  — Tara Brach

- We need community to ground us and return us to our shared identity as members of God's family.

  Saints cannot exist without a community, as they require, like all of us, nurturance by a people who, while often unfaithful, preserve the habits necessary to learn the story of God.[13]

  — Stanley Hauerwas

---

[12] Tara Brach, "Conversations That Matter: Satsang" allthatmatters.com, accessed December 7, 2014, https://allthatmatters.com/apps/mindbody/classes/705

[13] John Swinton, *Critical Reflections on Stanley Hauerwas' Theology of Disability: Disabling Society, Enabling Theology* (New York: The Haworth Pastoral Press, 2004), 74.

- We need community to connect us to stories and voices that we would not know on our own.

> *As humans, reality for us is largely based on other people's perceptions. If there's twenty bodies in your crawl space but you haven't been caught yet, you tell yourself you're still a birthday clown, and that's how you keep doing it.*[14]
>
> — Dan Harmon

- We need community to bring us to lives of authenticity where our burdens really can be shared and our joys really can be multiplied.

> *There are many forms of poverty: economic poverty, physical poverty, emotional poverty, mental poverty, and spiritual poverty. As long as we relate primarily to each other's wealth, health, stability, intelligence, and soul strength, we cannot develop true community. Community is not a talent show in which we dazzle the world with our combined gifts. Community is the place where our poverty is acknowledged and accepted, not as something we have to learn to cope with as best as we can but as a true source of new life.*
>
> *Living community in whatever form—family, parish, twelve-step program, or intentional community—challenges us to come together at the place of our poverty, believing that there we can reveal our richness.*[15]
>
> — Henri J.M. Nouwen

---

[14] Dan Harmon, "He likes to talk: extended Dan Harmon interview." Interview by Ryan Prendiville. San Francisco Bay Guardian Online, January 22, 2013, accessed April,24,2014,http://www.sfbg.com/pixel_vision/2013/01/22/he-likes-talk-extended-dan-harmon-interview

[15] Henri J.M. Nouwen, *Bread for the Journey: A Daybook of Wisdom and Faith* (New York: Harper Collins Publishers, 1997), 87.

Community Needs Us

It is a simple logical step from recognizing that we need community to grasp that community—likewise—needs us. Not only do we have things to receive from community, we have things to give. We know this. We know that good relationships are not parasitic in nature, where one benefits and the other is harmed. Authentic community is mutual symbiosis—everyone benefits. We may not always benefit at the same times or in the same ways, but our communal relationships necessarily require that we receive and that we give.

Truth be told, we could probably go a step further and say that our communal relationships should be obligate. Science uses this term to refer to those symbiotic relationships where organisms are dependent on each other for survival. My community and the relationships therein are obligate. I depend on them and they depend on me. This, like many of our conclusions, is not a giant leap. Rather, it is simply a statement of something we often take for granted.

We know that our lives are intertwined with other people. We know that decisions that others make and actions that others take impact our lives—and vice versa. We know that none of us exists in a vacuum—disconnected from others or the symbiotic impact our lives have on each other. Healthy and helpful community needs us to be conscious of this truth and contribute accordingly.

There is a quotation that is often attributed to Lilla Watson—a visual artist, scholar, and indigenous Australian activist. The quote is brilliant in and of itself: "If you have come to help me, you are wasting your time. But if you have come because your liberation is bound up with mine, then let us work together."[16] Right there, I just want to say, "Amen!" My liberation is bound up with yours, so let's work together toward freedom! But Watson lives out community even further by repeatedly refusing to take credit for this quotation, stating that she is "not comfortable being cred-

---

[16] Aboriginal activists group, Queensland, 1970s, accessed January 25, 2015, https://en.wikipedia.org/wiki/Lilla_Watson

ited for something that had been born of a collective process." Bam! Not only is the quote a statement about the intertwined nature of humanity, the citation of the quote drives the point home even further. She may have been the first person in her community to be quoted as saying that in Queensland in the 1970s, but she knows that such a conclusion and declarative truth was only born out of the consciousness of a collective. Her relationships and experiences with other people in community generated that quote. She did not generate it on her own.

That is the kind of "in your face" embrace of community that makes me feel like a ridiculous wimp. If I am a dude hanging out on the beach of community, Lilla Watson just emerged from swimming in the depths of the ocean, walked up the beach, and kicked sand in my face.[17] I can talk a good game but—damn!—Lilla Watson can back it up. Her commitment to community almost makes me not want to share these other quotes with you because their authors might be embarrassed to take credit for saying them after Lilla has pointed out that none of us comes up with anything on our own. Alas, I feel safe in the conclusion that were we to pose this question to the authors of the following quotes, they would agree wholeheartedly and confess that their wisdom was not original but communal. Thus, in community and for the sake of our communities, let us benefit from their collective wisdom.

We cannot seek achievement for ourselves and forget about progress and prosperity for our community.... Our ambitions must be broad enough to include the aspirations and needs of others, for their sakes and for our own.[18]

— César Chávez

---

[17] Clearly, this image is for effect. I do not know Lilla Watson, but she does not strike me as a bully or the kind of person who would actually kick sand in my face. Her commitment to communal life and embrace, however, does feel intimidatingly strong compared to my own.

[18] *Education of the Heart: Quotes by César Chávez,* United Farm Workers, under "Community" accessed September 15, 2014, http://www.ufw.org/_page.php?menu=research&inc=history/09.html

Independence is middle-class blasphemy. We are all dependent on one another, every soul of us on earth.[19]

— G.B. Shaw

Two heads are better than one, not because either is infallible, but because they are unlikely to go wrong in the same direction.[20]

— C.S. Lewis

First, we are challenged to rise above the narrow confines of our individualistic concerns to the broader concerns of all humanity.[21]

— Martin Luther King, Jr.

Community needs us to recognize that our lives are connected—that what I do or do not do, what I share or do not share, what I learn or fail to learn impacts the lives of other people. Our symbiotic relationships in community are both mutual and obligate. We benefit from our relational lives in community. We need those relational lives to survive. We need community and community need us.

"*When the Stranger says:*

> '*What is the meaning of this city?*
> *Do you huddle close together because you love each other?*'
> *What will you answer?*
> '*We all dwell together to make money from each other?*' *or* '*This is a community?*'

---

[19] George Bernard Shaw, *Pygmalion* (New York: CreateSpace Independent Publishing Platform, 2014), 65.

[20] C.S. Lewis, "Introduction" in *The Incarnation of the Word of God: Being the Treatise of St. Athanasius De Incarnatione Verbi Dei* (New York: Macmillan, 1947), 6–7.

[21] Martin Luther King, "Remaining Awake through a Great Revolution" (lecture, Morehouse College Commencement, Atlanta, GA, June 2, 1959).

Oh my soul, be prepared for the coming of the Stranger.
   Be prepared for him who knows how to ask questions.[22]

— T.S. Eliot

Community Is Not Optional

At this point, if you and I were seventh graders at my junior high in the mid-1980s and I said to you, "Community is not an option," your appropriate response would be a sarcastic, "No doy." I'm not really sure what "doy" was, but I believe it was related to "duh." In either case, you would be communicating that I was belaboring a point you already knew to be true. I get that. We have taken a pretty conclusive journey through the centrality of community and relationship in our lives. We have wrestled with the idea that we come from a relational and communal God. We have confronted the truth that we need community and relationship— that we do not do well without it. We have acknowledged that community needs us to contribute, to share, to give, and to receive. All of our lives are intertwined and related in ways we can see and recognize and in ways that are not immediately discernable. So when I say to you what my rabbi has taught me—that community is not optional—you are right to say, "No doy! I get it already!!"

Yet, there is still something with which we can wrestle here. It is possible for someone to disagree with what we have said thus far about community. It is possible to reject the notion that we come from a communal or relational God. You do not have to believe that *tzimtzum* and *perichoresis* are helpful descriptions of the divine. If we perceive God as a bearded, cosmic scorekeeper sitting alone on a cloud and not a relationship, it might seem easier to dismiss the importance of community and relationship. It might seem more logical to elevate the individual and hold our faith to be something private and personal. Herein lies the problem.

Faith presumes relationship. What does that mean? It means that

---

22   T.S. Elliot, *The Complete Poems and Plays 1909-1950* (New York: Harcourt Brace and Company, 1971), 103.

we can't have faith without relationship. Faith necessarily requires us to try to relate to something other than ourselves—a higher power, God, a spirit, another person, or all of the above. Whatever the case may be, faith requires relationship. And not in any sporadic or isolated instance, either—all the time and everywhere. Think of it this way: if our life of faith is the planet Earth, then relationships—our life in communion with others—are the weather. No matter where we go on earth or what time of day it is, there is weather. It may be calm weather—the kind that we don't really notice or think about, or it may be a raging tempest of a storm—the kind that scares us and causes us to hide. Hot, cold, windy, snowy, wet, dry, humid, mild, stormy, clear—wherever and whenever you are on earth, there is weather all around you. We exist in it all of the time. And in spite of what the Weather Channel may want us to believe, we don't control it, and it is not always predictable. True, there are patterns that we learn and study, but there are weather occurrences that seem to come out of nowhere.

The same is true of relationships. They are all around us all the time. We can no more exist apart from them than we can exist on Earth apart from the weather. Our ability to control relationships is equal to our ability to control the weather because they necessarily contain something beyond our control—another. Yes, like the weather, there are patterns that we can study and learn to live with harmoniously. But there are also relational behaviors that seem to come out of nowhere and defy explanation.

I know of no greater indicator to the communal and relational nature of the universe (and, thereby, its Creator) than the fact that we cannot exist apart from them. We are born of a physiological reproductive relationship. Don't miss that. You would not be here with us right now were it not for two people being in relationship to one another. However brief that relationship may have been, no relationship—no you.

And it didn't stop there. Upon being born, you immediately required the nurturing, protective relationships of others in order to survive. Nature is set up this way; it is nonnegotiable and irrefutable. We cannot come into existence without another person "making room" in themselves for us to exist. We cannot survive, once born, without the care of another. Without relationship, we do not exist. Without relationship, we do not live.

One of my spiritual directors frequently reminds me that human beings are the only creature in all of creation that are loved into walking. We do not emerge from the womb able to walk as most other mammals do. Most of the animals on earth have to get moving as soon as they are born or hatched—or else, they die. Their continued existence depends on their ability to move. Our continued existence depends solely on the care of another. When humans do learn to walk, it is because someone has modeled it for them, encouraged them, patiently helped them practice, picked them up when they wipe out, and encouraged them to try again. We are loved into walking—in relationship.

Community is not optional. It is hardwired into the very fabric of existence. We are never truly apart from relationship or community. We experience moments of isolation and loneliness, but even in those times, we are not truly alone.

We come from community.

We need community.

Community needs us.

Community is not optional.

So What?

How, then, could we ever believe that our faith was a private matter? How could we for one moment think that we live out our spiritual lives apart from others? We simply cannot. It is just not possible. Once more, when we try, it doesn't work. We are communal and relational beings—born of relationship, surviving in relationship, and only thriving in relationship.

Remember at the beginning of this chapter when we said we would hold on to our personal relationship with God? Recognize now that it is still there. Nothing has threatened it. You do have a personal, unique, one-of-a-kind relationship with the divine. Your heart is unlike any other that has ever been or will ever be. Therefore, it stands to reason that your relationship with God or Jesus or the divine is personal. Jesus taught, "God knows everything about you, even the number of hairs on your head" (Matt. 10:31). That sounds pretty personal to me.

Many of us also know that when we open ourselves up to a relationship with God, we are changed in profoundly personal ways. Our prayer, our confession, our wrestling, our spiritual growth can all be extremely personal and intimate. Yet, as we open ourselves up, we also learn that the personally intimate is not all there is to God. God is also communally intimate. We begin to understand that we are not alone—that we never have been and we never will be. We begin to apprehend the presence of community all around us—and our interdependence upon it.

This is not an either/or scenario. We are not choosing between a personal relationship or a communal relationship with the divine. This is a both/and situation. Our relationship with God is personal and communal. We don't sacrifice one for the other: we get it all, and we are called to give to it all.

When we are tempted to keep our faith to ourselves as a private matter, we must recognize the lie and remember the truth. Our faith is not private. We do not have an independent relationship with God. We need each other to shape, practice, and broaden our faith. We need to share what we have received, and we need to receive what others share. If we are to be like our God, we will make room for one another. We will recognize that the dance spins around us all. To live any other way would be like trying to change the weather with our mind.

> *Nor knowest thou what argument*
> *Thy life to thy neighbor's creed has lent.*
> *All are needed by each one;*
> *Nothing is fair or good alone.*[23]

— Ralph Waldo Emerson

---

[23] Ralph Waldo Emerson, *Nineteenth-Century American Poetry* William Spengmann, ed. "Each and All" (New York: Penguin Books, 1996), 31.

LIE 7

REAL FAITH IS BLIND BELIEF

Think of a flabby person covered with layers of fat. That is what your mind can become—flabby, covered with layers of fat till it becomes too dull and lazy to think, to observe, to explore, to discover. It loses its alertness, its aliveness, its flexibility, and goes to sleep. Look around you, and you will see almost everyone with minds like that: dull, asleep, protected by layers of fat, not wanting to be disturbed or questioned into wakefulness.

What are these layers? Every belief that you hold, every conclusion you have reached about persons and things, every habit and every attachment. In your formative years, you should have been helped to scrape off these layers and liberate your mind. Instead, your society, your culture, which put these layers on your mind in the first place, has educated you to not even notice them, to go to sleep and let other people—the experts: your politicians, your cultural and religious leaders—do your thinking for you. So you are weighed down with the load of unexamined, unquestioned authority and tradition.[1]

— Anthony de Mello

---

[1] Anthony De Mello, *The Way to Love: Meditations for Life* (New York: Random House, Inc., 1991), 61.

Have you ever felt guilty about doubting or questioning something about your faith? Have you ever suppressed or ignored your thoughts or ideas so as not to make waves or cause trouble in your church or faith community? When parts of your intellect or experience cannot be reconciled with what you are "supposed to believe," what do you do? Have you ever been told that faith believes without seeing or knowing—that it is a blind leap? Has such thinking ever failed you? Has that approach to faith always felt right?

The final lie that we will push through together in this book is the idea that real faith is blind belief. Put another way, faith involves the suspension of intellect. Hopefully, we have been wrestling with this lie all throughout this journey as we have sought to deconstruct bad or incomplete ideas and engage our intellect in the pursuit of understanding our faith. Even so, we still need to name and understand this lie so that we are better equipped to recognize it when we see it—or live it.

This lie tells us that our brains—our thinking and reasoning—get in the way of our faith and must therefore be sidelined for faith to be real or pure. This lie is sneaky. It has quietly crept its way into our lives and our culture. The results of this lie, however, are not quiet. The results range from fundamental extremists who are willing to completely, intellectually detach and blindly follow faith interpretations that call for intimidation or violence against those who do not believe to millions of faith survivors who feel forced to quietly abandon systems and doctrines that do not seem to include their lives. This lie can make faith seem ridiculously unhelpful and irrelevant. This lie can also make faith seem violent and cruel.

Though this lie can make loud reverberations throughout our society, strangely enough, this is a lie of keeping silent—a lie of quieting objections, running from arguments, and avoiding disagreements. It is a lie of punting away our intellect in order to keep the status quo. It is a lie of hiding that which we really think or struggle with because we don't want to appear weak in the faith. This is a lie of a small god—a god who can only be engaged through fairy-tale-like belief. The god at the center of this lie is so weak and insecure that it cannot withstand doubt, questions, argument, or dissent.

In a recent episode of *Real Time with Bill Maher*, Maher—the show's host and moderator—stated, "Faith is the suspension of critical thinking."[2] The depressing reality is that how Maher defines faith is directly related to how we faithful people are living our faith in the world. Maher doesn't arrive at such a conclusion without stimuli from the people around him. He has witnessed and experienced faith as the suspension of critical thinking. More and more, faith is perceived and is becoming the opposite of critical thought and reflection. Maher is accurately describing how many people perceive and experience faith in the public sphere.

So what should I do about it? Rather than dismiss Maher or attack him as an atheist—which we have already learned is not our job—I am compelled to take a good look in the mirror. Maher's statement causes me to self-examine.

Who is a greater threat to the preservation and continuance of my faith—the atheist who is disconnected from what he or she perceives is an inauthentic explanation of reality or the believer who has inherited and is promulgating a decontextualized, fairy-tale faith of blind belief and superstition? As we have already learned, the rejection of the God I profess says more about me than it does about God. I am the one professing. My life, my actions, my words are a testament to the presence of this God within me. If Maher looks at my life and sees blind belief and the suspension of critical thinking, that is not God's problem: it is my problem. I am living the lie that real faith exists without question, without doubt, and without reflection. In order for this lie to exist, that's exactly what must happen—I must blind myself. I must refuse to use my vision, experience, and mind to govern my relationship with the very God I profess gave me that same vision, experience, and mind.

Oftentimes, this lie relies on biblical literalism to create a diabolical

2   *Real Time with Bill Maher*, Season 12, Episode 18. Directed by Paul Casey. Written by Scott Carter, Adam Felber, Matt Gunn, Brian Jacobsmeyer, Jay Jaroch, Chris Kelly, Bill Maher, Billy Martin, and Danny Vermont, HBO, June 6, 2014.

faith cocktail that causes well-meaning people of faith to behave like drunken idiots. This is the lie that falsely tells us that our doubts, our questions, and our inability to reconcile the parts of our faith or God that don't make sense are all evidence of our weak faith—our failure to believe "with our whole heart."

The LORD Works in Mysterious Ways

One problem with boiling faith down to blind belief is that it causes our faith to seem disconnected from reality—out of touch with the world around us. Have you ever been in the midst of suffering and had someone throw an empty faith platitude at your feet? I am sorry to say that I have been on both sides of this equation. There have been times when I am hurting, struggling, trying to find a reason to hang on and someone in my life—usually someone within my faith family—will respond to my suffering with a bumper sticker like "Well, Darrell ... I know this is tough, but the LORD works in mysterious ways."

Before we rush to judgment, let me again confess that I have also done this to people. I have had someone invite me into the unspeakable darkness surrounding him or her and nervously responded with an empty faith platitude. The truth is, there is an honorable desire to help behind such platitudes. The problem is such bumper-sticker wisdom also usually originates in the disconnect caused by the lie that we must believe blindly in order to be faithful. When we are confronted with suffering and tragedy, the real questions have to deal with "Why did this happen?" or "Why did this happen to me?" Those are not fun questions to answer. When someone else invites us to join them in exploring those questions, intellect usually runs out the door, and we default to whatever Scripture we can remember and rip from its context—like "I know the plans I have for you, plans to prosper you and not to harm you" (Jer. 29:11).

Really? If the point of that Scripture is to assure me that God has no plans to let me experience anything other than prosperity and a harm-free life, then what is going on? Is God not paying attention? I have been harmed. I have not always prospered. I am sure you can say the same thing. Trying to reconcile our experiences to scriptural platitudes that are ripped out of context leads us to a number of hopeless conclusions, ranging from God being an absent-minded professor to our lives being unworthy of the aforementioned prosperity. So, instead of dealing with those extremely troublesome conclusions, we disconnect and act like our willingness to believe anyway is the measure of faith.

Friends, that is some wacky religion. No matter what your faith persuasion may be, if suffering and pain are seen merely as a test of what we are willing to endure and continue to blindly believe, that faith will ultimately fail you. The suspension of reflection and critical thought is not something to be admired and duplicated by the faithful. Such a faith leaves us with a God or reality that is either disconnected and aloof or, quite simply, cruel.

A few years ago, a friend of mine wrote an "open letter" to the church after walking through a tragedy with a family. My friend supported and stood with this family as the church surrounded them seeking to console and help. Funeral preparations, memorial service planning, the funeral, the reception, the grieving line—my friend was there for all of it. By the end of the week, my friend was fed up. He was directly experiencing the real questions and conversations the tragedy birthed, but he felt those same questions and conversations were being avoided in the church. No one was willing to confess that they couldn't explain it. No one was willing to cry out, "Why?!" With good and loving intentions, people lined up at the funeral to offer whatever platitude they thought best.

Following the reception, my friend sat down and wrote a letter—some of which is below. This writing is emotional and harsh. It is angry, which I think is a logical reaction to the emotional isolation and dishonesty with which so many of us "faithful" people operate in times of tragedy and confusion.

We act like a bunch of damn fools. "God works in mysterious ways?"
"His ways are higher than ours?" That may be true but shut the (——)

up! Dime store wisdom and Sunday school sayings don't help in the darkness. They get swallowed whole never to be heard from again. We need to show up and shut up. That's it. We have no answers, we never did. To pretend otherwise is a fraud.

Do we really expect faith to compete with the things that numb the pain if we don't validate the pain and sit in it ourselves? We squirm and flee from real discomfort and try to smooth things over with scripture sound-bites. We make God look like a disconnected (——).

I refuse to believe that God is afraid of the pain and wants to avoid it like we do. God doesn't try to Scripture the pain away, doesn't try to ignore it or hide it, doesn't try to numb it—and if he does, then that's not a god I want to know. I need a God who cries with me. I need a God that comes in, sits down in the middle of my (——) and says, *I'm here. However long this takes, wherever this goes, I'm here.* Why is that so (——) hard for us to do?[3]

Those words, though clearly written in anger and frustration, reveal the presence of the lie that we are called to believe blindly and without making too much of a fuss. To move through and past this lie, we need to step outside of our faith and see how that looks from the outside looking in. In a word, CRAZY.

In fact, when we express our relationship with God as a blind leap that requires the suppression of intellect, we're once again roaming around that "bat-guano crazy" region. A blind, thoughtless faith without intellect doesn't look helpful or desirable. An unreflective, unquestioned faith doesn't tell the story of God. It doesn't even appear to be about love, relationship, community, mercy, compassion, or connection. It just comes across as: how much are you willing to believe?

---

[3] I get that the language and attitude of this excerpt is harsh. Pain has the capacity to confront us with discomfort and tension—and our capacity to feel discomfort and tension means we are not numb, dead, or disconnected. It means we are in the game. So if we feel a little discomfort and tension when confronted with harsh criticism of our faith, that is not a bad thing.

If You Just Believe

This may seem a little harsh—and I apologize for the potential bubble bursting, but not everyone believes in Santa Claus.

Wait, what?!

That's right, there are people out there who think the whole Santa thing is a scam—that Santa sits on a throne of lies and smells like beef and cheese.[4] I'm getting ahead of myself, though—let me back up.

You may be familiar with the movie *The Polar Express* and the accompanying Josh Groban Christmas song "Believe" or even the Chris Van Allsburg book that inspired it all.[5] If not, allow me to give you the gist of this charming Christmas story: it is our belief that makes things real. After a dream-like experience at the North Pole with Santa Claus and the elves on Christmas Eve, the main character, who has been wrestling with his belief in Santa Claus, is given a present by the big man himself—a sleigh bell from Santa's sleigh. When he awakes on Christmas morning, wondering if it was all real or just a dream, he still has the bell! Here's the trick: the bell is empty—it has no visible clapper or marble to make it ring. Only those who believe in Santa can hear the ringing of the sleigh bell. To those who don't believe, the bell is silent.

Friends, I do not want to ruin Christmas or throw *The Polar Express* under the bus. My kids love *The Polar Express*. We watch it every year. The idea that we can find peace in believing—even when it doesn't make sense—is not a bad idea. However, when we let our definition of faith

---

[4] David Berenbaum, *Elf*, DVD, directed by Jon Favreau (Burbank, CA: New Line Home Entertainment, 2004).

Don't worry, Santa Claus is not one of the lies that we are attacking in this book. Santa is safe. You can count on Buddy the Elf to give you the straight dope on what Santa is or is not.

[5] Why in the world did I write this? I just created my own footnote nightmare by referencing a movie, a song, and a book all in one sentence. Here comes the fun...

Chris Van Allsburg, William Broyles, Jr., and Robert Zemeckis, *The Polar Express*, DVD, directed by Robert Zemeckis (Burbank, CA: Warner Home Video, 2005).

Glen Ballard and Alan Silverstri, "Believe," performed by Josh Groban, *The Polar Express Original Motion Picture Soundtrack*, CD Track 4, Warner Brothers, 2004.

Chris Van Allsburg, *The Polar Express* (New York: Houghton Mifflin, 1985).

stop there, we are headed for trouble. To be blunt, that kind of belief is something we do as children. That kind of belief is how we approach fairy-tales—or even *The Polar Express*. It is not a bad thing. Believing in things that are greater than ourselves and our understanding is a necessary part of our development. Such belief brings us to a place of humility and, hopefully, to awe and wonder. Some could argue—and I would agree—that it is where faith begins.

> At that time the disciples came to Jesus and asked, "Who is the greatest in the kingdom of heaven?" He called a child, whom he put among them, and said, "Truly I tell you, unless you change and become like children, you will never enter the kingdom of heaven. Whoever becomes humble like this child is the greatest in the kingdom of heaven."
>
> (MATT. 18:1–4)

There it is, right? This is the verse that gets used to tell us the "faith of a child" is the goal. But that is not what it says, is it? The text actually says that we should become *humble* like a child. That our belief should lead us to a place of humility, awe, and wonder—a recognition that there is something greater than ourselves. This text is about humility, not about blind faith. Have you known many children who weren't inquisitive? Who didn't ask a thousand questions about every possible detail? I have three children, and their ability to ask questions has repeatedly triumphed over me in victory. They investigate, explore, and question like ceaseless sponges, desperate to soak up information. How in the world did we ever arrive at the conclusion that to have faith like a child was to accept without questioning?

Faith, our spirituality, God—these things are not sleigh bells that only ring if you believe. We are allowed to question, to wonder, to doubt, to scrutinize. I realize it may seem like a minor detail, but we must recognize that it is not our blind belief that makes them real. They are real whether or not we believe in them. If God is a sleigh bell, that sleigh bell is a ring-a-ling, jing ting ting-a-ling regardless of what we believe or accept blindly.

God's power and presence and the realness of spirituality do not originate in our belief. We do not believe God into existence or believe our faith into substance. God is—whether we believe blindly or not. And isn't that the way it should be? Do we really want to have faith in a God who requires our belief in order to be real? Or do you want to trust in something that is so present, so strong, so good, that it just IS—no matter what?

It is not our blind belief that makes God real or that secures our faith. The truth is, we are not even called to such a standard. We are called to the humility of children. Wrestling with these truths confronts us with the place of belief in our lives and allows us to ask the question of what our belief actually does—or should do. Just because our belief doesn't make God real doesn't mean it doesn't have an impact. In fact, our beliefs have a profound impact on us. Imagine if you ran around with an empty sleigh bell in your pocket, insisting through the silence that it was ringing. Then imagine how you would feel if someone ran up to you with an empty bell they insisted was ringing and asked you if you heard it, too. Would you pretend to hear it even though you didn't? How would you feel about the person with the bell? How would you feel about the bell?

Let's Get Critical

In the first season of the HBO show *True Detective*, there is a scene where the two primary detectives of the series walk into a tent revival in rural Louisiana. One of the detectives—Rust—is a professed cynic, perhaps even an atheist. His partner, Marty, is a God-fearing Louisianan. This is an excerpt from their conversation as they enter the tent revival and observe the worshipers.

Rust: What do you think the average IQ of this group is here, huh?

Marty: Can you see Texas up there on your high horse? What do you know about these people?

Rust:	Just observation and deduction. I see a propensity for obesity, poverty…and again, for fairy-tales. Folks putting what few bucks they do have in the little wicker baskets being passed around. I think it's safe to say that nobody here is going to be splitting the atom, Marty.
Marty:	Some folks enjoy community—the common good.
Rust:	Yeah, well, if the common good's got to make up fairy-tales, it's not good for anybody. What's it say about life? You got to get together, tell yourself stories that violate every law of the universe just to get through the day? What's that say about your reality, Marty? Certain linguistic anthropologists think that religion is a language virus that rewrites pathways in the brain and dulls critical thinking.[6]

Okay, full disclosure—I edited out some of Marty's spicier responses to Rust because, while hilarious, they distract from the thinking I want us to see here. To be sure, the show *True Detective* and the two detectives in that conversation are caricatures. They may seem a bit exaggerated, but I think the conversation is still incredibly realistic. Marty is on the inside of the faith represented in that tent revival, and he doesn't want to question it—he just accepts it. Rust is disillusioned with organized religion and rightly so if we pay attention to what he describes.

Don't dismiss this example as not representative of your church or faith community. We don't have to be a tent revival to be accurately described by Rust's conclusion. Do I agree with Rust's conclusion that people of faith cannot be people of great intellect—capable of "splitting the atom"? Not at all. However, the stereotypical conclusion being made there comes from a real place. It comes from observing people of faith

---

[6] *True Detective*, "The Locked Room," Season 1, Episode 3. Directed by Cary Joji Fukunaga. Written by Nic Pizzolatto, HBO, January 26, 2014.

repeatedly dismissing their intellect in the interest of their faith—as if the two were mutually exclusive.

There is a precedent for what Rust describes. People of faith have gotten together and told stories that defy every law of the universe. We still do.

People of faith get together and tell a fairy-tale about creation, insisting that evolution is a fraud and the earth was created in six literal 24-hour days. This line of thinking completely misses the underlying truths of the creation story, instead doing mental gymnastics to place Adam and Eve in the Garden of Eden with dinosaurs and dismiss the science of carbon dating as heresy. What about the deeper truths of the creation poems?

What about the assertion that what makes every one of us more
    than dirt is the breath of God?
Or the divine statement that it is not good for us to be alone?
Or the idea that we were created from love and a creative desire
    for relationship and not from death and destruction?
How about the notion that the human capacity to forsake rela-
    tionship with God because we think we know a better way
    has always been?

Those are huge ideas that reach past time, geography, culture, language, and science. Those are notions that impact reality for everyone. How should we feel when instead of wrestling with such truths from the creation poems, we instead insist that the story exists only to provide historical facts, and therefore, the earth is only 6,000 years old?

If you are experiencing a pit in your stomach right now at the thought of your faith being represented that way, let me first say I get that reaction. Friends, I wish the above description were something I made up, but it is not. There have been televised debates between scientists espousing evolution and "creationists" arguing against evolution, carbon dating, and dinosaurs all in the name of defending the Scripture. It is the reduction of faith to the lowest possible denominator. Ironically, such stances proclaim, "Our faith is so *strong* we are willing to dismiss and ignore any-thing that contradicts our present understanding of our faith"—even if our present understanding of our faith is incredibly ridiculous.

I shudder to think what detached people think about faith or spiritu-ality while watching such debates. There is an entire world of chaos out there. People are starving, children are dying of thirst, human trafficking is at its all-time high, and there sit the "believers"—on a stage arguing with the science community about the precise dating of dinosaurs on earth.[7] This is what it looks like when we posit God and the life of faith as a sleigh bell without a clapper and tell those around us, "If you would just believe, you would hear the ringing." We look like detached, crazy people with a broken bell.

How about when the faithful insist that the LORD flooded the entire world and that one man and his family built a boat and literally gathered up at least a pair of every animal on earth and put them in the boat so that the earth could be repopulated after the flood? Keep in mind that we don't just insist with our words. We rebuild the boat (several times in different places), according to the biblical specifications, to prove that it could be done. We charter archeological digs, searching for the remains of Noah's Ark. Keep in mind the time, money, resources, and energy faithful people spend searching for empirical data that supports blind faith in a biblical story that was never written to provide empirical data.

How many relationships are destroyed—how many people are pushed away or rejected by our posturing of such a life of faith? Can a faith that detaches intellect from the spiritual life really help anyone? Seriously,

---

[7] Author Rob Bell tells a story about a friend of his who was in Israel for a meeting with a leading rabbi. They were sitting and drinking coffee, discussing various topics. When the discussion found its way to the creation story of Genesis, Rob's friend mentioned the position some people hold that the earth was created in six literal days. The rabbi paused and reflected quietly for a moment. He finally responded, "I've never thought of that." This rabbi—who has spent his entire adult life studying the Torah and most likely had the book of Genesis memorized—had never even considered the possibility that one would read the creation poems in Genesis and look for literal, empirical data. What should it tell us when the teachers and preservers of the stories of the Bible—the descendants of those who first told them and wrote them down—are astounded by our interpretations and conclusions?

what good is a spiritual zombie? If faith requires that I don't think, how does it change the world? How is it working toward the common good? As Detective Rust says, "If the common good's got to make up fairy-tales, it's not good for anybody."

Separating the Fairy-Tale from the Faith

Our spiritual lives have an inexorable need for critical thought because even the slightest amount of critical thought exposes the fairy-tales we are telling as facades. The fairy-tales aren't the truth: they are candy coating that we have confused for something good. Pay attention closely here: the fairy-tales are facades—not God, not faith, not the scriptures. Yet without critical thought and reflection on our faith, our beliefs, our scriptures, we will not be able to tell the difference. Instead of blindly accepting the fairy-tales, we have to do the work of getting to know that which our faith is actually built upon. This is a very important distinction. Blind leaps and swallowing fairy-tales without question is not faith—that is superstition. Faith believes that God, the scriptures, and the history of God's people are worthy of investigation, exploration, and critical thought and reflection. The strength or genuineness of our faith should not be measured by how much we are able to believe but by how we trust that the story of God demands and requires our questions and critical thoughts.

That is not a haphazard word choice—*requires* is the right word. Faith should *require* critical thought, reflection, introspection, and investigation. Faith should require questions. Faith should *require* that we understand the context of the writings we claim are the "Word of God." Faith should *require* that we discuss, debate, and argue over the meanings and impacts of different stories and truths in community. Faith should *require* conversation and consideration of perspectives beyond our own.

There has not been a day in my life where my faith didn't require such work from me. Which is not to say I always do the work, just that the sustaining, deepening, and strengthening of my faith requires it. Contrastingly, there have been very few times in my life where my faith required a blind leap. There have been plenty of obscured steps—times that required me to put my next foot forward in trust even when I didn't know if it would go well—but very few blind leaps off a cliff, not knowing how I would land. Herein lies an important distinction.

This lie is about the reduction of faith to simply a test of how much we are willing to believe without question or engagement. This lie is not about taking obscured steps forward toward God and other people. People take obscured steps forward every day, and doing so requires steadfast faith, hope, and love. There is a confidence-building beauty in taking and beholding obscured steps of faith as they are made toward God and other people. Coming out from under this lie does not mean that our lives will be filled with clarity and certainty. Life—whether lived in faith or not—will definitely still include obscured steps. There will be times when we're not sure, and we just have to step forward and do what we feel is the right thing right now. The Apostle Paul wrote about such realities in 1 Corinthians 13—a text commonly associated with weddings but strangely about much more than romantic love.

> Love never ends. But as for prophecies, they will come to an end; as for tongues, they will cease; as for knowledge, it will come to an end. For we know only in part, and we prophesy only in part; but when the complete comes, the partial will come to an end. When I was a child, I spoke like a child, I thought like a child, I reasoned like a child; when I became an adult, I put an end to childish ways. For now we see in a mirror, dimly, but then we will see face to face. Now I know only in part; then I will know fully, even as I have been fully known. And now faith, hope, and love abide, these three; and the greatest of these is love.
>
> (1 COR. 13:8–13)

Paul is testifying to the fact that there will be times where our prophecies and our knowledge can't take us any further—that as much as we may think we know or see, we simply can't grasp the whole of it. According to Paul, life necessarily includes obscured steps forward, and those steps must be made in faith, hope, and love.

What Paul doesn't write—anywhere in the Bible—is that faith is a blind leap. The measure of our faith does not lie in how much we are willing to suspend our intellect and accept. Our faith is engaged to and informed by the story of God, the people of God, and our own interaction with the divine. Accordingly, we develop what rabbi Emil Fackenheim referred to as "Midrashic Stubbornness," or an ability to perceive what is happening to us or around us as part of God's larger story.[8] According to Fackenheim, it is only through such stubbornness that the Jews can face and frame the horrors of the Holocaust while stepping forward in faith. That stubbornness tells us that no matter where the story may go, at the end of the story, we are with God.

That I believe is the opposite of a blind leap. That is a faith that is informed by what God has already done. That is a hope that believes God continues to intercede. That is a love that says, "I would rather experience death or discomfort than disconnect." I once heard N.T. Wright describe faith as essentially saying to God, "Wherever this goes, I'm with you." I love that. It is a simple yet profound statement. All at once, it recognizes that there will be obscured steps, but that no matter where those obscured steps go, we are safe and we are loved. That is not a blind leap. That is not a faith that is defined by what we believe. It is a faith defined by relationship and story.

That makes much more sense in my life. Even if I believe I have taken some blind leaps, I usually find that if I am honest, it is my retelling of my stories that has turned obscured steps into blind leaps. This is the faith equivalent of a fishing tale. With every recounting, the fish gets bigger. Furthermore, when I really look back on my journey and ponder the few blind leaps I think I have taken, I am not so sure that God asked me to take them—or that my faith demanded such leaps. It is more likely that I took those leaps on my own, and God lovingly leapt with me. It's as if my

---

[8] Emil Fackenheim, *God's Presence in History: Jewish Affirmations and Philosophical Reflections* (New York: New York University Press, 1970), 21.

selective memory of the event constructs a fairy-tale cozy to cover and obscure the real story. Over time the real story disappears, and all I am left with is the fairy-tale—the story I invented.

When we do the work—we protest, investigate, and explore the context of God's story—the cultural fairy-tales we have constructed on top of God's story crumble away. For example, the fairy-tale version of Creation reads Genesis 1 and 2 as literal and posits that the LORD created the entire universe in six 24-hour days. Such thinking runs into real problems with carbon dating, the theories of evolution, the fossil record, and dinosaurs. The truth is the fairy-tale doesn't even work by taking the Scripture literally. The scriptural poem that inspired the fairy-tale of creation says that the sun and moon were created on the fourth day. If time is calculated by the rotation of the earth and the earth rotates around the sun, how was time measured on the first three days before the sun existed? The only way the fairy-tale works is if it completely detaches from the Scripture that inspired it in the first place. The fairy-tale must leave the Bible and become its own story to survive.

It's not that critical thinking hurts the Bible. Critical thinking actually respects the scriptures enough to return to them—to push past the fairy-tale and discover what is really being said and why. Critical thinking moves through the fairy-tale narrative of Noah's Ark and finds a primitive people writing a story with which they were very familiar—a story of divine wrath and destruction. Many different cultures and tribes in the ancient Near East told that story. This time, however, the story is different. This God—who gets fed up with people's mishandling of the world—doesn't wipe everything out and start over. This God makes a covenant with the people—a promise that no matter how bad things get, there will always be hope. This God promises never to let divine wrath wipe everything out because this God is into relationship. In fact, this God even hangs the divine bow (think primitive weapon) in the sky to remind the people of the covenant. This God will not take up weapons against the people. This God promises to remain in relationship with them no matter what.

If we spend our time trying to figure out who went and got the penguins from Antarctica or how all those animals fit in that boat, we miss the whole dang point. This story does not exist to present us with a faith dare to see how far we are willing to go to believe. Faith is not measured by what fairy-tale stories we are willing to accept as scientific fact. This story exists as a progressive marker highlighting the journey of God's people getting to know God. This story exists—alongside all the other ancient flood narratives—to say this God is different. This God is a God of relationship—a God of covenant—a God who abounds in mercy and love.

A People Named Wrestle

One of the many unfortunate results of our expressed faith over the last few hundred years has most certainly been the dulling of critical thinking. We are afraid to question. We are afraid to doubt. We are afraid that unbelief will somehow result in an eternal penalty of some sort. Is that the way it should be? Do we believe in a God so small—in a faith so insecure—that it cannot handle questions or doubt—that it turns away from critical thinking?

The faith that has been passed down to us through thousands of years came through searchers—people who explored, struggled, risked, failed, doubted, and wrestled. That is not to say they never had to take an obscured step. In fact, I think that same history of faithful people arguing and questioning their faith also included times when no answers could be found and they moved forward anyway. Again, the problem is not that faith can include unknowing and uncertainty. The problem is that we think that blind leaps are all there is to faith. There most certainly are times in any life where the only way forward is to trust completely without complete understanding. Yet, even in those times when the answers don't come, we are never asked to suppress our intellect. We are never asked to stop asking the questions. We are never asked to stop wrestling.

Wrestling is who we are—the people of Israel are literally named for those who wrestle with the divine.

The same night, he got up and took his two wives, his two maids, and his eleven children, and crossed the ford of the Jabbok. He took them and sent them across the stream, and likewise everything that he had. Jacob was left alone; and a man wrestled with him until daybreak. When the man saw that he did not prevail against Jacob, he struck him on the hip socket; and Jacob's hip was put out of joint as he wrestled with him. Then he said, "Let me go, for the day is breaking." But Jacob said, "I will not let you go, unless you bless me." So he said to him, "What is your name?" And he said, "Jacob." Then the man said, "You shall no longer be called Jacob, but Israel, for you have striven with God and with humans, and have prevailed." Then Jacob asked him, "Please tell me your name." But he said, "Why is it that you ask my name?" And there he blessed him. So Jacob called the place Peniel, saying, "For I have seen God face to face, and yet my life is preserved."

(GEN. 32:22–30)

If you ascribe to any faith that finds its roots in the stories of Genesis and the Exodus, you are a descendant of wrestlers. You are a distant, perhaps adopted, relative of a people whose very identity comes from their calling to struggle with their relationship to the divine. Their name is a marker—a testament to the fact that the relationship with God requires questioning and engagement. They have wrestled to learn more of what God is like. They have wrestled to learn more of who they are. Jacob did not simply believe in the man with whom he wrestled. The story doesn't say that while alone in the night, Jacob encountered a man and his faith was so strong that he believed the man to be God or an angel of God. The story says that Jacob wrestled with the man all night. The story says that even after his hip was wrenched out of socket, Jacob refused to let go until he received a blessing—a new revelation, a new understanding.

That is in the DNA of faith: wrestling, questioning—pushing past pain and discomfort in pursuit of a greater understanding. It is our name. It is our identity. We are a people called to wrestle.

So What?

We started this journey tackling the lie of biblical literalism and seeing how, when confronted with aspects of God's story we cannot explain, we tend to responses of *fight*, *flight*, or *freeze*. As we near the end of the exploration, we should recognize that those same responses are at work in every lie we have faced. They are still at work in this lie. Fighting, in the sense of digging our heels in behind a certain belief or biblical interpretation, is not wresting. I know that seems nitpicky, but Jacob didn't fight God. That would have looked a lot different. Perhaps it would have looked like Jacob taking shelter behind a large rock and throwing stones or shooting arrows at the man in the night. In a fighting posture, the point is to overcome—to destroy the other. Fighting seeks to be right, to be the victor—to conform the other's will to our own. This is what we do when we search for the remains of the ark or debate scientists on television regarding creation. Fighting is not wrestling. The story does not tell us that Jacob sought to overcome or destroy the man. Jacob wasn't seeking to be right—to conform the man's will to his own. Jacob wanted a blessing. He wanted to know the name of the one with whom he wrestled.

Fleeing and freezing are not something Jacob did either. We know what these responses would look like as well. Jacob did not run at the sight of the impending wrestling match. He could have. He had sent all his people and possessions forward. At this point, he was traveling light and could have responded to the visit from the divine by turning tail and hauling arse out of there. This is what we do when we withdraw from the conversations and arguments of our times. And let's be clear. Withdrawal doesn't necessarily mean that we run away. We can freeze, too. We are complex beings, fully capable of being present and not present at the same time. We can be there and not be engaged. We can be at the scene of the wrestling but not actually wrestle. Anytime we choose not to engage, not to argue, debate, or investigate because we are afraid that our beliefs or our faith can't withstand the wrestling, we are not living out the faith we were given.

So, what does all of this mean in a practical sense? We must look around our own lives. We know the places where this applies. We all know the times when we suppress intellect—when we refuse to do the work, when we avoid the conversation, when we turn away from engagement or we dig our heels in behind what we believe. Sometimes we do this because we don't know what else to do. Sometimes we do this because we are afraid ... or lazy ... or tired ... or all of the above.

The practical application here is that while these reasons may be valid and have a real impact on our ability to engage our intellect with our faith, as people of wrestling, we cannot allow them to persist. We must explore and name our fears. We must study, listen, and learn in order to grow beyond our present understanding or confusion. We must also be purposeful about rest if we are to have continuing strength and stamina for struggling with our faith.

The Faith of Galileo

How about a specific example? We have described—and certainly we have all experienced—the unfortunate cultural disconnect between faith and science. In perhaps one of our most daft moves as faithful people, we have allowed, if not formed, the tragically ironic notion that science and faith are mutually exclusive. This idea is actually a raging symptom of the lie that faith is blind belief. As we discussed in the last chapter, the age of reason and science has challenged many of the fairy-tales historically associated with God or God's story. One unfortunate result of that progression has been the retreat of faith to dealing only with those things that cannot be questioned. Faith—which was previously an encompassing understanding of life *including* reason and intellect—began to withdraw to that which science and empiricism could never challenge, the realm of blind belief.

In essence, faith shrank. Instead of trusting that God and God's story could transcend and include new discoveries and developing understanding, we bifurcated our faith, thinking that we were protecting it.

Instead of loosening our grasp and entertaining new ideas that could expand our understanding, we tightened our fists and responded by treating science as an enemy that must be quartered off. To be clear, this is not a recent development. It is a trend that has been developing over the last several hundred years. It is a trend and a lie that has permeated our culture to the limiting of entire generations of faithful people who have been raised under the lie of a divided existence—the secular and the sacred. Well-meaning, devout people live their entire lives as though denying their intellect and believing that which makes no sense is the test of their faith.

Today, we all accept that the earth is not the center of the universe. At least, I hope we do. We have learned from scientific study that the earth is not even the center of our galaxy or our solar system. In fact, we have learned that our sun is the gravitational anchor of our solar system (hence the name "solar" system) and that the earth rotates around it. I am willing to bet that none of those scientific facts challenge your faith. Accepting that the earth is not the center of the universe most likely does not threaten you spiritually. Four hundred and fifty years ago, however, claiming that the earth rotated around the sun was seen as heresy—a threatening lie from which the faithful needed protection.

Galileo Galilei, the Italian astronomer, physicist, and philosopher who is widely accepted as the father of modern science, found himself near the beginning of the bad idea that science stands in opposition to faith. In the early seventeenth century, his writings in further study and support of the Copernican idea that the earth revolved around the sun conflicted with the Church doctrine that understood the earth to be the center of the creation. Where did the Church get such a doctrine? How did the faithful arrive at this orthodoxy?

In two words, interpretation and tradition.

At the time Galileo was writing, the accepted tradition posited that verses such as Psalm 93:1, Psalm 96:10, Psalm 104:5, and 1 Chronicles 16:30 were to be understood as asserting the earth as the center of the universe. As you read the scriptures below, recognize the interpretive leaps required to arrive at such a singular and concrete conclusion.

He has established the world; it shall never be moved;

(Ps. 93:1)

The world is firmly established; it shall never be moved.

(Ps. 96:10 / 1 CHRON. 16:30)

You set the earth on its foundations, so that it shall never be shaken.

(Ps 104:5)

These verses were interpreted as making empirical statements about the universe—that God had established the earth as literally stationary in the cosmos. Since the earth could not move, the thinking went, everything else in the heavens must rotate around it. Yep ... that just happened ... literally, like 400 years ago.

Into that juggernaut of thought enters Galileo. Galileo argued that *heliocentrism*—the idea that the sun is at the center of the universe—was not contrary to the Scripture and that the writers of the poetry in the aforementioned psalms never intended their verses to be interpreted as making literal and empirical statements about the placement of the planet Earth in the universe.

Unfortunately for Galileo, once his opinions moved from scientific observation to debating whether or not the Church was correctly interpreting Scripture, things began to get ugly. In 1616, at the instruction of Pope Paul V, Galileo was ordered to abandon the opinion that the sun is the center of the universe and to cease teaching, writing of, or defending the idea in any way.[9] To make a long story short, Galileo did not suppress his intellect nor would he see his pursuit of truth as threatening to

9   John L. Heilbron, *Galileo* (New York: Oxford University Press, 2010), 218.

his faith. His continued writings and defense of those ideas caused him to be threatened with torture and ultimately punished by the Church in 1633. Galileo was found guilty of holding ideas that were contrary to Holy Scripture and sentenced to house arrest for the remainder of his life. His writings on the subject were banned, and publication of any of his works was forbidden.[10]

Now, resist the temptation to roll your eyes at the Church. That is low-hanging fruit. Hindsight is 20/20, and the Church has owned its mistake with regard to Galileo. The ideas put forth by Copernicus and Galileo were incredible ideas at the time. They seemed counterintuitive to everything people had been taught and accepted about the nature of the universe. We do not arrogantly look to the wrestling between Galileo and the Church in order to condemn the Church. The Pope and the leaders of the Church were faithful people, just like Galileo. They were doing the best that they could with the narrative they had been given.

Galileo saw that narrative to be incomplete and worthy of reflection.

Galileo refused to suppress his intellect as if that were what faith requires.

Galileo believed in a God who was not threatened by the developing apprehension of a people trying to understand the universe—and sometimes getting it wrong.

To be sure, the Church really blew this one. The very people who were entrusted with the story of a "free God that desires the free worship of free people"[11] actually believed the best thing they could do in response to Galileo was to remove his freedom.

Yikes!

That is some epic and ironic failure! To be honest, though, that is a level of completely striking out with which I can identify. I have screwed up like that. I have been so afraid of new ideas that I have used

---

[10] Ibid., 308–317.

[11] Jonathan Sacks, *Yitro (5773) - The Politics of Revelation*, rabbisacks.org, accessed September 15, 2013, http://www.rabbisacks.org/covenant-conversation-yitro-the-politics-of-revelation/.

the Scripture, my God, and my faith to shut someone down. I—just like the Church leaders Galileo took to task—have been a prisoner of faith lies, too. I have created prisoners of war in the battle between my fear and my faith.

According to legend, as Galileo finished his forced recanting of the theory that the earth moved around the sun, he muttered the phrase, "And yet it moves." As much as that may inspire our righteous rebellion, I believe there is more going on in that statement. To me, that is a statement of continued wrestling. This man has just been obedient to the Church and the faith to which he ascribed—even when he believed them to be wrong. He is, however, not blindly obedient. He will maintain both his relationship to the faith and his intellect. He will continue to wrestle and, in doing so, invite others to do the same. That is the faith of Galileo. "And yet it moves" is far more interesting and compelling to me as a commitment to wrestle. The Church wrenched Galileo's hip, so to speak. He could have refused to recant. He could have turned his back on the faith. Instead, he remained in the relationship and in the struggle.

The legend and legacy of Galileo is an Ebenezer for us. It is a monument of standing stones that testify for future generations what happens when we juxtapose faith and science. When we accept blind belief and set science, reason, and empiricism up as an enemy to faith, we set faith up as an enemy to intelligence.

Science is the pursuit of truth through observation and empirical study. As people of faith, we should applaud and encourage the pursuit of truth in any form. Let's ask it this way: is there any truth out there that we have yet to discover that is outside of God? When Galileo asserted that the earth moved around the sun, was God surprised? If we believe in an ultimate reality—which we call God—is it possible for any truth to exist outside that reality? Put another way, is there any truth out there—discovered or not yet discovered—that does not belong to God? The answer has to be no. If it were possible for truth to exist outside of the ultimate reality, then that reality would not be ultimate. If it were possible for our discovery and exploration to surprise God, then that which we are calling God would not really be God.

It is a safe and humble posture to assume that any truth our brains can ever stumble upon is a truth with which God is already familiar. And if that's the case, shouldn't we be exploring? Shouldn't we be asking questions—thinking, debating, arguing in the pursuit of new understanding? Science, reason, empiricism—these things are not the enemies of faith because faith is not blind belief. Faith is wrestling. Faith is continuing to struggle in pursuit of new revelation and blessing. Faith is holistic. Faith is not only for things that are sacred because all of existence is sacred.

If the lie is that faith is blind belief and therefore must be separated from doubt, questioning, and exploration, then the truth is, those things were never to be separated in the first place. Faith is that which believes doubt, questioning, and exploration are supposed to be part of the relationship. Doubt, like faith, is transcendent. Doubt cannot be avoided nor eliminated from life—no matter how strong our faith is—because doubt is part of faith. Theologian Paul Tillich wrote, "If faith is understood as belief that something is true, doubt is incompatible with the act of faith. If faith is understood as being ultimately concerned, doubt is a necessary element in it. It is a consequence of the risk of faith."[12]

If you're mind cramped a little reading that Tillich quote, don't worry. Tillich is a heavyweight theologian who frequently causes brain cramps around the world. We should be able, however, to see the very lie we've been exploring within his words. If faith is simply our ability to believe the fairy-tale is true—to believe with all our heart that our sleigh bell does have a clapper—then doubt can't be a part of it. Just like Santa in *The Polar Express*—if our belief makes *it* real, then we can't possibly doubt or *it* will die. Yet if, as Tillich asserts, faith is concerned with things transcendent—the ultimate reality, the nature of the universe—then doubt comes with the territory.

Here's the kicker: what do we humans typically do with doubt? We

---

[12] Paul Tillich, *Writings on Religion* Robert P. Scharlemann, ed. (Berlin: Walter De Gruyter & Co., 1988), 240.

protest and investigate. We explore. We ask questions. We study and test in an effort to increase our understanding and decrease our doubt. And what does that sound like? Exploration, investigation, studying, testing—that's right, science. Science, in the end, is the pursuit of truth. Why in the world would the pursuit of truth stand juxtaposed to the life of faith? It wouldn't. Science and faith are related—siblings in the ultimate family—both trying to make sense out of the universe. And like science, faith—when rightly understood—is not about what you can blindly believe. It's about what you experience.

In a 2008 interview, astrophysicist and author Neil deGrasse Tyson commented on the history of misperception between faith and science.

> There's no tradition of scientists knocking down the door, the Sunday school door, telling the preacher what to teach. There's no tradition of scientists picketing outside of churches nor should there be some [emergent] tradition of religious fundamentalists trying to change the curriculum in the science classroom. There's been a happy coexistence for centuries. And for that to change now would be unfortunate.[13]

What should it mean to us as people of faith when we argue for separation and division while the scientists are arguing for an integrated consciousness? Are we repeating the mistakes of Galileo's accusers? Keep in mind that we don't have to be confronted with worldview-altering ideas to play that role. Anytime we close ourselves off to someone else's understanding in the name of preserving our faith, we are tragically misrepresenting the God we claim. Everything we believe, blindly or otherwise, must be held loosely enough to receive new information or new insight. The moment we wrap our clinched fist around a truth and close

---

[13] Neil deGrasse Tyson, *Neil deGrasse Tyson on Science and Faith*, bigthink.com, accessed September 4, 2012. http://bigthink.com/videos/neil-degrasse-tyson-on-science-and-faith

Okay, full disclosure here … I freaking love Neil deGrasse Tyson. If scientists had trading cards, I would trade every baseball card I own to get his rookie card. Legend.

ourselves off to reflection, we take something that was intended to be helpful and create a weapon.

The Difference Between Belief and Value

A belief is an acceptance of something as true or that something exists. It is a trust or confidence in someone or something. Compare that to a value, which is a principle, standard, or judgment of what is important in life. I have become increasingly disinterested in what people believe and increasingly interested in what people value. People believe all sorts of things for all sorts of reasons. Sometimes, we can't even tell each other why we believe what we believe. Even worse, we often claim to hold beliefs for which there is no evidence in our lives that we actually believe them. Friends, there are plenty of people who claim to believe in Jesus who look, live, and behave nothing like him. They believe in him, but they do not value what he valued. So what is that "belief" worth?

Contrastingly, when someone values something—I mean really values it—everyone around them knows it. Our values are expressed in our behavior. It's the difference between my having a belief in my kids or valuing my kids. I hope and pray that my life communicates that I value my children. I think if someone were to document a day in my life, they would be able to make some conclusions about what I hold as important after watching me. I don't know if they'd have an idea of what I believe, but they would know what I care about. This is not to say that beliefs aren't important because they are. Beliefs exist in the core of our being; they can help us define our world and our place in it. What we believe is important. Yet, we must face the reality that our beliefs present an incomplete, inconsistent, and developing picture. Our beliefs are dynamic—they change and evolve.

So when people want to talk to me about faith, I try to share the values faith has instilled in my life. Love, relationship, story, inclusion, forgiveness, exploration, rest—these are the things I have learned to value and that I continue to grow toward. These are the things that I hope my life communicates. What I believe is much more fluid than what I value. My beliefs can be radically changed by new information or experience. Think of it this way: when Galileo's studies allowed him to theorize about the earth's movement around the sun, what changed—his beliefs or his values?

At some point in Galileo's life, he believed—as he had been taught—that the earth was the center of the universe. Later, Galileo received new information and insight that caused his belief to change. When his belief shifted and he thought that the sun was the center of the universe, did his values change? Surely, I am no expert on what Galileo valued, but his life is a testament to the reality that he valued the pursuit of knowledge, truth, and exploration. The real kick in the backside, however, is that his response to his sanctioning by the Church also seems to reveal that he valued the Church, even when it was imprisoning him. His beliefs shifted—to the point of putting him at odds with the leaders of his faith, but his values remained rooted. Galileo valued relationship. Galileo valued faith. Galileo valued wrestling. His beliefs changed, his values did not.

So what do you value?

Think about it. Write down some responses. What values has your family passed down to you? What values have been passed to you by your faith? How have you seen those values growing or deepening throughout your life? My suspicion is that we will notice a consistency and development in our values—good or bad. Values seem to follow the overarching journey of our stories. Values seem to ooze out of us, regardless of what we claim to believe. Values are the real testimony of our faith—whether we like it or not.

When we hold faith up as a collection of blind beliefs—fairy-tales in which we are willing to believe—we show the world that we do not value intellect or critical thought. Even worse, our blind belief can be used to separate us from those who won't or can't believe. In such instances, our faith appears to value

... orthodoxy over love
... doctrine over relationship

... fairy-tales over story

... preservation over inclusion

... winning over forgiveness

... absolutes over exploration

... striving over rest

That faith is not helpful to anyone. That faith is a shell of what was handed down to us. It is a lie. It is not who we are called to be.

We are called to value love. We are called to value relationships with other people. We are called to value listening to God's story and the stories of others. We are called to value those at the margins and those in power—even when they try to exist exclusive of one another. We are called to treasure forgiveness when we receive it and give it away as often as possible. We are called to search—to value questions and doubt. We are called to value rest as a posture of humility in knowing that we all have a home and a family to which we belong.

We are called to keep all these things in tension to one another. If that sounds impossible, that's good. It is not something we can do alone—we need help. Nor is it something we ever conquer. It is something with which we wrestle. That is who we are.

When we reduce our faith or our scriptural stories to a blind leap of faith, we are in danger of sidestepping, or missing altogether, the great question we are being asked or the greater reality to which we are being invited to awaken. When we believe faith is simply a blind leap, our faith lies to us. There comes a moment when we can no longer keep quiet—when we can no longer ignore or turn a blind eye. When will that moment be?

Galileo's head was on the block
The crime was looking up the truth
And as the bombshells of my daily fears explode
I try to trace them to my youth

How long 'til my soul gets it right
Can any human being ever reach that kind of light
I call on the resting soul of Galileo
King of night vision
King of insight[14]

---

[14] Emily Saliers, "Galileo," performed by Indigo Girls, *Rites of Passage*, CD Track 2, Epic Records, 1992.

CONCLUSION

LIVING OUTSIDE THE LIES

This is what gives origin to your beliefs: fixed, unchanging ways of looking
at a reality which is not fixed and unchanging at all but in movement and
change. So it is no longer the real world that you interact with and love
but a world created by your head. It is only when you drop your beliefs,
your fears, and the attachments that breed them that you will be freed
from the insensitivity that makes you so deaf and blind to yourself and
to the world.[1]

— Anthony de Mello

You have to admit—that is a serious quote! What a way to start the conclusion, right? Anthony de Mello, the Indian Jesuit priest who wrote these words, was not known for beating around the bush. Straight to the point—"It is only when you drop your beliefs, your fears, and the attachments that breed them that you will be freed from the insensitivity that makes you so deaf and blind to yourself and to the world."

Wow!

How do you react to that statement? That's one of those statements that makes me want to sit down for a bit. Confronting the truth that I may

---

[1] De Mello, *The Way to Love*, 48.

be deaf and blind to the world and myself is not something I want to do on my feet. I need to sit for that kind of work.

Once I am seated, I can start to realize that removing the fear from my life sounds like a good idea. I would like to live a life with no fear. But then there are those other two things I have to drop—my beliefs and my attachments. That does not sound like fun. How do you feel about dropping your beliefs or your attachments? Does the thought of dropping your beliefs—even if they are the bad or incomplete ideas we have chronicled—make you nervous?

I get that. Me, too.

Anytime we grow accustomed to something, we have a hard time growing beyond it. That can even be the case with fear, injustice, imprisonment, and suffering. No person who ever lived aspired to be afraid. No one who has ever been born wanted to grow up to suffer injustice or be imprisoned. Yet, that is exactly what many of us do. We settle into suffering, oppression, and fear. We get used to it—so used to it that it begins to feel like home.

All we have done in this book is trace through seven commingled lies from which I struggle to be freed—seven incomplete ideas that caused me to live in and engender religious oppression and fear. Years ago, a friend of mine who had been praying for me looked up and said he had seen an image while he prayed. The image was of me sitting in a prison cell. The strange thing was that the door to the prison cell was not there. It had been removed. The cell was wide open, and yet I still sat there as though I were locked in.

De Mello's quote reminds of me of that prison cell. It reminds me that I have choices to make and that this journey is never complete. It forces me to reflect on my attachments, my fears, and my beliefs. Where am I sitting in a prison cell, believing there is a locked door when there is really no door at all? To what am I attached in that cell—what do I find comforting about it? If I do get up and walk out of that cell, what do I fear I will lose? What do I fear will happen if I embrace freedom? These are the kinds of questions with which we wrestle when we confront the lies of our faith.

There is another wonderful quote from a movie that was seen as a box-office flop. The quote—in my humble opinion—is so good, however, that I think of the movie as a success. The movie is *After Earth*, a sci-fi thriller starring Will Smith and his son, Jaden. It comes about as Smith is trying to communicate to his son, who is alone and in danger on another side of the planet. Trying to calm his hysterical son over the radio, Smith says,

> Recognize your power.
>
> You have the ability to create or cocreate what happens next.
>
> Fear is not real. The only place that fear can exist is in our thoughts of the future. It is a product of our imagination, causing us to fear things that do not at present and may not ever exist. That is near insanity.
>
> Now, do not misunderstand me. Danger is real, but fear is a choice.
>
> We are all telling ourselves a story.[2]

We are all telling ourselves a story, and we all possess the power to change that story. What stories are we telling ourselves? Where did we get these stories? Are they true? Do our stories point us toward freedom and the reality that there is no door on the cell? Or do our stories keep us comfortable where we are?

Spoiler Alert: There Is No Easter Bunny

When my boys were about seven years old, they determined that the Easter bunny was not real. This was not due to any great detective work on their part—just more of a casual observance. As long as they had been

---

[2] M. Night Shyamalan and Gary Whitta, *After Earth*, DVD, directed by M. Night Shyamalan (Culver City, CA: Sony Pictures Home Entertainment, 2013).

alive, their mother and I had worked for the church. That meant that Easter Sunday was not only a workday but quite a hectic workday for both of their parents. Now judge if you must, but we simply never had time for the Easter bunny on Easter Sunday morning. My wife and I would be at the church at the crack of dawn—with our twin boys in tow—gearing up for Easter worship services. This same effect was taking place in my older sister's home as well because she also worked for the church.

Each year, after all of the work was done, we would join my extended family for a late lunch at my parents' house around 2:00 PM. At some point during the lunch preparation, one of the uncles would duck outside to hide eggs around the yard when no one was looking. Then, after lunch, we would turn all the kids loose for an Easter egg hunt. Keep in mind that none of these kids ever had eggs hidden at their own houses. They never awoke to a visit from the Easter bunny on Easter Sunday. Moreover, when they would arrive at their grandparents' home in the afternoon on Easter, there were no eggs and no signs of a visit from the Easter bunny. Yet, somehow, after everyone had arrived—in the middle of the day—the Easter bunny would apparently arrive and hide eggs all over the yard. The veil of mystery was incredibly thin. I am sure it did not take any of the grandkids long to figure out what was going on.

However early my boys may have figured out the charade, they managed to keep their mouths shut about it until they were seven years old. As their seventh Easter approached, they were ready to discuss it. They had compared their Easter stories and experience with enough of their friends to recognize the disparity and finally asked their mother, "There is no Easter bunny, is there?"

Their mother, wanting to believe in the paper-thin mystery we had created said, "What do you mean?"

Undeterred, my son Sammy asked, "Isn't it just Uncle Keith who hides the eggs every year?"s

My wife, revealing her disdain for cross-examination, caved and confessed. "You're right. There is no Easter bunny. It's not real—it's Uncle Keith."

Now at this time—when my boys were seven and making this discovery—my daughter was two and approaching her third Easter. She was still all in. The Easter bunny was very real and certainly capable of popping by unseen in the middle of the afternoon to hide eggs for all the grandchildren. Accordingly, my wife told my sons that they had to keep this new information to themselves. She gave them a firm speech about not telling any of the other grandkids—especially their little sister—about their Easter scandal revelation. They agreed.

A few days later, my wife and I were in the car together with our kids, running some errands. We needed to go by my father's office to pick up some paperwork. The grandkids in our family call my father Bop. He is not particularly fond of the label, but that was the name the first grandchild uttered when trying to say "Grandpa," so it stuck, and my dad became Bop. With my daughter sandwiched in her car seat between her brothers in the backseat, we swung by Bop's office, and he came out to hand us the paperwork. While sitting in the parking lot, we rolled down the backseat window so my dad could see and talk to the kids for a while. As we were wrapping up and saying our goodbyes, my dad told all the kids that they had better come visit him next Sunday because he was expecting the Easter bunny to visit and hide some eggs. Sammy—armed with his newly-confirmed truth—began to tell Bop how he knew that was not true. He knew it was a scam, and he wasn't going to let Bop pull a fast one on him. But before he could finish his thought, my wife jumped in. "Sammy! Be quiet!" In a flash, you could see the seriousness of the situation wash over Sammy's face. You could tell he remembered that he promised his mother that he would not ruin anyone else's Easter by telling the secret. He had almost let the cat out of the bag, and he knew it. He got very still and very quiet.

We finished our goodbyes and drove away. My wife—wanting to make sure that Sammy knew what was going on—questioned Sammy.

"Sammy, do you know why I told you to be quiet? Do you remember what we talked about?"

Sammy nodded in agreement—but also a little bewildered as he uttered this brilliantly honest confession, "Yeah, but I didn't think you were talking about Bop. I thought he knew."

Somehow, I managed not to wreck the car as I fell hysterically to the floorboards in laughter over Sammy's conclusion. My son, who could no longer believe in the Easter bunny, overlooked his younger sister sitting next to him and deduced that it was his grandfather who believed. In six-plus decades on earth, Bop still hadn't figured out the truth. Sammy's view was that Bop was stuck in an Easter bunny prison cell with no door. How could he still believe in the bunny? What story was he telling himself in order to be content living inside that lie? As funny as that sounds, we all tell much stranger stories to ourselves, and few of them are as benign as a bunny that hides candy eggs.

Where the Freedom of the LORD Is, There Is Spirit

In the first century, the apostle Paul—no stranger to prison cells himself—wrote letters to the faith community he helped establish in Corinth. In what was known as the second of those letters, he describes to his friends how people can harden their minds and their hearts—in essence pulling a veil down over themselves so as not to see. He then makes this most compelling statement, "Now the LORD is Spirit and where the Spirit of the LORD is, there is freedom" (2 Cor. 3:17).

This is one of those statements people grow up with in the Christian church. It's in songs, Sunday school lessons, and sermons. It's on bumper stickers and billboards. "Where the Spirit of the LORD is, there is freedom." It makes sense. God is in the freedom business. That is what God is into—freedom. The library of the Bible represents a progressive story of people moving toward freedom at God's urging and by God's power and love. As Rabbi Jonathan Sacks teaches, "At the heart of Judaism is the idea—way ahead of its time, and not always fully realized—that the free God desires the free worship of free human beings."[3]

Yet, I think I misunderstood this idea for most of my life. For some

---

[3] Sacks, *The Politics of Revelation*.

reason, in my Western mind, I made this statement into a recipe. In essence, I believed that if I wanted freedom, I needed to pursue the Spirit. In other words, if I tried really hard to connect to the presence of God, I might catch a glimpse and thereby earn or access some freedom. Maybe if I worshiped hard enough or prayed hard enough, I could get the Spirit of God to dwell where I was, and the freedom would rub off on me.

Then one day, I found myself in a tough situation, and I called one of my mentors for some direction. After listening to me whine and describe my problem, my mentor said, "Darrell, where do you see the freedom in this situation?" I tried to answer that question as best I could by describing where I thought freedom could possibly exist amidst my circumstances. My mentor said, "Go there," and hung up the phone. It was like a light came on inside of me. Paul's statement became something completely new to me. Look for the freedom and go there—because that is where God is. Wherever you find freedom, you will also be accessing the Spirit of the LORD.

That idea really changes things when I find myself sitting in a prison cell. If I am not experiencing freedom, it's not God's doing. It's mine. God is in the freedom business. Wherever God's presence is, there will be freedom. This kind of freedom is not simply the ability to choose to do whatever the heck we want. That kind of freedom—or free will—is implicit in our reality. We always have that kind of freedom (unless it is oppressed by other human beings). The kind of freedom we are referencing here is more than free will. It is the kind of freedom that causes us to be fully alive—to connect, synchronize, and engage with something larger than ourselves and know intuitively that there is something more going on. This kind of freedom lies just below the surface and unites everything. It causes us to feel empowered, connected, and strong—not powerless, isolated, and weak. This kind of freedom warms us and inspires us—making our hearts race and our minds explode with possibilities. This divine freedom always—and I mean always, without exception—results in love.

Look around your life...

- Where do you see such freedom?
- Is it always in the places it is "supposed" to reside?
- Do you sometimes experience or witness freedom in situations or locations that are supposed to be "unbiblical" or "against God's will?"
- What does it mean if you experience divine freedom in situations or places of which you assumed God disapproved?
- Is your religion causing you to experience freedom? Is your doctrine?
- Do your beliefs lead you to freedom? Your attachments? Your fears?
- What does it mean if you are not experiencing divine freedom in the situations and places of which you assumed God approved?
- Is the story you are telling yourself—the story upon which you build your life—a story that leads to freedom?

Important ~~Words~~ Ideas

Asking these questions and looking for freedom through reflection, prayer, community, and study takes time, and it takes discipline. While there may certainly be lightning-bolt moments along the way, the more likely course will be a series of slowly progressive awakenings that string together one pearl at a time to form beautiful growth within us. In my experience, the recognition of a lie that may not initially seem to affect my life much is usually followed by an experiential unraveling that reveals the pervasive impact the lie truly has on my worldview and understanding. Furthermore, just because I have been able to recognize and wrestle some understanding from the lies in my faith does not mean I have them beat. I struggle with the faith lies every day.

Obviously, I don't struggle alone because community is not optional, and my faith is not a private matter. Moreover, I don't wrestle blindly or ignorantly as I have the stories of those who have gone before to guide me. That is really what the Bible is in the end—a library of progression that shares how others before us have wrestled and what they learned. The examples and templates from which we can learn don't stop with the last page of the Bible either. We are surrounded by stories. We walk amidst wisdom and revelation from lives lived like people walking through a downpour who cannot help but get wet.

In his letter to the Philippians, Paul—writing from prison—offers his friends some advice for the journey. He wrote, "Finally, Beloved, whatever is true, whatever is honorable, whatever is just, whatever is pure, whatever is pleasing, whatever is commendable, if there is any excellence and if there is anything worthy of praise, think about these things" (Phil. 4:8).

I hope that is what we have done here. I hope that these stories and ideas have pointed toward some important words that represent important ideas for the life of faith.

Whatever allows you to wrestle, whatever leads you to awakenings, whatever lets you tell and listen to stories, whatever causes you to give and receive love, whatever you find to be helpful along your path, if there is any inclusion and acceptance, and if there is that which builds and releases freedom, think about these things.

My prayer for this writing has been that it will cause the kind of questioning that leads to freedom. Freedom may be hard to spot in your circumstances. We don't always get a clear picture. Sometimes, we take obscured steps forward. For some of us, we may just see the slightest hint of dawn on the horizon. For others of us, we may not see it all—we may have to remember where the last dawn broke and move toward that memory, trusting in the God who desires our freedom. Wherever it may be in your life and circumstances, my prayer is that you will search for freedom and move toward it. That is where the Spirit of the LORD is.

Go there—and go in peace.

A ROHR-ing Epilogue

We find it hard to love imperfect things, so we imagine God is just as small as we are. One of the most helpful pieces of advice I ever received from Francis is found in the seventh chapter of the Rule of the Friars Minor. Here he tells us not to be surprised or upset by the sins or mistakes of others (and I would add, by our own sins and mistakes) because, he says, "such anger and annoyance make it difficult to be charitable." His analysis is that simple, that hard, and that true. If we expect or need things (including ourselves) to be perfect or even "to our liking," we have created a certain plan for a very unhappy life.[1]

— Richard Rohr

As I have worked on this project over the last few years, I have been sustained by a number of people. Most of them are the family and loved ones listed in the acknowledgments. Richard Rohr is not someone I know personally but someone whose writings and leadership have sustained me nonetheless. If you know Rohr, then you know what I am talking about here. If not, I encourage you to get to know him. In my humble estimation, Richard Rohr is one of a handful of spiritual parents

---

[1] Richard Rohr, *True Perfection is the Ability to Include Imperfection*, Richard Rohr's Daily Meditation, accessed June 16, 2015, http://myemail.constantcontact.com/Richard-Rohr-s-Meditation–True-Perfection-Is-the-Ability-to-Include-Imperfection.html?soid=1103098668616&aid=Di-DcOKA4V8

we currently have available to us, and we should be listening and follow-ing. I will be blunt here. Read Father Rohr's books. Watch his teachings online. Subscribe to the daily meditation from the Center for Action and Contemplation. Listen and follow.

There have been a number of times in this book when I have used Richard Rohr's thoughts to help explain or understand my own. At the risk of over-Rohr-ing you, I would like to offer one more as we go forth.

> Ironically, a prophet must be educated inside the system in order to have the freedom to critique that very system. You have to know the rules of any tradition, and you have to respect those rules enough to know why they do exist—and thus how to break them properly, for the sake of a larger and more essential value. This is what Martin Luther King, Jr. taught America and what Gandhi taught the British. Here is the key: you can only unlock systems from the inside.[2]

If any part of this journey has encouraged you or brought freedom, rejoice and bless the LORD. That is really all you need to do at this point. One of the mistakes I make repeatedly upon awakening to new revela-tions of freedom or consciousness is to assume that it is now my job to make sure everyone around me receives the same revelation. As Rohr points out, that is not necessarily the case. Rushing into my priest's office or my local church board meeting to tell them all their beliefs or doctrine are wrong is not going to help anyone.

In our journey, we have learned that there is not one right way to believe or behave and that we do not need to defend God or our faith. Now, we must trust that if we have truly awakened to revelation or free-dom, God will provide us with opportunities to grow and to share. We may, in fact, be given opportunities to teach against lies in the systems of

---

[2]   Richard Rohr, *Who Would Want to Be a Prophet*, Richard Rohr's Daily Meditation, accessed February 19, 2015, http://myemail.constantcontact.com/Richard-Rohr-s-Meditation–Who-Would-Want-to-Be-a-Prophet-html?soid=1103098668616&aid=O 32zgddYuTc

our faith, but we must do so, as Rohr states, "from the inside." Being on the inside necessarily requires love. To know a system, a church, a community well enough to understand the lies which imprison it and where those lies came from means that we are invested. When have you ever welcomed someone who wants to tear down something you care about? We will only be given opportunities to share our freedom in the systems where we have built, studied, listened, prayed, and loved.

We must remember that any worthwhile wisdom we have ever received was something to which we awakened when we were ready. Another way to say that is that we hang onto what's working for us. When our ideas or our faith stops working, we go searching—then we are open to awakening. My friend, Chris Estus, helps me to remember that I am not called to look forward with fear nor back with disdain. I do not need to fear the future—mine or yours. I do not need to be disgusted or ashamed of the past—mine or yours.

In 1897, Rev. W.L. Sheldon wrote a wise reflection that is often incorrectly attributed to Ernest Hemingway. "Remember that there is nothing noble in being superior to some other man. The true nobility is in being superior to your previous self."[3] We might trip up a little bit over that word "noble" but just substitute in the word *holy* or *righteous*. There is nothing righteous about thinking our beliefs or our faith is better than someone else's—that they would be better off if they believed or understood like us. True righteousness lies in humble and joyous reflection upon our own developing belief and faith. How good it is to be a work in progress.

Wherever a person is on the journey—that is where they are. And where they are is valid. It is how they will get to where they are going. It is not our job to push anyone down the path.

While finishing the writing of this book, I got to go to the Grand Canyon with my family—including my mother and father. Having been to the Grand Canyon before, my dad—who all now know as Bop—had some rules for his grandchildren. The rules were simple—three basic

---

[3]   W. L. Sheldon, "What to Believe: An Ethical Creed," *The Unitarian, Volume XII*, Frederick B. Mott, ed. (Boston: Geo H. Ellis, 1897), 270.

guidelines to govern our behavior whilst we all encountered the Grand Canyon together.

1. Don't jump in.
2. Take one step back.
3. Adapt.

By the time we arrived at the Grand Canyon, my father had so drilled these rules into all of our heads that we didn't even have to say them. He could just say "Rule 2," and everyone knew that someone in our party was getting too close to the edge of the Canyon and we all needed to take a step back. Granted, Rules 1 and 2 were very specific to not falling into the Grand Canyon while Rule 3 was much more vague and inclusive of the whiny behavior we all expect when traveling as a family. Still, the rules were poignant. They governed our time together well—and made us laugh a lot.

The more I thought about it, I realized that these rules had application beyond the Grand Canyon. This is typically the way my father works—he is brilliant that way.

So I share these rules with you here, at the end of our journey together, as a possible guideline on how to move forward. As we all seek to grow into freedom and share our awakening with others, we must always remember:

1. **Don't jump in.** Trust that the God who brought you here is still at work. We are not brought to new levels of freedom and truth so that we can respond with the anxiety and pressure of fixing everyone and everything around us. Relax.
2. **Take one step back.** As the wise rabbi Chris Estus has taught me, if we are depressed, we should get busy—if we are confused, we should do nothing. If we are depressed and confused, we should take a nap. Get your bearings. We don't have to create

opportunities to love others and share our stories. They will come—so let them. Rest.

3. **Adapt.** Let people be who they are and let them be where they are. Transcend and include—get to know people better rather than trying to make them better. What comes our way will probably look much different from what we planned for—which kind of puts all our planning and manipulating in perspective, doesn't it? Receive.

Richard Rohr teaches that great change only comes about through great love or great suffering, and great suffering is not the business to which we are called as people of faith. We are called to great love. Maybe that is where the three rules of the Grand Canyon lead.

Don't jump in … relax.
Take one step back … rest.
Adapt … receive.

If we do all that, love is inevitable.

ACKNOWLEDGMENTS

Having wrestled with the reality that faith—or life, for that matter—is not something we do alone, it should come as no shock that this writing would not exist were it not for many, many wonderful people to whom I owe a great debt of gratitude.

Without question, my thanks must begin with my wife, Stacy, and our children, Nathanael, Samuel, and Abigail. Their sacrifice of time and space for me to read and write spans decades—and their ability to share the journey with me with great intrigue, mercy, and love is what makes it all worth it. You are the joy of my heart.

The same must be said for my family. My parents, Darrell and Janet, started me on this journey and have always been there to inform and encourage the next step. My amazing sisters, Dinah and Frances, share and shake up the journey as we go—along with their beautiful families. Our extended family—a wild and wooly group of fellow travelers for whom I am extremely grateful—makes sure no part of this journey is too isolated or too boring.

My life is and always has been full of teachers who push and provoke—may it never cease! I bless the Source for Rev. Dr. David J. McNitzky, Rev. Dinah Shelly, Rev. Donna Strieb, Rev. Dr. Robert Gibbs, Dr. Alexander Shaia, Dr. Tom Fisher, Rev. Dr. Constance Cherry, Dr. A.E. Hill, Rev. Dr. Lynn Anderson, Rabbi Aryeh Scheinberg, Rev. Michael Crocker, Rev. Matt Scott, Rev. Robert Ortiz, Rev. Donna Bellamy, Rev. Ryan Jacobson,

Rev. Erika Forbes-Wilson, Rev. Stephanie Schlimm, Rev. Scott Heare, Rev. Rob Grimes, Rev. Janet Weatherston, Dr. Matthew Schlimm, Chris Estus, Chris DiSabato, Jeff Barker, Shay Forbes-Wilson, Ruth Ann Lind, Roger Lind, and Mary Parker.

I must give thanks for the light and love of the people with whom I get to work and serve day in and day out. The loving, inclusive, hard-working, servant-hearted, common-good-pursuing women and men of Alamo Heights UMC are the reason I love my job. Thank you all!

There are also those whose support through C3 and MORE not only shaped, prayed for, and paid for this writing, but also in countless ways informed any wisdom it contains with their own lives and service: Dave and Emily Angulo, Jennifer Bailey, Twyla Benson, Randy and Debbie Boggs, Bryan and Cindy Boynton, Scott and Nicole Boynton, Colin and Jordan Bryant, Bruce and Carol Cauley, Debbi Chesney, Michael and Ginna Crocker, Lemanda Del Toro, Jeff and Frances Downing, Jason and Tracy Echols, Chris and Pat Estus, Shay and Erika Forbes-Wilson, Leslie Halks, Joel and Cayce Harris, Ryan and Kylea Jacobson, Ben and Heather Keenan, Ed and Leslie Kinchen, Mitch Connell and Melissa Ludwig, A.J. and Kristin Navarro, Joe and Wendy McClellan, Craig and Molly McMahon, Kelly McMakin and Melissa Low, Donna Nicolson, Richard and Brooke Peacock, Evan and Diane Renz, Jack Rodgers, Bob & Nora Scott, Keith and Dinah Shelly, Derek and Cari Spielhagen, Wendy Taylor, Lawrence and Joanie Thames, Audrey Treviño, Chris and Amy Tsakopulos, Charlie and Pat Wiseman, Kevin and Carrie Workman, and Mike and Lil Yates.

The process of bringing this writing to publication would have been treacherously dark were it not for the guiding light and expertise of literary guru, Steve Green. I must also thank Scott Boynton, Patton Dodd, Alice Rhee, Gayle Timberlake, Tony Jones, and Paul Soupiset for their encouragement, direction, and (in Paul's case) a singularly awesome cover design.

My love and gratitude goes to all my fellow "wrestlers of the divine." For reasons that escape me, I have been covered in the blessing of fellow searchers, questioners, and protestors whose faith and spirit are far too important to leave on a shelf. To all the folks from Haven for Hope, the *Quadratos* journey, and "What is the Bible?"—thank you. Make no mistake, your wrestling and sharing filled these pages.

Lastly, I thank you—the reader. Your willingness to even pick up this book, let alone plow through my quirky writing and footnotes, is both humbling and inspiring. May your ability to ask and talk and be okay with "I don't know" keep the whole thing alive. Peace.

Hold On Loosely

Words and Music by Jeff Carsisi, Don Barnes and Jim Peterik
Copyright ©1981 by Universal Music – MGB Songs, WB Music Corp.
    and Easy Action Music
All Rights for Easy Action Music Administered by WB Music Corp.
International Copyright Secured All Rights Reserved
Reprinted by Permission of Hal Leonard LLCC

Needle and Thread

Written by Ryan O'Neal
©2006 Wine and Song Music (BMI) on behalf of itself and Asteroid
    B-612
International Copyright Secured All Rights Reserved
Used By Permission

Galileo

Words and Music by Emily Saliers
Copyright © 1992 GODHAP MUSIC
All Rights Controlled and Administered by SONGS OF UNIVER-
    SAL, INC.
All Rights Reserved Used by Permission
Reprinted by Permission of Hal Leonard LLC

Suggested Reading By Chapter

We are all mere beggars telling other beggars where to find bread.

— Martin Luther

The thing about coming out from under incomplete or inconsistent ideas is that we often rush to replace our old ideas with new ones. It's as if the old story—the one which we had accepted for so long—is gone and we immediately need a new story. The truth is there are lots of stories. Probably the best advice I can give anyone looking to do further study or reading is to relax, take your time, and let every story that unfolds before you draw you into relationship. Therein also lies the key, I think, to discerning those narratives that are helpful from those that are not. If a narrative of faith, idea, or theology creates fear and anxiety within you and does not draw you into relationship with God or with other people, leave it and move on. There are far too many good stories, ideas, and theology to get mired down in those that are not helpful.

That being said, below is a list of writers and theologians that I have found to be extremely helpful on my journey. This list is by no means exhaustive nor is it meant to exclude the thousands of other great stories and storytellers out there. If anything, this list represents a snapshot of those ideas and stories that have introduced me to a deeper narrative of faith and a deeper experience of freedom. Journey on.

LIE 1: The Bible Is Only the Literal Word of God

- *What Is the Bible?: How an Ancient Library of Poems, Letters, and Stories Can Transform the Way You Think and Feel About Everything* by Rob Bell (© HarperOne, 2017).
- *Getting Involved With God: Rediscovering the Old Testament* by Ellen F. Davis (© Rowman and Littlefield Publishers, Inc., 2001).
- *The Bible Tells Me So: Why Defending Scripture Has Made Us Unable to Read it* by Peter Enns (© Harper Collins Publishers, 2014).
- *This Strange and Sacred Scripture: Wrestling with the Old Testament and Its Oddities* by Matthew Richard Schlimm (© Baker Publishing Group, 2015).
- *Heart and Mind: The Four-Gospel Journey for Radical Transformation* by Alexander John Shaia with Michelle L. Gaugy (© Morning Star Publishing, 2015).

LIE 2: God Is Angry and Doesn't Like Me—Especially When I Sin

- *Did God Kill Jesus?: Searching for Love in History's Most Famous Execution* by Tony Jones (© Harper Collins Publishers, 2015).
- *The Way to Love: Meditations for Life* by Anthony De Mello (© Random House, 1991).
- *Eager to Love: The Alternative Way of Francis of Assisi* by Richard Rohr (© Franciscan Media, 2014).
- *Original Blessing: Putting Sin in Its Rightful Place* by Danielle Shroyer (© Fortress Press, 2016).
- *The Good and Beautiful God: Falling in Love With the God Jesus Knows* by James Bryan Smith (© InterVarsity Press, 2009).

LIE 3: The Devil Is God's Counterpart

- *The Divine Comedy: The Inferno, The Purgatorio, and The Paradiso* by Dante Alighieri Translated by John Ciardi (© New American Library, 2003).
- *The Screwtape Letters* by C.S. Lewis (© Harper Collins Publishers, 2001).
- *Paradise Lost* – Dover Giant Thrift Editions by John Milton (© Dover Publications, Inc., 2005).
- *The Devil: Perceptions of Evil From Antiquity to Primitive Christianity* by Jeffrey Burton Russell (© Cornell University Press, 1977).
- *The Life of Saint Teresa of Avila by Herself* by Teresa of Avila (© The Penguin Group, 1957).

LIE 4: I Am Supposed to Protect and Defend God and My Faith

- *Accidental Herod: Becoming a Leader You Can Live With* by David McNitzky (© Quarry Press, 2014).
- *Falling Upward: A Spirituality for the Two Halves of Life* by Richard Rohr (© Jossey-Bass, 2011).
- *God Talk in America* by Phyllis Tickle (© Crossroad, 1997).
- *Exclusion and Embrace: A Theological Exploration of Identity, Otherness, and Reconciliation* by Miroslav Volf (© Abingdon Press, 1996).
- *Renovation of the Heart: Putting On the Character of Christ* by Dallas Willard (© NavPress, 2002).

LIE 5: There Is One Right Way to Believe and One Right Way to Behave

- *The Storytelling Church: Adventures in Reclaiming the Role of Story in Worship* by Jeff Barker (© Parson's Porch Books, 2011).
- *Pastrix: The Cranky, Beautiful Faith of a Sinner and Saint* by Nadia Bolz-Weber (© Jericho Books, 2014).

- *Grounded: Finding God in the World – A Spiritual Revolution* by Diana Butler Bass (© HarperOne, 2015).
- *A Generous Orthodoxy: Why I am a missional, evangelical, post/protestant, liberal/conservative, mystical/poetic, biblical, charismatic/contemplative, fundamentalist/Calvinist, Anabaptist/ Anglican, Methodist, Catholic, green, incarnational, depressed-yet-hopeful, emergent, unfinished Christian* by Brian D. McLaren (© Youth Specialties, 2004).
- *We Are the Ones We Have Been Waiting For: Inner Light in a Time of Darkness* by Alice Walker (© The New Press, 2007).

LIE 6: Faith Is a Private Matter

- *Journey to the Common Good* by Walter Brueggemann (©Westminster John Knox Press, 2010).
- *A Failure of Nerve: Leadership in the Age of the Quick Fix* by Edwin H. Friedman (© Seabury Books, 2007).
- *The Wounded Healer: Ministry in Contemporary Society* by Henri J. M. Nouwen (© Image Books, 1979).
- *Future Tense: Jews, Judaism, and Israel in the Twenty-first Century* by Jonathan Sacks (© Random House, 2009).
- *From Tablet to Table: Where Community is Found and Identity is Formed* by Leonard Sweet (© NavPress, 2015).

LIE 7: Real Faith Is Blind Belief

- *Beyond Fundamentalism: Confronting Religious Extremism in the Age of Globalization* By Reza Aslan (© Random House, 2010).
- *Daring Greatly: How the Courage to Be Vulnerable Transforms the Way We Live, Love, Parent, and Lead* by Brené Brown (© Avery, 2012).
- *God's Presence in History: Jewish Affirmations and Philosophical Reflections* by Emil Fackenheim (© New York University Press, 1970).

- *The Meaning of the Bible: What the Jewish Scriptures and Christian Old Testament Can Teach Us* by Douglas A. Knight and Amy-Jill Levine (© Harper Collins Publishers, 2011).
- *The Divine Embrace: Recovering the Passionate Spiritual Life* by Robert E. Webber (© Baker Books, 2006).

I think I'd be remiss if I didn't also give a shout-out to the Bible translators who have worked so hard to take the Bible from black and white to color. I'm not saying these Bible translations are the "right" ones or that others are the "wrong" ones—you should know this by now. What I am saying is that it is good to be immersed in different translations and I have been blessed to swim in the Bibles below.

- *The Jewish Bible: Tanakh: The Holy Scriptures – The New JPS Translation According to the Traditional Hebrew Text* by The Jewish Publication Society (©Jewish Publication Society, 1985).
- *NIV Cultural Backgrounds Study Bible: Bringing to Life the Ancient World of Scripture* by Craig S. Keener and John H. Walton (©Zondervan, 2016)
- *NIV First-Century Study Bible: Explore Scripture in Its Jewish and Early Christian Context* by Kent Dobson (© Zondervan, 2014).
- *The Message: The Bible in Contemporary Language* by Eugene H. Peterson (© NavPress, 2005).
- *The Voice Bible: Step Into the Story of Scripture* by Ecclesia Bible Society (© Thomas Nelson, 2012).
- *The Renovaré Spiritual Formation* Bible by Richard J. Foster, Dallas Willard, Walter Brueggemann, and Eugene H. Peterson (© Harper San Francisco, 2005).

SOURCES CONSULTED

A History of Christian Worship: Ancient Ways, Future Paths. Directed by Tom Dallis. USA: Ensign Media. 2010. DVD.

Aboriginal activists group. *Queensland, 1970s*. https://en.wikipedia.org/wiki/Lilla_Watson (accessed January 25, 2015).

After Earth. Directed by M. Night Shyamalan. USA: Sony Pictures Home Entertainment. 2013. DVD.

Almond, Steve. *Against Football: One Fan's Reluctant Manifesto*. Brooklyn, NY: Melville House Publishing, 2014.

American History X. Directed by Tony Kaye. USA: New Line Home Entertainment. 1999. DVD.

Back to the Future. Directed by Robert Zemeckis. USA: Universal, 2002. DVD.

Ballard, Glen and Alan Silvestri. *Believe*. Performed by Josh Groban. CD. Warner Brothers. 2004.

Barnes, Don, Jeff Carlisi, and Jim Peterik. *Hold On Loosely*. Performed by 38 Special. CD. A&M Records. 1980.

Bell, Rob. "Part 11: How We Got It," *What is the Bible?* http://robbellcom.tumblr.com/post/67479672681/what-is-the-bible-part-11 (accessed March 5, 2015).

Bell, Rob and Kristen Bell. *The Zimzum of Love: A New Way of*

Understanding Marriage. New York: Harper Collins Publishers, 2014.

Berry, Wendell. *The Art of the Commonplace: The Agrarian Essays of Wendell Berry*. Berkley, CA: Counterpoint Press, 2002.

Blazing Saddles. Directed by Mel Brooks. USA: Warner Home Video. 1997. DVD.

Brach, Tara. "Satsang," *Conversations That Matter*, https://allthatmatters.com/apps/mindbody/classes/705 (accessed December 7, 2014).

BrainHQ.com. "Scrambled Text." http://www.brainhq.com/brain-resources/brain-teasers/scrambled-text (accessed October 1, 2015).

Crisp, Oliver D. "Problems with Perichoresis" *Tyndale Bulletin*. 56.1: 2005.

De Mello, Anthony. *The Way to Love: Meditations for Life*. New York: Random House, Inc., 1991.

Dogma. Directed by Kevin Smith. USA: Columbia TriStar Home Entertainment. 1999. DVD.

Donne, John. *Devotions Upon Emergent Occasions and Death's Duel*. New York: Knopf Doubleday Publishing, 1999.

Edwards, Jonathan. "Sinners in the Hands of an Angry God. A Sermon Preached at Enfield, July 8th, 1741," Reiner Smolinski, editor. http://digitalcommons.unl.edu/cgi/viewcontent.cgi?article=-1053&context=etas (accessed October 29, 2015).

Elf. Directed by Jon Favreau. USA: New Line Home Entertainment. 2004. DVD.

Elliot, T.S. *The Complete Poems and Plays 1909–1950*. New York: Harcourt Brace and Company, 1971.

Emerson, Ralph Waldo. *Nineteenth-Century American Poetry*. William Spengmann, ed. New York: Penguin Books, 1996.

Every Good and Perfect Gift: Devotional Thoughts on the Gift of the Savior. Uhrichsville, OH: Barbour Books, 2014.

Fackenheim, Emil. *God's Presence in History: Jewish Affirmations and Philosophical Reflections.* New York: New York University Press, 1970.

Foster, Richard. *Celebration of Discipline.* New York: Harper Collins Publishers, 1998.

Going Clear: Scientology and the Prison of Belief. Directed by Alex Gibney. USA: HBO Documentary Films. 2015. DVD.

Hawking, Stephen. *A Brief History of Time.* New York: Bantam Books, 1988.

Heilbron, John L. *Galileo.* New York: Oxford University Press, 2010.

Jefferson, Thomas. *The Jefferson Bible: The Life and Morals of Jesus of Nazareth Extracted Textually from the Gospels in Greek, Latin, French and English.* Washington D.C.: Smithsonian Books, 2011.

Jones, Tony. *Did God Kill Jesus?: Searching for Love in History's Most Famous Execution.* New York: HarperCollins Publishers, 2015.

King, Martin Luther. "Remaining Awake through a Great Revolution," Lecture. Morehouse College Commencement, Atlanta, GA, June 2, 1959.

Lewis, C.S. *The Incarnation of the Word of God: Being the Treatise of St. Athanasius De Incarnatione Verbi Dei.* New York: Macmillan, 1947.

Lincoln, Abraham. "First Inaugural Address," *abrahamlincoln-online.org,* http://www.abrahamlincolnonline.org/lincoln/speeches/1inaug. htm. (Accessed April 22, 2015.)

Mannering, Ellisha Rader. "Stephen Hawking Says He's An Atheist," *WebPro News,* http://www.webpronews.com/stephen-hawking-says-hes-an-athiest-2014-09 (accessed September, 30, 2014).

McSwain, Stephen B. *The Enoch Factor: The Sacred Art of Knowing God*. Macon, GA: Smyth & Helwys Publishing, Inc., 2010.

Miller, Donald. *Blue Like Jazz: Nonreligious Thoughts on Christian Spirituality*. Nashville, Tenn: Thomas Nelson, Inc., 2003.

Nouwen, Henri J.M. *Bread for the Journey: A Daybook of Wisdom and Faith*. New York: Harper Collins Publishers, 1997.

O Brother, Where Art Thou? Directed by Joel Coen and Ethan Coen. USA: Buena Vista Home Entertainment. 2000. DVD.

O'Neal, Ryan. *Needle and Thread*. Performed by Sleeping at Last. CD. Sleeping at Last. 2006.

Olson, Roger E. "Is God 'A Being' or 'Being Itself?'" *My evangelical Arminian theological musings*.
http://www.patheos.com/blogs/rogereolson/2015/05/is-god-a-being-or-being-iself/ (accessed August 4, 2015).

Peterson, E.H. *The Message: The Bible in Contemporary Language*. Colorado Springs, CO: NavPress, 2002.

Prendiville, Ryan. "He likes to talk: extended Dan Harmon interview." *San Francisco Bay Guardian Online,* January 22, 2013.
http://www.sfbg.com/pixel_vision/2013/01/22/he-likes-talk-extended-dan-harmon-interview (accessed April, 24, 2014).

Rohr, Richard. "Jesus as Paradox," *Richard Rohr's Daily Meditation*.
http://myemail.constantcontact.com/Richard-Rohr-s-Meditation–Jesus-as-Paradox.html?soid=110309866
8616&aid=oce_J7-8kkI (accessed July 29, 2014).

_____. "Prophets: Self Critical Thinking," *Richard Rohr's Daily Meditation*.
http://myemail.constantcontact.com/Richard-Rohr-s-Meditation–Archetypal-Religion.
html?soid=1103098668616&aid=JJ-SgyYu2H0 (accessed February 17, 2015).

_____. "True Perfection is the Ability to Include Imperfection," *Richard Rohr's Daily Meditation*.
http://myemail.constantcontact.com/Richard-Rohr-s-Meditation–True-Perfection-Is-the-Ability-to-Include-

Imperfection.html?soid=1103098668616&aid=Di
-DcOKA4V8 (accessed June 16, 2015).

_____. "Who Would Want to Be a Prophet?" *Richard Rohr's Daily Meditation.*
http://myemail.constantcontact.com/Richard-Rohr-s-
Meditation–Who-Would-Want-to-Be-a-Prophet-.
html?soid=1103098668616&aid=O32zgddYuTc (accessed
February 19, 2015).

_____. "Jesus: Human and Divine," *Richard Rohr's Daily Meditation.*
http://myemail.constantcontact.com/Richard-
Rohr-s-Meditation–Love–Not-Atonement.
html?aid=iXa_UNn2YaQ&soid=1103098668616 (accessed
March 20, 2015).

Sacks, Jonathan. *Covenant & Conversation – Genesis: The Book of Beginnings.* Jerusalem: Koren Publishers, 2009.

_____. *Future Tense: Jews, Judaism, and Israel in the Twenty-first Century.* New York: Random House, Inc., 2009.

_____. "The Politics of Revelation," *rabbisacks.org,*
http://www.rabbisacks.org/covenant-conversation-yitro-the-
politics-of-revelation/ (accessed September 15, 2013).

Saliers, Emily. *Galileo.* Performed by Indigo Girls. CD. Epic Records. 1992.

Seay, Chris. ed. *The Voice Bible: Step Into the Story of Scripture.* Nashville, TN: Thomas Nelson, Inc., 2012.

Shaia, Alexander and Michelle L. Gaugy. *Heart and Mind: The Four-Gospel Journey for Radical Transformation.* Eugene, OR: Wipf and Stock Publishers, 2015.

Shaw, George Bernard. *Pygmalion.* New York: CreateSpace Independent Publishing Platform, 2014.

Shroyer, Danielle. *Original Blessing: Putting Sin in Its Rightful Place.* Minneapolis, MN: Fortress Press 2016.

Star Trek II: The Wrath of Khan. Directed by Nicholas Meyer. USA: Paramount Home Video. 1982. DVD.

Star Wars: Episode VI – Return of the Jedi. Directed by Richard Marquand. USA: Twentieth Century Fox Home Entertainment. 2005. DVD.

Teresa of Àvila. *The Life of Teresa of Jesus: The Autobiography of Teresa of Àvila.* Translated by E. Allison Peers. New York: Image Books, 2004.

Shakespeare, William. "Romeo and Juliet," *Norton's Anthology.* Chicago: Hampton Publishers, 2004.

Sheldon, W.L. "What to Believe: An Ethical Creed," *The Unitarian, Volume XII,* Frederick B. Mott, ed. Boston: Geo H. Ellis, 1897.

Suk, John. "A Personal Relationship with Jesus?" *Perspectives: A Journal of Reformed Thought.* http://perspectivesjournal.org/blog/2005/11/16/a-personal-relationship-with-jesus/(accessed July 2, 2014).

Swinton, John. *Critical Reflections on Stanley Hauerwas' Theology of Disability: Disabling Society, Enabling Theology.* New York: The Haworth Pastoral Press, 2004.

The Polar Express. Directed by Robert Zemeckis. USA: Warner Home Video, 2005. DVD.

The Lion King. Directed by Roger Allers and Rob Minkoff. USA: Buena Vista Home Entertainment, 1995. DVD.

The *Usual Suspects.* Directed by Bryan Singer. USA: PolyGram Video, 1995. VHS.

This is Spinal Tap. Directed by Rob Reiner. USA: MGM Home Entertainment, 2004. DVD.

¡*Three Amigos!* Directed by John Landis. USA: HBO Home Video, 1995. DVD.

Tillich, Paul. *Writings on Religion.* Robert P. Scharlemann, ed. Berlin: Walter De Gruyter & Co., 1988.

Tyson, Neil deGrasse. "Neil deGrasse Tyson on Science and Faith," *bigthink.com,* http://bigthink.com/videos/

neil-degrasse-tyson-on-science-and-faith (accessed
September 4, 2012).

UFW.org. "Education of the Heart: Quotes by César Chávez,"
http://www.ufw.org/_page.php?menu=research&inc=history/09.
html (accessed September 15, 2014).

Van Allsburg, Chris. *The Polar Express.* New York: Houghton
Mifflin, 1985.

Webber, Robert E. *Who Gets to Narrate the World? Contending
for the Christian Story in an Age of Rivals.* Downers Grove, IL:
Intervarsity Press, 2008.

_____. Editor. *The Complete Library of Christian Worship,* VIII
Volumes. Peabody, MA: Hendrickson Publishers, 1993.

Wright, N.T. *Acts for Everyone: Part One.* Louisville, KY:
Westminster John Knox Press, 2008.

ABOUT THE AUTHOR

Rev. Dr. Darrell Smith is a teacher, writer, and an aspiring integral theologian who has served in the Alamo Heights United Methodist family of churches since 1999.

He attended Texas A&M University, the Perkins School of Theology, Wayland Baptist University, and the Robert Webber Institute for Worship Studies and holds degrees in English, Speech Communication, Christian Ministry, and Worship Studies.

He founded and serves as a director of C3—a non-profit organization committed to conversations and connections that serve people and the common good.

Darrell's exploration—and at times protest—of religion and spirituality has led him to homeless shelters, prisons, refugee ghettos, and recovery groups as well as universities, temples, synagogues, and mosques. He has supported relief efforts in Central and South America and worked with such organizations as Renovaré, Apprentice, and Kairos Prison Ministry. Darrell lives with his wife and three children in San Antonio.

darrellsmith.org
chapter3ministries.org